国家哲学社会科学项目
"英语专业基础阶段内容依托式教学改革研究"项目组

《圣经》与文化

The Bible & Culture

主　编：常俊跃　李文萍　赵永青
本书编校主要参与者：
　　　　夏　洋　白苡萱　范　蕊　谷湘琴
　　　　吴慧丹　薛少静　付　慧
对本项目教材编校有贡献的其他教师：
　　　　李莉莉　吕春媚　高璐璐　霍跃红
　　　　姚　璐　傅　琼　刘晓蕖　黄洁芳
　　　　范丽雅　赵秀艳　王　磊

图书在版编目(CIP)数据

《圣经》与文化/常俊跃,李文萍,赵永青 主编. —北京:北京大学出版社,2011.9
(21世纪CBI内容依托系列英语教材)

ISBN 978-7-301-19224-5

I. 圣… II. ①常… ②李… ③赵… III. ①英语—阅读教学—高等学校—教材 ②圣经—研究 IV. H319.4:B

中国版本图书馆CIP数据核字(2011)第134801号

书　　　名：《圣经》与文化
著作责任者：常俊跃　李文萍　赵永青　主编
责 任 编 辑：孙　莹
标 准 书 号：ISBN 978-7-301-19224-5/H·2888
出 版 发 行：北京大学出版社
地　　　　址：北京市海淀区成府路205号　100871
网　　　　址：http://www.pup.cn
电　　　　话：邮购部 62752015　发行部 62750672　编辑部 62754382　出版部 62754962
电 子 邮 箱：zbing@pup.pku.edu.cn
印 刷 者：三河市博文印刷有限公司
经 销 者：新华书店
　　　　　787毫米×1092毫米　16开本　14.25张　380千字
　　　　　2011年9月第1版　2017年1月第3次印刷
定　　价：30.00元

未经许可,不得以任何方式复制或抄袭本书之部分或全部内容。
版权所有,侵权必究　举报电话：010-62752024
　　　　　　　　　　电子邮箱：fd@pup.pku.edu.cn

前　言

《〈圣经〉与文化》是在内容依托教学理念指导下,依托国家哲学社会科学项目"英语专业基础阶段内容依托式教学改革研究"推出的系列英语内容依托教材之一,是大连外国语学院优秀教学成果一等奖、辽宁省优秀教学成果一等奖、第六届国家级优秀教学成果奖获奖成果的重要组成部分。这套系列教材的推出具有重要的理论意义和现实意义。

随着我国英语教育的快速发展,英语专业长期贯彻的"以技能为导向"的课程建设理念及教学理念已经难以满足社会的需要。现行英语专业教育大、中、小学英语教学脱节,语言、内容教学割裂,单纯语言技能训练过多,专业内容课程不足,学科内容课程系统性差,高低年级内容课程安排失衡及其导致的学生知识面偏窄、知识结构欠缺、思辨能力偏弱、综合素质发展不充分等问题日益凸显。

针对上述问题,国家哲学社会科学项目"英语专业基础阶段内容依托式教学改革研究"以内容依托教学(CBI)理论为指导,确定了如下改革思路:

(一)打破传统教学理念,改革英语专业教学的课程结构。在不改变专业总体培养目标和教学时限的前提下,对课程结构进行革命性的变革,改变传统单一的语言技能课程模式,实现内容课程——语言课程的融合,扩展学生的知识面,提高学生的语言技能。

(二)开发课程自身潜力,同步提高专业知识和语言技能。内容依托课程本身也同时关注内容和语言,把内容教学和语言教学有机结合。以英语为媒介,系统教授专业内容;以专业内容为依托,在使用语言过程中提高语言技能,扩展学生的知识面。

(三)改革教学方法,全面提高语言技能和综合素质。依靠内容依托教学在方法上的灵活性,通过问题驱动、输出驱动等方法调动学生主动学习,把启发式、任务式、讨论式、结对子、小组活动、课堂展示、多媒体手段等行之有效的活动与学科内容教学有机结合,提高学生的语言技能,激发学生的兴趣,培养学生的自主性和创造性,提升思辨能力和综合素质。

本项改革突破了我国英语专业英语教学大纲规定的课程结构,改变了英语专业基础阶段通过开设单纯的听、说、读、写四种语言技能课提高学生语言技能的传统课程建设理念,对英语课程及教学方法进行了创新性的改革。首创了有英语专业基础阶段具有我国特色的"内容—语言"融合的课程体系;率先开发了适合英语专业基础阶段的内容依托课程;系统开发了英语国家史、地、社会文化、欧洲文化、中国文化、跨文化交际、《圣经》文化教材;以英语为媒介,系统教授专业内容;以内容为依托,全面发展学生的语言技能;扩展学生的知识面,提高学生的综合素质,以崭新的途径实现英语专业教育的总体培养目标。

经过七年的酝酿、准备、实验,内容依托教学改革取得了鼓舞人心结果。

(一)构建了英语专业基础阶段内容依托课程与语言课程融合的课程体系。新的课程体系改变了传统单一的听、说、读、写语言技能课程模式,实现了内容依托课程和语言技能课程两种模块的融合;语言技能课程包含综合英语、听力、语音、写作,内容课程包含了美国历史文化、美国自然人文地理、美国社会文化、英国历史文化、英国自然人文地理、英国社会文化、澳新加社会文化、欧洲文化、中国文化、跨文化交际、《圣经》与文化;语言技能课程密切关注听、说、读、写技能的发展,内容依托课程不仅关注系统的学科内容,而且也关注综合语言技能的培养。在课程外和课程内两个层面把内容教学和语言教学有机结合,通过内容教学培养学生综合语言运用能力,扩展学生的知识面，提高学生的综合素质和多元文化意识，从根本上改变英语专业学生知识面偏窄、综合素质偏低的问题。

（二）系统开发了相关国家的史、地、社会文化以及跨文化交际课程资源。在 **CBI** 教学理论的指导下，在实施内容依托教学的关键期——英语专业的第一学年，成功开出了美国和英国的历史、地理、社会文化等课程。第二学年开出澳新加社会文化、欧洲文化、中国文化、跨文化交际、《圣经》与文化等课程。内容依托教材改变了传统的组织模式，系统组织了教学内容，设计了新颖的栏目板块，设计的活动也丰富多样，实践教学中受到了学生的广泛欢迎。此外还开发了开设课程所需要的大量资源。在北京大学出版社的支持下，系列教材已经陆续出版。

（三）牵动了教学手段和教学方法的改革，取得了突出的教学效果。在内容依托教学理论的指导下，教师的教学理念、教学方法、教学手段得到更新。通过问题驱动、输出驱动等活动调动学生主动学习，把启发式、任务式、讨论式、结对子、小组活动、课堂展示、多媒体手段等行之有效的活动与学科内容教学有机结合，激发学生的兴趣，培养学生自主性和创造性，提高学生的语言技能，提升思辨能力和综合素质。曾有专家教师担心取消专门的英语泛读课以及缩减基础英语精读课会对阅读技能发展产生消极影响。实验数据证明，内容依托教学不仅没有对学生的语言技能发展和语言知识的学习产生消极影响，而且还产生了多方面的积极影响；在取消专门英语阅读课的情况下，阅读能力发展迅速；内容依托教学对学科知识的学习产生了巨大的积极影响。

（四）提高了教师的科研意识和科研水平，取得了丰硕的教研成果。项目开展以来，团队对内容依托教学问题进行了系列研究，活跃了整个教学单位的科研气氛，科研意识和科研水平也得到很大提高。课题组已经撰写研究论文17篇，在国际、国内学术研讨会交流12篇，在国际学术期刊 *World Englishes*、国内外语类核心期刊《外语与外语教学》、《中国外语》、《教育理论与实践》等发表研究论文9篇。

教学改革开展以来，每次成果发布都引起强烈反响。在2008年3月的第三届中国外语教学法国际研讨会上，与会的知名外语教育专家戴炜栋教授等对这项改革给予关注，博士生导师蔡基刚教授认为本项研究"具有导向性作用"。在2008年5月的"第二届全国英语专业院系主任高级论坛"上，研究成果得到知名专家博士生导师王守仁教授和与会专家教授的高度评价。在2008年7月的中国英语教学研究会东北地区年会上，改革的系列成果引起与会专家的强烈反响，研究论文获得3个优秀论文一等奖，3个二等奖，1个三等奖。在2008年11月在中国英语教学研究会年会上，成果再次引起与会专家的强烈反响，博士生导师石坚教授等给予了高度评价。在2008年10月和12月，本项改革成果分别获得大连外国语学院教学研究成果一等奖和辽宁省优秀教学成果奖一等奖，而且还被辽宁省特别推荐参评国家教学成果奖。在2009年5月的"第三届全国英语专业院系主任高级论坛"，本项改革成果再次赢得专家同行们的关注和赞誉。2009年10月"中国英语教学研究会2009年会"上，中国英语教学研究会会长、中国外语教育研究中心主任文秋芳教授和我国外语教学指导委员会主任戴炜栋教授对我们的教学研究所取得的成果给予高度肯定和赞扬。2011年5月"以内容为依托的外语教学模式探索研讨会"更是得到来自全国专家、学者的关注，大家共同探讨了大学阶段内容依托教学这一重大课题。

目前，该项成果已经在全国英语专业教育领域引起广泛关注。它触及了英语专业的教学大纲，影响了课程建设的理念，引领了英语专业的教学改革，改善了教学实践，必将对未来英语专业教育的发展产生积极影响。

本项改革开展过程中得到了全国各地专家的关注、支持和帮助。衷心感谢戴炜栋教授、王守仁教授、文秋芳教授、石坚教授、蔡基刚教授、杨忠教授等前辈们给予的关注、鼓励、指导和帮助，

前言

衷心感谢大连外国语学院校长孙玉华教授、赵忠德教授、杨俊峰教授及其他各位领导的大力支持，感谢大连外国语学院教务处刘宏处长、姜凤春副处长以及工作人员们在改革实验中给予的大力支持，感谢大连外国语学院科研处张雪处长和工作人员们给予的热情帮助，感谢大连外国语学院英语学院的领导全力支持和同事们的无私帮助以及团队成员的共同努力。同时也真诚感谢为我们内容依托教学改革提供丰富教学材料的国内外专家们。特别感谢的是北京大学出版社富有远见的张冰主任和刘强助理，没有他们对新教学理念的认同，没有他们对英语专业教育的关注和支持，这套教材不可能如此迅速地面世。

《〈圣经〉与文化》的出版具有它特殊的背景。在现代社会，《圣经》经常被标注为"西方之书"，被认为是西方文化的一部分。而事实上《圣经》并非仅是西方之书，基督教也并非只是西方的宗教。全世界有33%的人信仰基督教，在英美的很多学校，《圣经》都是贯穿义务教育的学校必开课程。在美国众多家庭中，《圣经》更是家庭必备之书，《圣经》以及与此相关的文化影响英语国家的政治、经济、文化以及社会生活的每个角落。随着国际交流的频繁，了解各国文化尤显重要。西方社会的文化产品，诸如电影、原版小说、电视剧等等在国内已经越来越普遍。而这些文化产品本身都或多或少的与《圣经》以及相关文化相关。为了更好地让广大英语爱好者系统、深入地了解《圣经》与文化知识，我们特地为英语专业高级阶段的学生编写了《〈圣经〉与文化》这本教材。教学实验发现，该教材还是需要学生有一定英语语言积累。因此，它的读者群体确定为具有一定英语基础的英语专业三年级以上的学生、水平相当的大学公共英语的学生或社会上的英语爱好者。总体来看，本教材具备以下特色：

(一) 打破了传统的教材建设理念

本教材改变了"为学语言而学语言"的传统教材建设理念，在具有时代特色且被证明行之有效的内容依托教学理论指导下，改变了片面关注语言知识和语言技能忽视内容学习的作法。它依托学生密切关注的《圣经》与文化内容组织学生进行语言交际活动，在语言交流中学习有意义的知识内容，既训练语言技能，也丰富相关知识，起到的是一箭双雕的作用。

(二) 涉及了系统的相关内容

《〈圣经〉与文化》共分十五单元。包含了衣物、食品、家庭、婚姻、人物、社会、城市、节日、教育、价值观、《圣经》对美英社会文化的影响等人们感兴趣的话题。

(三) 引进了真实的教学材料

英语教材是英语学习者英语语言输入和相关知识输入的重要渠道。本教材大量使用真实、地道的语言材料，为学生提供了高质量的语言输入。此外，为了使课文内容更加充实生动，易于学生理解接受，编者在课文中穿插了大量的插图、表格、照片等真实的视觉材料，表现手段活泼、形式多种多样，效果生动直观。

(四) 突出了学生的主体地位

本教材每一单元的主体内容均包括 Before You Read、Start to Read、After You Read、Read More 四大板块，不仅在结构上确立了学生的主体地位，而且系统的安排也方便教师借助教材有条不紊地开展教学活动。在 Before You Read 部分，读者可以对本单元的主要内容进行自测，通过自测激发自己对单元内容的好奇心和学习热情。Start to Read 是每个单元的重点，通过对主课文的学习，读者可以对每单元的内容有一个总体了解。然后，在 After You Read 部分对课文练习的完成，进一步深化对单元内容、以及英语语言知识的学习。除主课文之外，每单元 Read More 还配有两篇辅助阅读材料，这些阅读材料有助于读者对单元内容的进一步了解和掌握。这种设计改变了教师单纯灌输、学生被动接受的教学方式，促使学生积极思考、提问、探索、发现、批判，培养自主获得知识，发现问题和解决问题的能力。

(五) 提供了多样的训练活动

为了培养学生的语言技能和综合素质，本教材在保证文化知识体系完整的前提下，在关注英语语言知识训练和相关知识内容传授的基础上精心设计了生动多样的综合训练活动。教材在每一单元都精心设计了旨在对学生在语法、词汇、篇章结构、语言功能等方面进行全面严格的基本技能练习。同时，编者通过参阅大量国外资料，设计出与《圣经》与文化是相关的、学生参与度极高的课堂和课外活动。多样化的活动打破了传统教材单调的训练程式，帮助教师设置真实的语言运用情境，组织富于挑战性的、具有意义的语言实践活动，培养学生语言综合运用能力。这些活动的设置成为本教材的亮点之一，它使得课堂教学得以延伸，也能激发学生的学习热情，这也是CBI教学理念在本教材中的最好体现。

(六) 推荐了经典的学习材料

教材的这一特色在于它对教学内容的延伸和拓展。在每个章节的For Fun部分，编者向学生推荐相关网站、经典的影视作品和文学作品等学习资料。读者对某一方面的内容产生了兴趣，可以轻松地浏览编写在每单元最后的参考网站，欣赏推荐的电影，对自己感兴趣的内容进行更深层次的挖掘。这不仅有益于学生开阔视野，也使教材具有了弹性和开放性，方便不同院校不同水平学生满足不同层次的需求。

作为一项探索，我们团队成员虽然为打造这套级精品教材做出了巨大努力，但由于水平所限，教材中难免存在疏漏和不足，希望全国各地的同仁不吝赐教，希望亲自体验内容依托教学的同学积极提出改进意见和建议，以期不断完善教材，为提高英语专业教育的质量共同努力。

编者
2010年2月于大连外国语学院

Contents

Unit 1	Clothing and *the Bible*	1
	Text A Clothing	2
	Text B Cloak and Tunic	6
	Text C Sackcloth	7
Unit 2	Food and *the Bible*	11
	Text A Food, Diet and Health	11
	Text B Food	16
	Text C Diet	18
Unit 3	Family Life and *the Bible*	23
	Text A Family Life	24
	Text B Parents and Children	28
	Text C How to Strengthen Your Family Ties	30
Unit 4	Marriage and *the Bible*	33
	Text A Types of Marriages	34
	Text B Jewish Wedding	38
	Text C Jewish Wedding Customs and Their Origins	41
Unit 5	Women and *the Bible*	45
	Text A Old Testament Post-creation Views	46
	Text B Daughters of Eve	50
	Text C Stories of the Women	52
Unit 6	Shepherds and *the Bible*	55
	Text A Shepherds	56
	Text B Shepherd Leader	61
	Text C Shepherds' Implements	62
Unit 7	Prophets and *the Bible*	66
	Text A The Prophet Isaiah	67
	Text B The Prophet Jeremiah	71
	Text C Ezekiel the Prophet	72
Unit 8	Slaves and *the Bible*	76
	Text A The General Picture of Slavery	76
	Text B Treatment of Slaves	81
	Text C Slavery and *the Bible*	83

Unit 9 Weapons and Warfare and *the Bible* ... 87
- Text A Weapons ... 88
- Text B Alternative Weapons ... 93
- Text C War ... 94

Unit 10 City and *the Bible* ... 99
- Text A Cities ... 99
- Text B A Biblical Theology of the City ... 104
- Text C Bible Archaeology: Sodom and Gomorrah ... 106

Unit 11 Holidays and *the Bible* ... 109
- Text A Jewish Holidays ... 110
- Text B Purim in Bible Times ... 115
- Text C Holiday Customs ... 116

Unit 12 Education and *the Bible* ... 120
- Text A Christianity's Influence on Education ... 121
- Text B Education in Old Testament Times ... 125
- Text C Education in New Testament Times ... 127

Unit 13 The Power of Dreams and *the Bible* ... 131
- Text A Four Main Dreams in *the Bible* ... 131
- Text B What does *the Bible* Say about Dreams? ... 136
- Text C Dream Interpretation ... 137

Unit 14 Jewish Values ... 141
- Text A Jewish Impact on the Civilization of America ... 141
- Text B The Jewish Influence on the Great Seal ... 147
- Text C Number Thirteen ... 149

Unit 15 Bible's Impact on English & American Culture ... 153
- Text A English Culture and *the Bible* ... 154
- Text B American Literature and *the Bible* ... 159
- Text C *The Bible*'s Influence on American Culture ... 161

Appendix I: List of Biblical Names ... 165

Appendix II: 参考答案 ... 166

Appendix III: Famous Bible Stories ... 177
- Abraham ... 177
- Adam and Eve ... 178
- Bartimaeus ... 179
- Crossing the Red Sea ... 180

Daniel and the Lions	181
David and Goliath	182
Feeding of the 5000	184
Food and Water in the Desert and the First Covenant	184
Gabriel Visits Mary	186
Jesus and Nicodemus	186
Jesus and Peter	187
Jesus and the Children	188
Jesus Calms a Storm	188
Joseph and His Brothers—Part I	189
Joseph and His Brothers—Part II	190
Noah's Ark	194
Pharaoh's Dreams	196
Parable of the Sower	198
Peter Denies He Knows Jesus	198
The Ascension	199
The Baptism of Jesus	200
The biblical Account of Creation	200
The Birth of Jesus	201
Moses and the Burning Bush	203
The Coming of the Holy Spirit	203
The Death and Resurrection of Jesus	204
The First Passover	205
The Good Samaritan	207
The Good Shepherd	208
The Last Supper	208
The Lost Sheep and the Lost Coin	209
The Parable of the Talents	210
The Plagues	210
The Prodigal Son	214
The Temptation of Jesus	215
The Ten Commandments Given to Moses	216
The Word Becomes Flesh	216
Zacchaeus	217

Appendix IV: 参考的主要文献和网站 ·········· 218

Unit 1
Clothing and *the Bible*

> There is much to support the view that it is clothes that wear us and not we them; we may make them take the mould of arm or breast, but they would mould our hearts, our brains, our tongues to their liking.
> —Virginia Woolf

Unit Goals

- To gain a general knowledge of clothing in *the Bible*
- To develop a right attitude towards clothing in *the Bible*
- To get acquainted with some basic cultural concepts concerning clothing in *the Bible*
- To learn useful words and expressions about clothing in *the Bible*
- To improve English language skills and western culture awareness

Before You Read

I. Please match the words in the box with the pictures. And then figure out who wears them.

circlet	sandals	anklets	headwear	ephod
veil	bracelets	loin cloth	cloak	

II. Form groups of three or four students. Try to find, on the Internet or in the library, more information about clothing in the Bible. Get ready for a 5-minute presentation in class.

Start to Read

Text A Clothing

Merchants bringing silk and finely woven **fabrics** would travel in caravans over vast distances from as far away as India. Fine linen was imported from Egypt. In Palestine, clothing was frequently made of linen from locally grown flax. Everyday clothes were made from an ordinary quality **linen**; priests wore more expensive linen. Wool could easily be made into clothing by semi-**nomadic** people, but **flax** for linen could be cultivated only by a settled community.

The poor often wore coarse clothing made from goat or camel hair, which was rough and very uncomfortable. Also known as sackcloth, it was often worn as a sign of **penitence**. It also served as a blanket for **warding off** the cold at night. Cotton was known in Egypt and elsewhere and in Roman times a form of local wild silk was obtainable. Fine gold wire gave luxury to **garments**, while different colors were obtained from plant or animal sources: red from an insect, yellow from a flower, **saffron** from the stigma of a crocus, and purple from the Murex mollusk. Purple dye, renowned for its color, became a symbol of royalty and wealth.

The clothing of most people was simple in style. The **loin** cloth was worn by men of all social levels from an early period, with the later addition of an outer and inner garment. The inner garment of wool or linen had an opening for the neck and arms, and generally had long sleeves. Often belted at the waist, it fell either to the knees or ankles. The outer garment, cloak or **mantle**, generally made of animal skin or wool, was almost square, with openings for the arms, and was worn **draped** over one or both shoulders. As a man was considered naked unless he was wearing his cloak, he was forbidden to lend or pledge it. At night he removed it for use as a blanket. Jesus' undergarment was woven without **seam** and would have been worthless if cut into pieces. That was why Roman soldiers at his **crucifixion** decided to cast lots to see who should have it.

Fine linen with elaborate **embroidery** was used for outer clothing by the wealthy. Kings sometimes wore an additional garment similar to the priest's vest-like **tunic** or **ephod**. Both kings and priests wore an elaborate headdress to symbolize their status. The **adornment** of such garments contrasted sharply with the simplicity of most people's dress.

Most women in biblical times wore simple white clothing, although blue or black homespun was sometimes seen. Wealthy women wore garments of brightly dyed fine linen, often in scarlet or purple, and elaborately decorated with embroidery, jewels, and gold or silver detail. Such garments were also worn on **festive** occasions and at weddings. The undergarment worn by a woman was similar to a man's except that it was higher at the neck and normally fell to the ankles. Headwear, although rarely mentioned in *the Bible*, was probably like the **prayer-shawl** sometimes seen today, and was held in place by a cord. Women often wore a veil that was held in place by a **circlet** of coins that may have formed part of their dowry. Jewelry was normally designed in gold, sometimes with semi-precious stones inset. As early as 2,700 B.C., the royal graves at Ur give evidence of a high quality of design and craftsmanship in jewelry. Gold chains were popular, as were circlets, anklets, bracelets, and pins for clothing or hair. Footwear generally consisted of open leather sandals.

After You Read

Knowledge Focus
I. Pair Work: Discuss the following questions with your partner.
(1) Where did people get silk and fine linen?
(2) What are the differences in wearing clothes between priests and semi-nomadic people?
(3) How did people obtain colors? Why did Joseph's color coat arouse his brother's jealousy?
(4) What's the worth of Jesus' seamless clothes?
(5) How did the wealthy people decorate their clothes?
(6) How did women dress themselves in biblical times?

II. Solo Work: Tell whether the following statements are true or false according to the knowledge you learned.
(1) It is generally acceptable for a woman to wear traditionally male clothing, while the converse is unusual. ( )
(2) Clothing is only the reflection of gender differentiation, social status and religious aspects. ( )
(3) In the modern west, women are more likely to wear makeup, jewelry, and colorful clothing, while in very traditional cultures women are protected from men's gazes by modest dress. ( )
(4) Kilts were previously worn as normal clothing by women in Scotland. ( )
(5) Trousers were once seen as exclusively male clothing, but are nowadays worn by both sexes. ( )

Language Focus
I. Build your vocabulary.
A. Write the correct word next to its definition.

| crucifixion | nomadic | seam |
| embroidery | penitence | festive |

(1) _____ remorse for one's past conduct
(2) _____ patterns or pictures that consist of stitches sewn directly onto cloth
(3) _____ (of groups of people) tending to travel and change settlements frequently
(4) _____ offering fun and gaiety
(5) _____ the act of executing by a method widespread in the ancient world; the victim's

hands and feet are bound or nailed to a cross
(6) _____ joint consisting of a line formed by joining two pieces

B. Use the proper forms of the words to complete the sentences.
  (1) Christmas is an important religious _____ which is mainly celebrated in the heart of the Christian.
  (2) _____ is something that enervates our spirit, causing a greater loss than loss itself and making good words!
  (3) The Kazakh are a semi- _____ people who raise sheep and yaks for their main food source.
  (4) It is a type of folk _____ craftwork created by workwoman in the ancient time.
  (5) The _____ of Jesus Christ was, for its day, only a routine execution.
  (6) The tailor stitched the split _____ in seconds.

II. Fill in the blanks with the proper forms of the words.
  (1) Everything that is needed for the building and furnishing of a house is well made, inexpensive, and immediately _____ (obtain).
  (2) The _____ (royalty) wedding was an occasion of great festivity.
  (3) The lady appeared with a _____ (luxury) fur coat.
  (4) We believe that _____ (penitence) sinners are regenerated solely by God's grace and justified through faith in Jesus Christ.
  (5) We must _____ (cultivation) our own garden and find the joy of doing it in our own heart.
  (6) The minister _____ (crucifixion) by the press for his handling of the affair.
  (7) It is _____ (consider) of you to make so much noise when people are asleep.
  (8) The new house is not _____ (similar) to our old one except that it is a bit bigger.

Comprehensive Work
I. Group work
  1. Work in group of four and share ideas with your group members.
    (1) Clothing taboos tend to be central to every culture on earth and to contain some details which are very inflexible. Try to list some clothing taboos in UK, USA or China.
    (2) Read the following passage and present your point of view about this. What implications can be reflected from this passage?
      There have been cultures like the English and North American culture of Victorian times, which required men to cover only their genitals and buttocks but required women to hide their entire torso and the full length of their "limbs" behind several layers of cloth nearly all the time. Indeed, Victorian culture was so obsessed with "limbs" that, in a proper Victorian home, the legs of household furniture, which were considered a part of the feminine sphere of influence, were covered with petticoats lest men should be moved to lust after chairs.
  2. Read the following poem and discuss the functions of clothing.
    Dresses for breakfasts, and dinners, and balls;
    Dresses to sit in, and stand in, and walk in;
    Dresses to dance in, and flirt in, and talk in;

Dresses in which to do nothing at all;
Dresses for Winter, Spring, Summer, and Fall.

—William Allen Butler, "Nothing to Wear"

II. Pair Work: Discuss the following questions with your partner.
(1) Does *the Bible* have a dress code?
(2) What are the functions of clothing?
(3) Should women wear pants to church? What about hats and veils?
(4) Is it a sin for a woman to wear pants?
(5) What is proper to wear to church?

III. Essay Writing
Lee Mildon once said: "People seldom notice old clothes if you wear a big smile." Write a short essay to explain your understanding of it.

IV. Solo Work
1. Put in the missing words.

   Clothing is an aspect of human physical appearance, and like other aspects of human physical appearance, it has social significance. All societies have dress codes, most of which are unwritten but understood by most members of the society. The dress code has built in rules or signals indicating the m_____ being given by a person's clothing and how it is worn.

   Wearing expensive clothes can communicate w_____, the image of wealth, or cheaper access to quality clothing. All factors apply inversely t_____ the wearing of inexpensive clothing and similar goods. The observer sees the resultant, expensive clothes, but may incorrectly perceive the extent to which these factors apply to the person observed. Clothing can convey a social message, even if none is intended.

   If the receiver's code of interpretation differs from the sender's code of communication, misinterpretation follows. In every culture, current fashion governs the manner of consciously constructing, assembling, and wearing clothing to convey a social message. The rate of change of fashion v_____, and so modifies the style in wearing clothes and its accessories within months or d_____, especially in small social groups or in communications media-influenced modern societies. More extensive changes, requiring more time, money, and effort to effect, may span generations. When fashion changes, the messages communicated by clothing change.

2. Proofreading and error correction.

   In most cultures, gender differentiation of clothing is considered appropriate for men and women. The differences are in styles, colors and fabrics.

   In Western societies, skirts, dresses and high-heeled shoes are usually seen as woman's clothing, while neckties are usually seen as men's clothing. Trousers   (1) _____
   were once seen as exclusively male clothing, but are nowadays worn by both sexes. Male clothes are often more practical (that is, they can function well under a wide variety of situations), so a wider range of clothing styles is available for   (2) _____

females. Males are typically allowed to bare their chests in a greater variety of public places. It is generally acceptable for woman to wear traditionally male clothing, while the converse is unusual.

In some cultures, sumptuary laws regulate that men and women are required to wear.

Islam requires women to wear hijab, or modest clothing. What qualifies as "modest" varies in different Muslim societies; however, women are usually required to cover more of their bodies than men are. Articles of clothing worn by Muslim women for purposes of modesty range from the headscarf to the burqa.

Men should sometimes choose to wear men's skirts such as togas or kilts, especially on ceremonial occasions. Such garments were (in previous times) often worn as normal daily clothing by men.

Compared to men's clothing, women's clothing tends to be attractive, often intended to be looked at by men. In the modern West, women are more likely to wear makeup, jewellery, and colorful clothing, while in very traditional cultures women are protected from men's gazes by modest dress.

(3) _____
(4) _____
(5) _____

Read More

Text B Cloak and Tunic

Our knowledge of the clothing worn by people in *the Bible* comes primarily from the Scriptures themselves, as well as from illustrations on various monuments, seals and plaques that have been found. Findings in grave and tomb remains by archaeologists have also provided direct evidence.

Although there was a general similarity, in appearance and what the items were called, there were always easily-detectable differences in men and women's clothing. The Lord had commanded that male and female Israelites were to wear different forms of clothing, and made it very clear how He felt about those who did otherwise—"A woman must not wear men's clothing, nor a man wear women's clothing, for The Lord your God detests anyone who does this." (Deuteronomy 22:5). Generally, Biblical clothing consisted of—

For Men—

- The Inner Tunic—a long piece of plain cotton or linen cloth as an undergarment for the upper body, but sometimes reaching all the way down to the ankles. It was usually not worn when the weather was very warm.
- The Tunic-coat, or *Ketonet*—a shirt-like garment worn over the inner tunic in cool weather, or next to the body without the inner tunic when warm. It usually had long sleeves and extended down to the ankles.
- The Belt, or Girdle—made of leather, from 2 to 6 inches wide,

sometimes with a shoulder strap when heavier articles were being carried from it.
- The Cloke, or Mantle—a robe worn over all of the other items of clothing as an outer garment for warmth and appearance.
- The Headdress—worn chiefly as a protection against the sun. The Hebrew version could, depending upon circumstances, be a cap, a turban, or a head scarf.
- Shoes or Sandals—shoes were made from soft leather, sandals from harder leather.

For Women—
- The Inner Tunic—a long garment reaching all the way down to the ankles. It was usually of a finer quality cotton, linen or silk.
- The Outer Tunic—a full-length garment, again of finer quality than the men's version, and almost always enhanced with fine needlework and/or multicolor threads.
- The Belt, or Girdle—made of colorful silk or wool, sometimes with a fringe from the waist nearly to the ankles.
- The Cloke—warm and durable for protection against cool weather, and usually more intricate.
- The Headdress—a lighter and finer quality than the men's version, and always more colorful. Women also usually had elaborate plaiting or other arrangement of their hair, which tended to be long.
- Shoes or Sandals—shoes were made from soft leather, sandals from harder leather.

Questions for discussion or reflection.
(1) What kind of materials are they made of: the inner tunic, outer tunic, belt shoes and sandals?
(2) What is the function of headdress?
(3) Are there any differences between the outer tunic worn by men and women?

Text C Sackcloth

Being clothed in sackcloth has several meanings in *the Bible*. They are all somewhat similar, but they have nuances that we need to consider.

Sackcloth was worn by those who were in **mourning**. Recall in Ezekiel 9 that the angel was supposed to mark all those who sighed and cried for all the troubles of Jerusalem. That is a sign of woe, of mourning, or of being sorry for the fall of this once great nation or for their sins.

Sackcloth also can mean **repentance**, as an outward sign of the inner repentance of a person. Therefore it also has another meaning of being **humble**. A repentant person should be a humble person. He has seen his sins and turned from them.

Another meaning is **austerity.** This is one that the world often sees in John the Baptist and Elijah, that they were "poor" men. However, that is not necessarily the case. Austerity does not necessarily mean that one is poor. It can mean though that a person leads a simple lifestyle, and that he has

removed the frills that complicate his life. Wearing sackcloth, then, could mean a person has stripped down to the simplest essentials of his physical life.

Of course, the one that goes with this would then be **poverty**, yet not necessarily physical poverty (a lack of money) but spiritual poverty (poor in spirit). This is a fine way of looking at the wearing of sackcloth in the case of the Two Witnesses—and frankly, of Elijah and John the Baptist. They were ready to be filled and given the riches of God because they had considered themselves lowly and needy. They knew they needed what only God could give. They were poor in spirit.

However, all of these meanings could apply to the Two Witnesses: They mourn for the troubles this world is going through; they are repentant and humble; they are austere, not having any of the frills and complications that clutter other people's lives—they have stripped themselves of the things that would weigh them down so that they can run; and they are certainly poor in spirit.

Questions for discussion or reflection.
(1) When do people wear sackcloth according to Text C?
(2) What are the meanings of dressing in sackcloth?

Notes

(1) **The Seamless robe of Jesus (or Holy Tunic):** It is the robe said to have been worn by Jesus during (or shortly before) his crucifixion.

According to the Gospel of John, the soldiers who crucified Jesus did not divide his tunic after crucifying him, but cast lots to determine who would keep it because it was woven in one piece, without seam.

(2) **The Eucharist:** It also called Holy Communion, Sacrament of the Table, the Blessed Sacrament, or The Lord's Supper, and other names, is a Christian sacrament or ordinance, generally considered to be a commemoration of the Last Supper, the final meal that Jesus Christ shared with his disciples before his arrest and eventual crucifixion. The consecration of bread and a cup within the rite recalls the moment at the Last Supper when Jesus gave his disciples bread, saying, "This is my body", and wine, saying, "This is my blood".

(3) **Sackcloth and ashes:** (*slightly formal*)

If you wear sackcloth and ashes, you show by your behaviour that you are very sorry for something you did wrong.

In the past, clothes made of sackcloth (= a rough cloth) were worn by the Jews in religious activities to show that they were sad or sorry for the things they had done wrong.

References of sackcloth and ashes in classic literature:

And a hermit's got to sleep on the hardest place he can find, and put sackcloth and ashes on his head, and stand out in the rain, and —

Tom Sawyer by Twain, Mark

Some of his low places he found lifted to ideals, some of his ideas had sunk to the valleys, and lay there with the sackcloth and ashes of pumice stone and sulphur on their ruined heads.

Pudd'n'head Wilson by Twain, Mark

This Mary Dyer had entered the mint-master's dwelling, clothed in sackcloth and ashes, and seated herself in our great chair with a sort of dignity and state.

Grandfather's Chair by Hawthorne, Nathaniel

Book to read
Please read *the Bible* to learn about the sackcloth:

Genesis 37:34	Psalm 69:11
2 Samuel 3:31	Daniel 12:7
1 Kings 21:27	Joel 1:13
Esther 4:1	Jonah 3:8
Jonah 3:5	Revelation 1:5
2 Kings 19:1	Revelation 12:6
Nehemiah 9:1	Revelation 13:5

Movie to See
Joseph

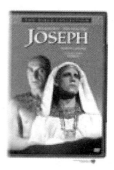

Joseph, the favorite son of Jacob, is sold into slavery by his jealous half-brothers. Sent to work in Egypt, Joseph's ability to interpret dreams makes him popular in the Pharaoh's court. But it is Joseph's faith in God which helps to rescue him when he's falsely accused and imprisoned.

Song to Enjoy

Here is part of the lyrics of "Joseph's Coat". Find the audio and enjoy the song. You can complete the lyrics while listening.

,

by Jacob

Joseph's mother, she was quite my favorite wife
I never really loved another all my life
And Joseph was my joy because
He reminded me of her
Narrator
….

Joseph's charm and winning smile
Failed to slay them in the aisle

And his father couldn't see the danger
He could not imagine any danger
He just saw in Joseph all his dreams come true
Jacob wanted to show the world he loved his son
To make it clear that Joseph was the special one
So Jacob bought his son a coat
A multi-colored coat to wear
….
Brothers

Quite the smoothest person in the district

Joseph & Female Ensemble

I look handsome, I look smart
I am walking work of art
Such a dazzling coat of colours
How I love my coat of many colours

Narrator, Joseph, Ensemble & Children

It was red and yellow and green and brown
And scarlet and black and ochre and peach
And ruby and olive and violet and fawn
And lilac and gold and chocolate and mauve

Unit 2
Food and *the Bible*

> Civilization is mostly the story of how seeds, meats, and ways to cook them travel from place to place.
> —Adam Gopnik
>
> Food is a central activity of mankind and one of the single most significant trademarks of a culture.
> —Mark Kurlansky

Unit Goals

- To understand some basic cultural concepts concerning food in *the Bible*
- To understand the Biblical verses related to food
- To learn some rules governing foods which are permitted and those which are forbidden in *the Bible*
- To learn useful words and expressions about food in *the Bible*
- To improve English language skills and western culture awareness

Before You Read

(1) Culture can be reflected from food. Would you please think over which food can typically represent your local culture?
(2) The Garden of Eden is a paradise without hunger. We are quite familiar with the famous article written by Tao Yuanming（陶渊明）"The Story of Peach Blossom Spring"（《桃花源记》）. When the fisherman came to the dreamy world, he was treated with wines and chicken. Please exchange your opinion with your partner about food preparation when a guest visits you.
(3) Form groups of three or four students. Try to find, on the Internet or in the library, more information about food in *the Bible*. Get ready for a 5-minute presentation in class.

Start to Read

Text A Food, Diet and Health

On most biblical occasions, it is the women's domain to prepare food. They pound the grains in **mortars** or use hand mills. From barley they prepare the grits, sometimes after roasting the **barley**. They **grind** the wheat and then bake bread, cake, or biscuits. Bread is **leavened** or unleavened. Butter and cheese are made from the milk of cows and sheep. Meat is boiled in a **cauldron** or roasted on a fire and seasoned with herbs and spices.

Meanings of Food in the Biblical Text

Food is **integral** to communicating the biblical message. Food characterizes situations and persons, and it structures and marks the dramatic development of the text. Metaphors frequently consist of **gastronomic** terms, and many of Jesus' parables are connected with food. Two important culinary fantasies active in modern texts or imaginations are **Cockaigne** and **cannibalism**.

Naming is a simple way to convey something about a person. Biblical figures often have figurative names, many derived from food. Adam, the ancestor of all humankind, is made "from red clay," a soil good for growing certain crops. Adam is described in a close relationship to agriculture, and the moment he leaves paradise he starts farming: "So the Lord God drove him out of the garden of Eden to till the ground from which he had been taken". Names like Leah, Rachel, Rebecca, and Tamar express the qualities of the women bearing them. Leah, which means "wild cow", and Rachel, which means "mother sheep", become the mothers of the twelve tribes. Tamar, "date palm," is the name of a number of influential women from Genesis to Matthew. The women important to Israel are named after animals and plants fundamental to subsistence in the Near East, part of everyday experience, and available, tame, and reliable. They guarantee survival, and they provide milk, meat, and fruit. In contrast, women and men named after wild animals, often favorite game animals, do not play any important role in the history of Israel. Associated with sexual situations, their names indicate they are beautiful, elegant, charming, and erotic. Examples include Dishon which means "gazelle"; Hoglah, "partridge"; and Zipporah, "bird".

A person's character is revealed in his or her good behavior at table. A negative figure is usually depicted as lacking good table manners, such as eating and drinking too much, consuming **impure** food, choosing a wrong seat according to the hierarchy, and general **immoderateness**. Frequently such people are killed, and their bodies become food for the dogs. Good and ideal people eat and drink moderately. They are modest and **hospitable**, and they carefully choose their food and their company at table.

Feasts and fasts not only structure the year of the commuity and the life cycles of individuals, they also mark climaxes and happy events, for instance, when people meet after a long separation, on the occasion of a wedding, before people part for some time, and when a war is won. Plenty of food and drink is typical of every feast, often indicating that the story is over and everything went well. Hunger moves people from one place to another, as when Abraham moves to Egypt, when Jacob's family does the same, and when hunger brings David's pious ancestor Ruth to the family. Fasting marks turning points, as when the **sterile** Hannah prays, fasts, and finally conceives Samuel when the warriors fast before the decisive battle, they will win.

The **recurrent** combination of "milk and honey" can be called a biblical recurring theme and is one of the best-known biblical gastronomic metaphors. Milk and honey are highly valued products, symbols of the wealth of a country. The land God promised to Abraham and his children, usually identified with Canaan, "is a land flowing with milk and honey". The cup is a metaphor for life or death, and the cup of the **Eucharist** is the **culminating** point in the New Testament. Psalms 23 is the poetically outstanding citation of the metaphor for the relation between Israel and God, the shepherd and his herd.

Pictures of the other world are deeply rooted in worldly experiences, of which food and eating and drinking are most important. Good and evil, heaven and hell are described with abundance of excellent food and drink or with hunger, starvation, and cannibalism respectively. The Promised Land Canaan is expected to produce plenty of food, and paradise is the place without hunger. The Garden of Eden is described in contrast to the place where Adam must work hard to eat his bread. The garden is lost forever, but after death the good will be rewarded.

After You Read

Knowledge Focus

I. Pair Work: Discuss the following questions with your partner.
(1) Do you know any meanings of food in *the Bible*?
(2) Biblical figures often have figurative names derived from food. Would you please list some names and try to explain their meanings?
(3) How can a person's character be revealed in his or her behavior at table?
(4) How is food prepared in *the Bible*?
(5) Feast and fasts mark climax and happy event. Can you give any examples to illustrate this?
(6) Why do people long to live in the Promised Land, the Paradise or the Garden of Eden?

II. Solo Work: Tell whether the following statements are true or false according to the knowledge you have learned.
(1) The Promised Land Jerusalem is expected to produce plenty of food, and paradise is the place without hunger. ( )
(2) Milk and honey are highly valued products, symbols of the wealth of a country. ( )
(3) Feasts and plenty of food mark climaxes and happy events. ( )
(4) Hunger moves people from one place to another, as when Abraham moves to Egypt, and Joseph's family does the same. ( )
(5) Three bad table manners are eating and drinking too much, consuming impure food, and choosing a wrong seat according to the hierarchy. ( )
(6) The women important to Israel are named after wild animals and plants. ( )
(7) Ruth, which means "mother sheep," become the mothers of the twelve tribes. ( )
(8) Women and men named after wild animals, often favorite game animals, do not play any important role in the history of Israel. ( )
(9) Adam is described in a close relationship to agriculture. ( )
(10) Good and ideal people do not eat or drink at all. ( )

Language Focus

I. Build your vocabulary.

A. Write the correct word next to its definition.

| gastronomic | culinary | leaven | cauldron |
| cannibalism | hierarchy | grit | culminate |

(1) _____ the eating of human flesh by another human being
(2) _____ the adjective of gastronomy, of a style of cooking or eating.
(3) _____ a large kettle or boiler
(4) _____ any system of persons or things ranked one above another
(5) _____ of or relating to a kitchen or to cookery
(6) _____ to reach the highest point, summit, or highest development
(7) _____ coarsely ground grain
(8) _____ to add a rising agent to

B. Use the proper forms of the words to complete the sentences.

(1) Paavo Nurmi lit the Olympic flame in a _____ on the field.
(2) There are many fine shadings of status through the social _____.
(3) _____ studies various cultural components with food as its central axis.
(4) Although Sally pursued a career as an accountant, she has excellent _____ skills.
(5) Many _____ tribes believed that consuming one's enemy would allow them to obtain and absorb the spirit and skills of the victim.
(6) Corn and corn-based feeds and foods are of concern, including cornmeal and corn _____.
(7) This process should _____ in the introduction of the single currency by the end of the century.
(8) For seven days, let your food be _____ bread; from the first day, no leaven is to be seen in your houses.

II. Fill in the blanks with the proper forms of the words.

(1) Scientists have _____ (abundance) evidences to conclude that cars have a harmful effect on the environment.
(2) The company's guests at LG are entertained in the corporate _____ (hospitable) area.
(3) The writer's _____ (depict) of the horror of war won her a worldwide reputation.
(4) His wife divorced him after the _____ (reveal) that he was having an affair.
(5) In the English Speech Contest, Lizzy and Sarah came first and third _____ (respect).
(6) Because of the earthquake, millions of people face _____ (starve) unless a vast emergency aid programme is launched.
(7) Our new managing director has reorganized the company a bit, but nothing has _____ (fundament) changed.
(8) Due to the economic crisis, we need to cut down on our fuel _____ (consume) by having fewer cars on the road.
(9) _____ (figure) speaking, it was a blow right between the eyes.

(10) Resumption of the talks is _____ (indicate) of an improving relationship between the countries.

Comprehensive Work
I. Group Work

Form groups of three or four students. Please share the stories of the following women with your group members: Sarah, Delilah, Dinah, Esther, Hagar, Miriam, Bathsheba and Rebecca.

II. Pair-Work: Work with your partner and consider the following question.

Many eating customs in *the Bible* have been kept in the west. How are they kept on some important occasions?

III. Essay Writing

If you were what you eat, what are you? Food is at once the stuff of life and a potent symbol; it binds us to the earth, to our families, and to our cultures. The aroma of turkey roasting or the taste of green tea can be a portal to memories, while too many Big Macs can clog our arteries. The chef is an artist, yet those who pick oranges or process meat may be little more than slaves. In your essay, you may explore many of the fascinating issues that surround food as both material facts and personal and cultural symbol.

IV. Solo Work

1. Put in the missing words.

The story of Judith in the book of "Judith" exemplifies the meaning the Israelite society accorded to food. The behavior of the two protagonists presupposes their respective fates. Judith, the shining heroine who finally s_____ the Israelites from the Assyrian siege, always drunk the right things. She fasts except on religious feasts, she only eats pure food, and she is never point. On the other hand, Holofernes (荷罗孚尼), the commander in chief of the Assyrian army, is a glutton and drunkard who gives dinner parties every day. This is the starting p_____ for Judith's project to rescue her people. She goes to Holofernes's tent dressed in her best clothes and prettily adorned, but she sits a_____ her own table and consumes her own pure food, only pretending to be his guest. Holofernes is blinded by the beauty of the Israelite lady and does not realize she is not truly participating in his party. He eats and drinks u_____ he is so drunk that he is incapable of seducing her. When he falls asleep, Judith cuts his head o_____. Deprived of their leader, the Assyrians withdraw, and Judith is celebrated as the savior of the Israelites.

2. Proofreading and error correction.

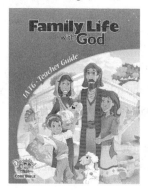

It is doubtful if families in Bible times had any meal comparable to our breakfast either for children or parents. If the father worked in the field, he would probably take a light lunch, as would children who tended herds or flocks. That a meal would include flat cakes or loaves, olives, figs, and curds or cheese from goats' milk. The young children would help to prepare an early dinner, the main daily meal. This mealtime was essentially a family occasion, and probably started in time to take advantage of whatever daylight remained. Conversation would continue into the evening by the light of small oil lamps. The evening meal would include bread or cakes from hand-grown grain, often barley, goats' cheese or curds, along with vegetables such as lentils, beans, peas and leeks. Although vegetables were not always available, they added variety to the meal when present. Salt, garlic, and possibly vinegar were used for flavoring. Wine, frequently well watered, was drunk with the meal.

(1) _____
(2) _____

Food was cooked in olive oil, with honey used as a sweetener. The problem with these meals, in other than wealthy families, was that they were extremely monotonous despite of the wife's cooking skills. However, the exhausted and hungry family members were probably more concerned with variety than with the fact that there was food on the table. Meat was rarely eaten except before a sacrifice, since at other times the animals were too valuable for the poor to consider slaughtering for food. The wealthy fared better in enjoying kid's (young goat) meat or venison, or a fatted calf for special feasts. Pheasants, turtledoves, quails, pigeons, and partridges were also eaten, and several varieties of fish were available.

(3) _____
(4) _____
(5) _____

Read More

Text B Food

Food and drink are everywhere in *the Bible*. Among the best-known scenes are the Last Supper, the feeding of the five thousand, the feast for the lost son, and the wine miracle in Cana from the New Testament and the first Pesach meal in Egypt; Abraham's sacrifice of Isaac, for whom a wild goat was **substituted**; the manna in the desert; and the recurring mention of the land flowing with milk and honey from the Old Testament. The function of food in *the Bible* is twofold. First, it offers information on what was produced and consumed in the area in biblical times, including how food was prepared and its meaning; second, it conveys messages to the reader.

Attitudes toward food in *the Bible*:

Scientific interest in food in *the Bible* always has focused on, among other things, sacrifice and **abominations**. The biblical sacrificial animal is rarely burnt entirely, as indicated in the descriptions

The feeding of the five thousand

of some specific sacrifices in Numbers 28 and 29 or Abraham's sacrifice. The majority of a sacrifice is consumed either by those who offer the sacrifice or by the priests. Each food offering (the meat) is accompanied by a grain offering (flour and olive oil) and a drink offering (preferably wine, but in some cases beer is acceptable). Sacrifices, usually offered at feasts, distribute precious animal protein evenly among the population and over time. A feast occurs on each new moon, and others follow in the middle of at least every second month.

The nature of the sacrifice follows the rules of purity described in Leviticus. No restrictions apply to the **consumption** of plants, but elaborate rules govern animal food. Animals are divided into three groups: animals on land, creatures in the water, and birds. Of these only a small sample are considered clean: "You may eat any animal which has a parted foot or a cloven hoof and also chews the cud; . . . all those that have fins and scales," and birds with two legs who fly and do not eat carcasses. The purity rules **conform** with the animals well adapted to the local climate and easily domesticated. Furthermore the food taboos keep the Israelites distinct from other peoples of the region, supporting their group identity. When Christianity starts to convert other peoples, the strict food rules become an obstacle and therefore are removed. According to Acts 10 it was revealed to Peter that nothing is unclean.

Meat is always in the foreground of biblical narratives on food, and it is the highly esteemed center of any festive meal, religious or secular. During their wanderings in the wilderness, the Israelites yearn for the flesh-pots of Egypt; in 1Samuel 2:12–17 the priests demand a piece of good roast from the sacrifice instead of being content with whatever their forks catch from the cauldron; it is a sign of honor to be fed a piece of meat by the host; and meat is essential to a covenant.

Nevertheless, the staples are cereals (barley, wheat, emmer, spelt, millet, and sorghum). Barley, the most important, is mainly consumed as grits (porridge); wheat is valued higher and is baked into bread. The highly valued fruits include olives for oil, which is easy to store, and dates, which provide energy. Vegetables (leek, orache, onion), pulses (fava bean, pea, lentil, chickpea), fruits (apple, fig, pomegranate, melon, mulberry, grape), and herbs and spices (cassia, cinnamon, coriander, cumin, dill, garlic, ginger, laurel, mint, mustard, saffron, turmeric) are abundant.

Questions for discussion or reflection.
(1) How many groups can animals be divided into?
(2) How much do you know about sacrifice from Text B?
(3) What is the role of meat in *the Bible*?

Text C Diet

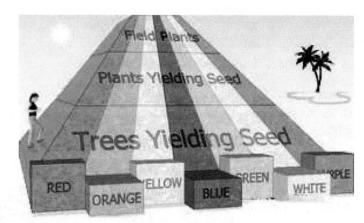

Four Bible Food Groups

1. Trees

2. Plants

3. Field plants

4. Clean meat

Bible foods and the pyramid:
　　The biblical diet pyramid displays the **proportional** relevance of the four food groups listed above. For a healthy and abundant life, those foods nearer the base merit more focus and consideration.
　　The Bible indicates that fruit, vegetables, nuts, whole grains and legumes are the foundation of a healthy diet. Herbs, exercise, water and sunshine are also essential for happiness. Safe, clean meat, by-products and vegetable oils are optional.
　　From Genesis to Revelation, food plays a vital role in the Biblical account. The forbidden fruit is elemental the fall of mankind from grace, and Jesus ate broiled fish when He appeared to His disciples after the Resurrection—evidence that He had indeed risen bodily from the dead.

Original food for man in the Bible:
　　In the beginning before man sinned, it was plants, seeds, cereals, legumes, fruits, nuts:
　　And God said, "Behold, I have given you every plant yielding seed which is upon the face of all the earth, and every tree with seed in its fruit; you shall have them for food." (Genesis 1:29)
　　The following explanation of Genesis 1:29 is given according to foods as we know them today:
　　Every plant yielding seed:
　　—Grains: wheat, corn, rye, barley, rice, oats, millet, etc.

—Seeds: sunflower, sesame, flax, pumpkin seeds, etc.
—Legumes: soybeans, lentils, peas, peanuts, other beans, etc.
—Vegetables: eggplant, okra, bell peppers, squash, green beans, pumpkins, cucumbers, tomatoes, melons, etc.
—Fruits: citrus fruits, sweet fruits, palm fruits, etc.
—Nuts: almonds, pecans, cashews, brazil, walnuts, etc.

So, God originally intended man to eat plants and fruits. And after the sin of Adam, green herbs were added and mankind lived extraordinarily long lives, 912 years on average, for over 1,700 years. Only after the drastic changes of a global flood and the addition of a meat-eating diet did man's life-span diminish.

And what was the original food for animals?

Originally it was "every green herb", "And to every beast of the earth, and to every fowl of the air, and to every thing that creepeth upon the earth, wherein there is life, I have given every green herb for meat: and it was so" (Genesis 1:30). So, Adam and Eve and the generations following, all the way up to Noah, were vegetarians and all the animals and birds and reptiles were green herb eaters.

Green herb is added for man:

Although vegetables (green herb) were not part of the Original Diet given to man, they were intended for animals, but they were added to man's diet after he sinned, and are part of his diet today.

After man sinned, he was driven out of the Garden of Eden, and no longer had access to the wonderful tree of life. Man had to gain his livelihood by tilling the earth, and the "herb of the field" (originally food for the animals) was added to his diet.

In Genesis 3:17–19 "And unto Adam He said... And you shall eat the herb of the field".

Herbs (vegetables):
Leaf: beet greens, brussels sprouts, cabbage, collard, etc.
Flower: globe artichoke, broccoli, cauliflower.
Root: carrots, beets, potatoes, turnips, etc.

When Daniel and his 3 friends were faced with a decision not unlike ours today, they chose a diet with just vegetables and water. And "At the end of the ten days they looked healthier and better nourished than any of the young men who ate the royal food." King Nebuchadnezzar's choice food was very similar to the Standard American Diet (SAD), with plenty of meat, fish, eggs... and Daniel an his friends, Hananiah, Mishael, and Azariah, were found even ten times better in matters of wisdom and understanding.

Meat and fish is added for man:

After the Flood, in Genesis 9:3 "Every moving thing that lives shall be food for you. I have given you all things, even as the green herbs. But you shall not eat flesh with its life, that is, its blood."

At the time of the flood, the earth's soil and climate was dramatically altered. In many places on earth it would not be possible to obtain enough food from plant sources during all times of the year. It was at this time that God gave man permission to each animal flesh... "every moving thing"! Animals, birds, fish, reptiles, insects...

Yet even in this God gave instruction that the blood must be drained from the carcass before eating it.

Milk and honey:

The Bible speaks pretty well about Milk and Honey:

"...and I have come down to deliver them out of the hand of the Egyptians, and to bring them up out of that land to a good and broad land, a land flowing with milk and honey".

God's idea of the ideal land is one with milk (**protein**) and honey (**carbohydrates**)! Anyone who calls you to a diet that curses honey and milk is a Bible heretic.

Moderation... no gluttony:

"The glutton shall come to poverty... and put a knife to your throat if you are given to gluttony." (Proverbs 23:2, 20)

"Let your moderation be known unto all men. The Lord is at hand". (Philippians 4:5)

Weight Watchers has simply applied this Bible principle to their program. Food did not make people fat—people's sin made them fat! They have to confess their sin of gluttony and be now ready to start giving that fat back to God.

Questions for discussion or reflection.

(1) What food can people eat according to Genesis in Text C?

(2) Can you get any implications on how to eat from Text C?

Notes

(1) **Cockaigne or Cockayne:** Cockaigne or Cockayne is a medieval mythical land of plenty, an imaginary place of extreme luxury and ease where physical comforts and pleasures are always immediately at hand and where the harshness of medieval peasant life does not exist. Specifically, in poems like The Land of Cockaigne, Cockaigne is a land of contraries, where all the restrictions of society are defied (abbots beaten by their monks), sexual liberty is open (nuns flipped over to show their bottoms), and food is plentiful (skies that rain cheeses). Writing about Cockaigne was a commonplace of Goliard verse. It represented both wish fulfillment and resentment at the structures of asceticism and dearth.

(2) **Judith:** It is the fourth book of the *Old Testament* Apocrypha in those versions of *the Bible* following the Greek Septuagint (generally Roman Catholic and Orthodox versions). Judith is included with the Apocrypha in the King James Version; it does not appear in the *Hebrew Bible*.

For Fun

Book to Read

Read *the Bible*:

(1) The first Pesach meal in Egypt (Exodus 12:1-13, 12:16).

(2) Abraham's sacrifice of Isaac (Genesis 22:1-19).

(3) Ten banquets in the Book of Esther: 7:1-10; 8:17; 9:17; 9:18-32.

Unit 2 Food and the Bible

Movie to See
The Revolutionary Life of Jesus Christ (1998)

The miracles and teachings of Jesus Christ are further highlighted in the second part of video series *The Life of Jesus the Revolutionary*. This Christian produced feature stars John Kay Steel as Jesus of Nazereth, and focuses on the various miraculous feats achieved during his short life, including healing the sick, giving sight to the blind, and casting out demons.

Song to Enjoy

Here is part of the lyrics of "The Last Supper". Find the audio and enjoy the song. You can complete the lyrics while listening.

The Last Supper
by Grave Digger

Well done my friend, thanks for the offer
We'll catch him at night to end this game
Take these thirty dimes in a coffer
Meet us at midnight, please hold the flame

Believe my days are counted
I feel the evil breath
The liar sits right by my side
His eyes are full of fear and pride

It's my last supper
After this I will die
It's my last supper
My own sacrifice

Welcome my friends, come celebrate with me
You are invited to take a place
Feast and drink as much as you will
Before they start the race of death

Believe my days are counted
I feel the evil breath
The liar sits right by my side
His eyes are full of fear and pride

It's my last supper
After this I will die
It's my last supper
My own sacrifice

My end is near

21

Come pray with me
My fortune is over
But love can be

Whenever I die
Please let me fly
Remember me
And love can be

Believe my days are counted
I feel the evil breath
The liar sits right by my side
His eyes are full of fear and pride

....

Unit 3
Family Life and *the Bible*

> In family life, love is the oil that erases friction, the cement that binds closer together, and the music that brings harmony.
> —Eva Burrows

Unit Goals

- To gain a general knowledge of family in *the Bible*
- To develop a right attitude towards family in *the Bible*
- To learn some basic cultural concepts concerning family in *the Bible*
- To learn useful words and expressions about family in *the Bible*
- To improve English language skills and western culture awareness

Before You Read

I. Are you familiar with the family problems in *the Bible*? Please try to identify the following pictures.

   1. Jacob and Esau   2. Hagar and Ishmael
   3. Joseph and his brothers   4. Cain and Abel

     A   B   C   D

II. Form groups of three or four students. Try to find, on the Internet or in the library, more information about the family life of Abraham and Jacob in *the Bible*. Get ready for a 5-minute presentation in class.

Start to Read

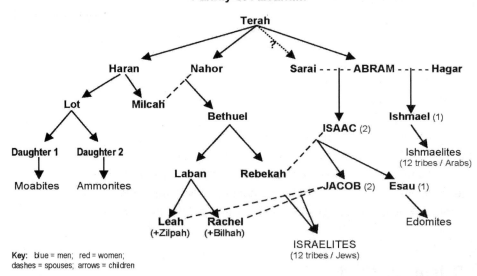

Family of Abraham

Key: blue = men; red = women; dashes = spouses; arrows = children

Throughout human history, the family has been the foundation of society. Within a strong, well-functioning family, we can fulfill our physical and emotional needs. Strong family ties provide us the love and security we need for a happy life. Children grow into well-adjusted adults through example, instruction and discipline. Chores and responsibilities are shared for the good of all.

The family of biblical times had the husband as "lord" of the household and the wife as his helper. The husband worked diligently to provide material needs and protection while the wife worked **diligently** at domestic chores. In these *New Testament* passages, the need for a strong, healthy marriage is expressed in terms of the idealized family of the ancient world:

> Wives, in the same way be **submissive** to your husbands so that, if any of them do not believe the word, they may be won over without words by the behavior of their wives, when they see the purity and **reverence** of your lives. Your beauty should not come from outward **adornment**, such as **braided** hair and the wearing of gold jewelry and fine clothes. Instead, it should be that of your inner self, the **unfading** beauty of a gentle and quiet spirit, which is of great worth in God's sight. Husbands, in the same way be considerate as you live with your wives, and treat them with respect as the weaker partner and as heirs with you of the gracious gift of life, so that nothing will hinder your prayers. (NIV, 1 Peter 3: 1–4, 7)

Contemporary marriages may follow the biblical model or may be quite different. **Regardless** of how we divide the roles and responsibilities in our marriages, we must be sure the marriage fulfills its essential family functions and provides a loving environment for children to grow into responsible adults.

Unselfish love is the "glue" that holds families together. In marriage we must subdue our own egos and selfish pride for the sake of the family. The Apostle Paul states it eloquently in this passage from First Corinthians:

Love is patient, love is kind, and is not jealous; love does not brag and is not arrogant, does not act unbecomingly; it does not seek its own, is not provoked, does not take into account a wrong suffered, does not rejoice in unrighteousness, but rejoices with the truth; bears all things, believes all things, hopes all things, endures all things. (NAS, 1 Corinthians 13:4–7)

Divorce is a genuine tragedy. It often leaves the marriage partners **embittered** and **disillusioned**. It robs the children of the love and security of a healthy family and denies them a good role model for their own future marriages.

We need to make an effort each and every day to keep our marriages strong and not let them drift toward divorce. We must put aside our anger, forgive our spouse a million times over, always be faithful, subdue our own pride and ego, and always let love guide our actions.

In the Old Testament Law, a man was allowed to divorce his wife if he found something **indecent** about her. (Wives did not have the same privilege.) Jesus saw the **injustice** and pain of divorce, and said that neither husband nor wife should separate from the other.

Unfortunately, some marriages cannot and should not be saved. A **viable** marriage is a contract of mutual love and respect, as reiterated in Ephesians:

However, each one of you also must love his wife as he loves himself, and the wife must respect her husband. (NIV, Ephesians 5:33)

When one partner seriously violates the marriage contract, as by emotional, physical or sexual abuse, the marriage cannot endure. None of us should feel obligated to endure an **abusive** relationship.

After You Read

Knowledge Focus
I. Pair Work: Discuss the following questions with your partner.
   (1) What roles do husband and wife play in the family according to *the Bible*?
   (2) What is the relationship between husband and wife?
   (3) How do you understand the passage of love by Paul?
   (4) Does *the Bible* allow man to divorce his wife?
   (5) Who should provide family income and who should care for the home?

II. Solo Work: Tell whether the following statements are true or false according to the knowledge you learned.
   (1) Both the man and the woman can get divorced if they are not satisfied with their marriage. (   )
   (2) Inner self is valued instead of outer ornament.   (   )

(3) In order to maintain our marriage, we each have to lessen our pride. ( )
(4) A broken marriage fails to give children a good role model for their own future marriages. ( )
(5) Wives must be obedient to their husbands in everything. ( )

Language Focus

I. Build your vocabulary.

A. Write the correct word next to its definition.

submissive	reverence	unrighteousness	
subdue	eloquent	brag	adornment

(1) _____ failure to adhere to moral principles
(2) _____ to show off
(3) _____ a profound emotion inspired by a deity
(4) _____ inclined or willing to submit to orders
(5) _____ a decoration of color or interest that is added to relieve plainness
(6) _____ to overcome, bring under control
(7) _____ expressing yourself readily, clearly, effectively

B. Use the proper forms of the words to complete the sentences.

(1) He criticized the school for trying to _____ individual expression.
(2) In the decoration in the study a few artwork, handicraft can rise to _____ action.
(3) These students have _____ for their teacher.
(4) Their early training programs them to be obedient and _____.
(5) These concepts are more _____ explained in much greater detail by Cliff Hall in the framework documentation.
(6) She _____ that she could run faster than I.
(7) If you have not been faithful in the use of _____ wealth, who will entrust the true riches to you?

II. Fill in the blanks with the proper forms of the words.

(1) It was the custom that men _____ (braid) their hair only after they married.
(2) They stand ready to fill the empty chairs left by the exhausted and _____ (embitter) old guard.
(3) The Puritans were _____ (disillusion) soon after they came to the new colony.
(4) But if anyone thinks that he is behaving _____ (unbecoming) to his virgin daughter, if she is past the bloom of youth and thus it must be so, let him do what he wishes, he does not sin; let them marry.
(5) It is not possible because the biology of the form holds in place the very violence and _____ (abusive) that plagues mankind.
(6) Instead, it should be that of your inner self, the _____ (fade) beauty of a gentle and quiet spirit, which is of great worth in God's sight.
(7) He is always welcomed because he dresses well and behaves gracefully, _____ (considerate) and politely, giving other a good impression.
(8) The husband will not have his wife talking _____ (indecent) before their children.

Comprehensive Work

I. Group work: Work in group of four and share ideas with your group members.

1. What are the duties of the husband, wife, parents, and children?
2. How important are love and commitment in marriage?
3. Who should exercise authority as head in the home?
4. Unselfish love is the "glue" that holds families together. Please examine your family life and share your understanding of this with your partner.
5. How should family members treat one another according to *the Bible*?

II. Essay Writing

1. **Please read the following paragraph from *the Bible* and design an action formula for strengthening your family.**

   Ephesians 6:1-4, "Children, obey your parents in the Lord: for this is right. Honour thy father and mother; which is the first commandment with promise. That it may be well with you and you may live long on the earth. Fathers, provoke not your children to wrath: but bring them up in the nurture and admonition of the Lord."

2. **What's your understanding of the following quotation? Write an essay to air your point of view.**

   Your family and your love must be cultivated like a garden. Time, effort, and imagination must be summoned constantly to keep any relationship flourishing and growing.

   —Jim Rohn

III. Solo Work

1. Put in the missing words.

   Children should be taught right habits: personal cleanliness, to eat what is set before them, to come when c_____, to listen to instructions, to answer respectfully his parents, and to perform routine family chores.

   You can punish your children in LOVE! Punishment should never be only negative, but always be accompanied by p_____ teaching. Negative punishment is a sin; it provokes your children to wrath.

   The greatest key to learning is discipline. Teach your child to listen to your instructions. Such self-discipline is the k_____ to success in life.

   Children should be t_____ together, the husband and wife working as a unified t_____. If one parent is missing, action should be taken to expose the child to responsible adults of his or her own sex.

2. Proofreading and error correction.

    When a child is born, two or three local musicians are usually waiting outside to know if the new arrival is a boy or a girl. If the former, they immediately beat the drum, and play upon whatever instruments they have, accompanying the din with improvised rhymes complimentary to the dignity of the family, and prophetic of the career lies before the son and heir. But the moment they learn from the silence and sad looks of the visitors that a daughter has been thrust upon the family, the drum is shouldered, and the musicians walk away. Music at such a time would be an unpaid affront. The grandmother sometimes refuses to visit daughter who has thus brought discredit on the family. When natural affection and financial interest pull in opposite directions, victory too often goes to the later. But God's ink does not lose color although it is applied to such poor paper, and in spite of this disappointment at the beginning, the little daughter's claims to family love are soon more full recognized.

(1) _____

(2) _____

(3) _____

(4) _____

(5) _____

    The idea of the Eastern family as a business syndicate, as much as a sanctuary of affection, is expressed in the Koran, which said, "Wealth and sons are the ornaments of life." Thus also in Psalm 127:3-5, the family circle is compared to a quiver, and the sons are arrows ready for service. Their father can command attention in the council of the elders at the city gate.

Read More

Text B Parents and Children

    The single most important function of the family is the raising of children. The family provides for the physical needs of children and teaches them how to grow into well-adjusted, responsible adults.

    Schools can teach the knowledge and skills needed to earn a livelihood, but children learn their values primarily from the example and teaching of their parents. As parents we must both practice and preach our values.

    Of course, the parents' instruction does no good if the child rejects it. Our parents may not be perfect, but they have loved and cared for us, and they deserve our respect. *The Bible* advises children to honor and obey their parents:

Children, obey your parents; this is the right thing to do because God has placed them in authority over you. Honor your father and mother. This is the first of God's **Ten Commandments** *that ends with a promise. And this is the promise: that if you honor your father and mother, yours will be a long life, full of blessing. (TLB, Ephesians 6:1–3)*

Listen to your father's advice and don't despise an old mother's experience. Get the facts at any price, and hold on tightly to all the good sense you can get. The father of a godly man has cause for joy—what pleasure a wise son is! So give your parents joy! (TLB, Proverbs 23:22–24)

In addition to instruction and a good example, children need discipline to grow into responsible adults. Through discipline, children learn the consequences of their actions and learn to control their behavior:

Discipline your son and he will give you happiness and peace of mind. (TLB, Proverbs 29:17)

Teach a child to choose the right path, and when he is older, he will remain upon it. (TLB, Proverbs 22:6)

The verse above and a few similar ones are sometimes used to justify a harsh parenting style based on corporal punishment. However, the dominant theme of *the Bible* is not to beat one's children, but rather to "teach a child to choose the right path" through instruction and discipline. Beating with a rod is an example of how discipline may have been practiced in Old Testament times. Unfortunately, beating and spanking embitter the child and teach him or her to control others by physical force. The child may change his or her behavior out of fear but does not learn self-control.

Fortunately, modern parenting methods offer us a better alternative. The methods of natural and logical consequences teach self-control and values without causing bitterness between parent and child. In New Testament times, the harsh Old Testament teachings about discipline are replaced with verses such as these:

Fathers, do not embitter your children, or they will become discouraged. (NIV, Colossians 3:21)

And now a word to you parents. Don't keep on scolding and nagging your children, making them angry and resentful. Rather, bring them up with the loving discipline the Lord himself approves, with suggestions and godly advice. (TLB, Ephesians 6:4)

A strong and supportive family bonds husband and wife in a union of love and mutual respect. It is our refuge from the pressures and disappointments of the world and is the instrument for giving our children the things they need most: protection, love, training and discipline. The more we cultivate strong family ties, the more fulfilling our lives will be.

Questions for discussion or reflection.

(1) What is the significance of listing "Honor your father and your mother" in Ten Commandments?

(2) How do you understand the following words about family life?

And now a word to you parents. Don't keep on scolding and nagging your children, making them angry and resentful. Rather, bring them up with the loving discipline the Lord himself approves, with suggestions and godly advice. (TLB, Ephesians 6:4)

Text C How to Strengthen Your Family Ties

The challenge of strengthening family life depends upon gaining knowledge about strong, healthy families. We might ask what we can learn from strong, healthy families that can be applied to our own family. Studies have demonstrated that strong families are characterized by four qualities.

Number one is the expression of appreciation. We like to be around people who show us appreciation. However, we often fail to express appreciation to our spouses and children. One study showed that only 20 percent of a family's time was spent in having fun or saying nice things to each other. To change this, a family must begin to look for each other's strengths. Try best not to miss an opportunity to give each other a sincere compliment. It is important to let others know, "You are important to me I care about you . . . You have many contributions to offer to the world".

An outstanding example of the expression of appreciation is found in the **Apostle** Paul's letter to the Thessalonians. The first chapter of Thessalonians is a hymn of praise and thanksgiving for the faith, love and **steadfastness** of the **Thessalonians**. Paul certainly expressed his appreciation for these members of the family of God.

Second, an outstanding characteristic of strong families is the great amount of time they spend together. They work and play together. They enjoy being together, even if they are not doing anything in particular. Life today has become very much a "rat race". Family living can be improved by not allowing our lives to become overly **fragmented**. Strong families intentionally cut down on the number of outside activities and involvements in order to minimize fragmentation of their family life. When you find yourself becoming so busy that you are not spending time with your family, it is time to look at what you're doing that's taking you away from your family. You may find that some of those involvements are not so important after all. Try to keep you family "number one" in terms of how you spend your time.

Third, strong families spend a lot of time in family discussion and in talking out problems as they come up. There are quarrels in every family, but by getting things out in the open and talking about them, the problem can usually be identified and the best alternative for resolving the conflict can be chosen.

Successful marriage and family relationships are characterized by positive, open channels of communication. It is not just communication perse which contributes to the strength of a family, but communication of a positive nature, marked by a frequent expression of appreciation toward each other.

Christianity emphasizes values such as commitment, respect, and responsibilities for the needs and welfare of others. These values contribute to good interpersonal and family relationships.

Commitment is the fourth quality of a strong family. A strong family is committed to helping and making each other happy. Their actions are geared toward promoting each other's welfare. Time and energy are invested in the family. Individual goals are frequently sacrificed for the welfare of the family.

Questions for discussion or reflection.
(1) What are the qualities of strong families?
(2) Do you think quarreling is a way of communication?

Notes

A rat race: It is a term used for an endless, self-defeating or pointless pursuit. It conjures up the image of the futile efforts of a lab rat trying to escape whilst running around a maze or in a wheel. In an analogy to the modern city, many rats in a single maze expend a lot of effort running around, but ultimately achieve nothing (meaningful) either collectively or individually.

The rat race: It is a term often used to describe work, particularly excessive work; in general terms, if one works too much, one is **in the rat race**. This terminology contains implications that many people see work as a seemingly endless pursuit with little reward or purpose. Not all workers feel like this. It is the perceived Conventional Wisdom, for example, that those who work for themselves are generally happier at work.

For Fun

Book to Read

East of Eden was written by American writer John Steinbeck (1912—1968) in 1952. Steinbeck's inspiration for the novel comes from the fourth chapter of Genesis, verses one through sixteen, which recounts the story of Cain and Abel. The title, ***East of Eden***, was chosen by Steinbeck from Genesis, Chapter 4, verse 16: "And Cain went out from the presence of the Lord, and dwelt in the land of Nod, on the east of Eden".

Steinbeck's allusion to Cain and Abel is furthered by the naming of the Trask family; the first letters of the names of the brothers are in match throughout the generations (Charles and Adam, Caleb and Aaron).

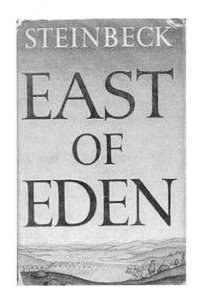

Movie to See
Abraham—One Man, One God

This 50-minute video tells all about the life and enduring faith of Abraham. Learn why Christians, Jews and others revere the purity of Abraham's belief that God is always loving and would always stand by him. Scholars are interviewed who have spent their professional lives searching for proof that Abraham truly existed. They discuss what they have learned from the 1,500 cuneiform tablets discovered at the ancient city of Ebla. The narrator repeats the basic Old Testament story in which Abraham was asked to sacrifice his son. Viewers will hear many things that can help them decide whether they fully believe that it was Abraham's covenant with God that led to the birth of Israel.

Song to Enjoy

Here is part of the lyrics of "A Family Is What You Make It". Find the audio and enjoy the song. You can complete the lyrics while listening.

A Family Is What You Make It
by Jim Rule

I used to believe that a family
Was a mom, and a dad, and 2.3 kids,
and a great big station wagon or a mini van
And a house and a dog and a cat.
But now that I've seen lots of families,
I know it's not always like that.

Chorus:
Because a family is what you make it.
It's you and your loved ones, whoever they are.
You've got to give and take it.
With understanding and love, your family's gonna go far.
With understanding and love, your family's gonna go far.

I used to believe I was normal
Now I don't know what that means.
'Cause if your family keeps you cozy and warm all right

and fits you like a pair of your favorite jeans
That's what's important. That makes it right,
Snug as a bug on a cold winter's night.
Someone to love you and someone to fight
for your right to be just who you are.
With understanding and love, your family's gonna go far.
With understanding and love, your family's gonna go far.
....

Unit 4

Marriage and *the Bible*

> In the end, of course, like the sea to a sandcastle, time sweeps over marriage, whether through death or betrayal. The bit of respite marriage affords is, however, all the Eden one needs for happiness.
>
> —Proverb

Unit Goals

- To gain a general knowledge of marriage in *the Bible*
- To develop a right attitude towards marriage in *the Bible*
- To learn some basic cultural concepts concerning marriage in t*he Bible*
- To learn useful words and expressions about marriage in *the Bible*
- To improve English language skills and western culture awareness

Before You Read

I. You can use the Internet and other resources to learn more about the wedding customs in America and China. Then finish the following exercises.

1. Match the western wedding customs with their meanings.

    (1) the white dress   A. perfection and never-ending love
    (2) the wedding ring   B. purity
    (3) something old   C. optimism and hope for the bride's new life ahead
    (4) something new   D. continuity with the bride's family and the past
    (5) something borrowed   E. love, modesty, and fidelity
    (6) something blue   F. an item from a happily married friend or family member, whose good fortune in marriage is supposed to carry over to the new bride
    (7) a silver sixpence
         G. wealth and financial security

2. Match Chinese wedding customs with their meanings.

    (1) Proposing   A. 迎亲
    (2) Birthday matching   B. 纳征
    (3) Presenting betrothal gifts   C. 请期
    (4) Presenting wedding gifts   D. 问名
    (5) Selecting the wedding date   E 纳吉
    (6) Wedding ceremony   F. 纳彩

II. Form groups of three or four students. Try to find, on the Internet or in the library, more information about the following wedding types. Get ready for a 5-minute presentation in class.

1. weekend wedding
2. white wedding
3. military wedding
4. civil wedding
5. sneak wedding
6. same-sex wedding
7. destination wedding

Start to Read

Text A Types of Marriages

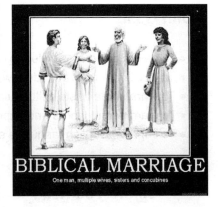

We have found eight types of marriages mentioned in *the Bible*: The standard nuclear family describes how a man leaves his family of origin, joins with a woman, **consummates** the marriage and lives as a couple. There were quite a few differences between the customs and laws of contemporary North Americans and of ancient Israelites. In ancient Israel, inter-faith marriages were theoretically forbidden. However, they were sometimes formed.

Children of inter-faith marriages were considered illegitimate. Marriages were generally arranged by family or friends; they did not result from a gradually evolving, loving relationship that developed during a period of courtship.

Polygynous marriage: A man would leave his family of origin and join with his first wife. Then, as finances allowed, he would marry as many additional women as he desired. The new wives would join the man and his other wives in an already established household. **Polygyny** was practiced by members of the Church of Jesus Christ of Latter-day Saints until it was suspended in the late 19th century. It is still practiced by separated **fundamentalist Mormon** groups.

Levirate Marriage: The name of this type of marriage is derived from the Latin word "levir," which means "brother-in-law". This involved a woman who was widowed without having borne a son. She would be required to leave her home, marry her brother-in-law, live with him, and engage in sexual relations. Their first-born son was considered to be sired by the deceased husband.

A man, a woman and her property—a female slave: As described in Genesis 16, Sarah and Abram were **infertile**. Sarah owned Hagar, a female slave who apparently had been purchased earlier in Egypt. Because Hagar was Sarah's property, she could dispose of her as she wished. Sarah gave Hagar to Abram as a type of wife, so that Abram would have an heir. **Presumably**, the arrangement to marry and engage in sexual activity was done without the consent of Hagar. Hagar conceived and bore a son, Ishmael. This type of marriage had some points of similarity to polygamous marriage, as described above. However, Hagar's status as a human slave in a plural marriage with two free individuals makes it sufficiently different to warrant separate treatment here.

A man, one or more wives, and some concubines: A man could keep numerous **concubines**, in addition to one or more wives. These women held an even lower status than a wife. As implied in

Genesis 21:10, a concubine could be dismissed when no longer wanted. According to Smith's *Bible Dictionary*, "A concubine would generally be either (1) a Hebrew girl bought...[from] her father; (2) a **Gentile** captive taken in war; (3) a foreign slave bought; or (4) a Canaanitish woman, bond or free." They would probably be brought into an already-established household. Abraham had two concubines; Jacob: 1; Saul: 1; David: at least 10 and Solomon: 300!

A male soldier and a female prisoner of war: Numbers 31:1–18 describes how the army of the ancient Israelites killed every adult Midianite male in battle. Moses then ordered the slaughter in cold blood of most of the captives. Only the lives of 32,000 women—all virgins—were spared. Some of the latter were given to the priests as slaves. Most were taken by the Israeli soldiers as captives of war.

A male rapist and his victim: Deuteronomy 22:28–29 requires that a female virgin who is not engaged to be married and who has been raped must marry her attacker, no matter what her feelings were towards the rapist. A man could become married by simply sexually attacking a woman that appealed to him, and paying his father-in-law 50 shekels of silver. There is one disadvantage of this approach: he was not allowed to subsequently divorce her.

A male and female slave: Exodus 21:4 indicates that a slave owner could assign one of his female slaves to one of his male slaves as a wife. There is no indication that women were consulted during this type of transaction. The arrangement would probably involve rape in most cases. In the times of the Hebrew Scriptures, Israelite women who were sold into slavery by their fathers were slaves forever. Men, and women who became slaves by another route, were limited to serving as slaves for seven years. When a male slave left his owner, the marriage would normally be terminated; his wife would stay behind, with any children that she had. He could elect to stay a slave if he wished.

After You Read

Knowledge Focus

I. Pair Work: Discuss the following questions with your partner.

(1) How many types of marriages can be found according to *the Bible*?
(2) What is the meaning of "levirate marriage"? Can you give an example in *the Bible*?
(3) What is the relationship between Sarah and Hagar? How about the status of *Hagar*?
(4) What is the meaning of "concubine" according to Smith's *Bible Dictionary*?
(5) Why does a male rapist marry his victim? Please tell the story of "The Rape of Dinah" in Genesis 34.

II. Solo Work: According to the marriage types mentioned above, write T if the statement is true and F if it is false.

(1) A female who became a slave not sold by her father, was limited to serving as slaves for seven years. ( )
(2) The marriage between Hagar and Abram belongs to polygamous marriage. ( )
(3) A male rapist must marry his victim and can never divorce her. ( )
(4) All female prisoners of war were given to their owners as wives according to the passage. ( )
(5) All these eight types of marriages reveal the lower social status of women. ( )

Language Focus

I. Build your vocabulary.

A. Write the correct word next to its definition.

| consensual | dismiss | perpetrator | sire |
| transaction | dispose | infertile | pare |

(1) _____ someone who has committed a crime, or a harmful act
(2) _____ to get rid of someone or something
(3) _____ the act of transacting within or between groups
(4) _____ with the willing agreement of all the people involved
(5) _____ to become the father of a child
(6) _____ to cut away the outer layer from something
(7) _____ no longer productive
(8) _____ to formally ask or order someone to leave

B. Use the proper forms of the words to complete the sentences.

(1) We need to monitor the _____ of smaller deals.
(2) It took a mere five minutes for the world champion to _____ of his opponent.
(3) The _____ of the massacre must be brought to justice as war criminals.
(4) The woman alleged rape, but Reeves insisted it was _____.
(5) At the age of 70, he married a much younger woman and went on to _____ two more children.
(6) Apple _____ contests are held in several communities.
(7) Since the birth of Louise Brown, assisted-reproduction technologies have made remarkable progress in helping _____ women and men become parents.
(8) The defending lawyer asked that the charge against his client _____.

II. Fill in the blanks with the proper forms of the words.

(1) A huge supply of knowledge is at your _____ (dispose) at the library.
(2) In Britain, half of all violent crime is _____ (perpetrator) by people who have been drinking alcohol.
(3) Frankly speaking, Andy is more of an angler _____ (theory) than practically.
(4) After the _____ (dismiss) of the cook, we had to make our meals ourselves.
(5) Children who are _____ (legitimate) can nevertheless inherit from their parents.
(6) He will _____ (presume) resign in view of the complete failure of his policy.
(7) We have discussed these plans on _____ (number) occasions.
(8) There are few _____ (indicate) that the economy is on an upswing.
(9) It is _____ (conceive) that knowledge plays an important role in our life.
(10) Animals bred in _____ (captive) would probably not survive if they were released into the wild.

Comprehensive Work

I. Group Work: Form groups of three or four students. Please retell the stories of the following pictures to your group members. Then identify their marriage patterns according to Text A.

Abraham and his wives **Judah and Tamar** **David and his wives**

II. Essay Writing

In the Genesis account, God created human being male and female, and intended them for relationship with each other. Marriage creates a tie so close it transforms the married couple into "one flesh" (Genesis 2:24), each other's closest human bond. The influence of Genesis on Jewish and Christian traditions of marriage is apparent in the wedding ceremonies of many Jews and Christians. Please write about the different marriage customs of the Jewish and the Christian.

III. Solo Work

1. Put in the missing words.

In virtually all religions, marriage is a life-long u_____ between two or more people and is established with ceremonies and rituals. The people are most commonly one man and one woman, though some religions have p_____ polygamous marriages and some faiths and denominations recognize same-sex marriages. In marriage, Christians see a picture of the relationship between Jesus Christ and His Church. In Judaism, marriage is so important that remaining u_____ is deemed unnatural. Islam also recommends marriage highly among other things. It helps i_____ the pursuit of spiritual perfection. Marriage is also seen as a foundation of the structure of society, and considers it both a physical and social bond that endures into the afterlife. Hinduism sees marriage as a sacred duty that entails both religious and s_____ obligations.

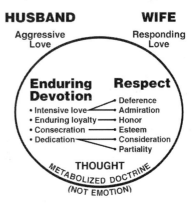

2. Proofreading and error correction.

Seal, Cord, and Staff

Three insignia (标记) are often found in Ugaritic (乌加里特人的) literature. The seal, cord, and staff are the insignia of a prominent man in Babylon as well as Canaan and Israel. "The signet ring or cylinder seal is used to sign contracts; the staff has markings carved on it which are particular to the owner." The seal was carried on a cord around the neck and used by rolling it on a soft clay document. The insignia are very valuable to their owner.

Tamar requires pledge of Judah because he is a stranger. With his signet ring or seal and staff, it is possible for her to identify with certainty the father of her child. While probably having little object value, the pledge is invaluable to her in this sense. Verses 20 to 23 function to explain how the three insignia remain in Tamar's possession like she had intended. When the recognition of his tokens reveal Tamar to be the prostitute, Judah acknowledges her as the mother of his offspring. "...her position in society is regular. She now becomes a true member of the patriarchal clan." She must wait until the last moment, however, and as is obvious from the narrative takes great personal risk.

(1) _____
(2) _____
(3) _____
(4) _____
(5) _____

Read More

Text B Jewish Wedding

The Jewish wedding is a Jewish religious marriage ceremony. A marriage once consisted of two distinct events—the **betrothal** and the actual act of marriage. Both are performed in the presence of a minimum of two witnesses.

1. Betrothal

In biblical times, a woman was legally regarded simply as property, and the betrothal was **effected** simply by purchasing her from her father. The girl's consent is not explicitly required by any biblical law; neither however, is there explicit permission to ignore it. *The Bible*, doubtless on the basis of ordinary human

affection, on one occasion portrays a parent as giving their daughter some choice in the matter; but the arrangements about the marriage, and especially about the purchase price, were made with her father.

The price paid for the woman is known by the Hebrew term *mohar*. *The Bible* gives very little indication of the usual range of value for a *mohar*. In the Deuteronomic Code, the only value given is that for a woman with whom the groom has already had sexual intercourse, namely a *mohar* of silver

worth fifty shekels. However, biblical narratives indicate that it could also take the form of personal service, as with the description of Jacob's service to Laban, or by prowess in war, as with the description of David's exchange of a hundred foreskins (each representing a slaughtered enemy) to obtain Michal in marriage.

2. Wedding preparations

It is customary in some areas to have a feast in honour of the bride's and groom's parents (in addition to the week-long period of feasting in honour of the marriage). This feast occurs before the marriage; specifically, on the day before the *shabbat* before the marriage (in other words, the preceding Friday), or on the *shabbat* before that. This additional feast was called *spinnholz* (meaning spindle).

3. Timing of the wedding

In the classical era, it was considered preferable for virgins to be married on a Wednesday, and widows on a Thursday; later the traditional time for widows came to be Friday afternoon. This custom is still practiced in parts of the East, and in the Caucasus a bride is always married on a Wednesday. The bride and groom wore special clothing during the act of marriage. The exact nature of this clothing isn't specified, and subsequent Jewish traditions vary substantially. The biblical account of the marriage of Isaac and of Jacob, and Jeremiah, imply that when a bride was in the presence of her groom, she was covered in some way. This lasted from the period before the marriage, until the marriage procession had taken her to the groom's house. The bride has a ritual bath up to two days before the wedding, typically during the night. In a few traditions, the groom also ritually bathes, or has an ordinary bath, before the wedding.

4. The Act of Marriage

The biblical portrayal of the marriages of Isaac and of Samson suggests that marriage could occur at any point after the betrothal, including immediately afterwards, whenever the groom desires; the betrothal, after all, is merely a purchase.

(1) Companions and Guests

The account of Samson's marriage, in the "Book of Judges", suggests that the groom was accompanied in the procession by his friends. Similarly, a psalm suggests that the bride was accompanied by her friends.

(2) The marriage procession

A feast was sometimes held before the groom's procession began, at which the procession's participants would gather; in other cases he would be led by the community elders, or the wise men. The procession also includes some customs: lighting, breaking the glass, music and dance, and fertility symbolism.

(3) Formal marriage ceremony

In most parts of *the Bible*, there is no mention of a formal marriage ceremony. However, in the Book of Tobit (which is not regarded as valid by Judaism), there is mention of a marriage contract. In this book's account of Tobias' marriage, once the marriage contract has been signed, the bride's room is prepared for the **consummation** of the marriage, which implies that signing the contract constituted an act of marriage. The wedding ceremony includes choosing the location of the ceremony, signing of the marriage contract, unveiling of the bride, giving the wedding blessings and so on.

(4) The feasting

In the biblical account of Jacob's marriage, and in that of Samson's, the celebration of the marriage is implied to last for a week. In later Judaism, the standard duration for marriage feasting also came to be a week, usually beginning on the evening following the wedding. As with many cultures, most of the costs of the feast are now usually borne by the bride's father. During the wedding night meal, the men and women are sometimes customarily **segregated**; among the Cochin Jews the men sit on one side of the bride and groom, while the women sit on the other. It is in keeping with the joyous occasion of a wedding that the invitees dance in front of, entertain and praise the new couple. During the main feast, there are several dances.

(5) Form of songs

Following the precedent set by the riddle in the Biblical account of Samson's wedding, it is also traditional for some wedding songs to take the form of riddles. Mournful songs are also sometimes customary. The Talmud contains mournful wedding-songs grieving about the destruction of the Temple in Jerusalem.

(6) Presents

The biblical account of the marriages of Isaac and of Jacob, indicates that it was sometimes customary for the bride to be given presents. Although in the account of Isaac's wedding these are given at the betrothal, as if they were an act confirming the betrothal arrangement, in the account in the Book of Judges of the wedding of Samson, these are clearly a gift. In most parts of *the Bible*, there is no indication that the concept of a dowry existed. It is true that in the account of Jacob's weddings, his two brides are each given slaves by their father. But these gifts remain the personal property of the bride, and do not pass to the groom.

On the next Shabbat after the wedding, it was traditional for the biblical account of Isaac's marriage to be read to the groom, usually at the synagogue, during the morning prayer service. This tradition ceased within Europe during the seventeenth century (and hence it is not customary in America), but in Asia it continues, sometimes with slight variations.

Questions for discussion or reflection.
(1) What happens before a Jewish wedding?
(2) What does the Jewish wedding consist of?
(3) Are there any Jewish wedding dress/attire traditions?
(4) Who pays for the wedding in Jewish tradition?

Text C Jewish Wedding Customs and Their Origins

Pre-reading exercise:
The following are basic Jewish wedding customs. Read Text B and find their origins and symbolic meanings.

	Origins	Symbolic meaning
veiling the bride		
torches and candles		
male wears skullcaps		
bridal canopy		
honor attendants		
bride circling the groom		
the Seven Blessings		
breaking of a glass		

    Traditional Jewish weddings are replete with a variety of rituals. The origins of these traditions find their roots in both Bible-related customs, traditions carried down through generations, and **vestiges** of superstitious beliefs. A widespread belief not only in the Jewish community, but throughout the world, is that demons or evil spirits are especially prolific and present during times of joy and life-cycle events such as wedding. Many wedding customs, with Jewish customs being no exception, have at least a part of their origins in an attempt to ward off the envy and rage of the spirit world and the belief that the bride needed protection against the evil eye.

    The custom of veiling the bride is traditionally explained by the reference to Rebecca in (Genesis 24:65) "Rebecca took her veil and covered herself" upon her first meeting Isaac. Popular legend attributes the *badecken* to the Biblical story of Jacob and his wives. After working seven years for permission to marry Rachel, Jacob was tricked on his wedding day into marrying Leah, instead. To avoid such a mishap, according to legend, the groom "checks" to be sure than it is, indeed, his bride, before her veil is lowered over her face.

    There once was a widespread belief that demons were frightened of fire and scared away by light. This belief formed the basis for many couples, of a variety of religious backgrounds, to walk down a protective **aisle** of torches and candles. The custom continues today in many Jewish weddings where two candles are carried to escort to bride and groom to the wedding canopy. The more traditional explanation explains that the **numerical** value for the Hebrew word candle has the same value as the biblical phrase in (Genesis 1:28) "Be fruitful and **multiply**."

    During Jewish ceremonies, it is traditional that males wear skullcaps, as a head covering. The covering of the head is a demonstration of the awareness that there is something which is infinitely

above our intellect and symbolizes our sense of respect and humility in the presence of such a Being.

The bridal **canopy** is perhaps the central tradition at most Jewish weddings. Usually it is made of ornamented satin, or velvet—supported by four poles. Marriage ceremonies in the Middle Ages customarily took place outdoors, as an omen that the marriage should be blessed with as many children as stars in the heavens. To make a space separate from the surrounding marketplace, the rabbis sanctioned the use of a canopy. Time and creativity have "turned it into" a variety of other similar structures. The original meaning of the word was "room" or "covering" from the phrase in *the Bible*: "Let the bridegroom go forth from his chamber and the bride out of her pavilion" (Joel 2:16). The canopy symbolizes the new Jewish home that the couple creates together. It may also have origin is in the reference in *the Bible* to the bridal **bower** in which the newlywed couple were confined at the end of the wedding ceremony. In the Middle Ages the custom evolved into a cloth, or outer covering, that was spread over the bridal couple as a means of protecting them from demonic harm and the evil eye. Some believe that it is **reminiscent** of the tents of the ancient Hebrews.

The tradition of having Honor Attendants also has some Jewish roots. Legend has it that Michael and Gabriel, two angels, attended the "wedding" of Adam and Eve. Honor attendants are thus considered to be model friends of the bride and groom.

Hakafot, is the custom of the bride circling the groom, in some traditions seven times, in some three. This circling is bride's way of demonstrating how central the groom is to her thoughts and to her very being. Another interpretation is based on the belief that evil spirits seek to keep the young couple from the fulfillment they look for in their marriage. The "walking around" may serve to protect the husband from the demons which seek to find him. The seven *hakafot* corresponds to the seven marriage blessings.

The Seven Blessings mark the completion of the wedding ceremony. The blessings are recited over wine or grape juice. It is the seven blessings that join the new couple to their community. A "new custom" has been added to add even more symbolism. Their two mothers and then the two fathers pass the wine **goblet** to the bride. This symbolizes the joining not only of the bride and the groom, but also of their two families. It should be noted that in Hebrew and in **Yiddish** there are specific words to "name"  the relationship between the bride's and groom's families, as apposed to the somewhat **pejorative** and perhaps distancing expression "in laws".

Almost every Jewish wedding ends with the traditional breaking of a glass. The traditional explanation is that the smashing of the glass adds a social component to the ritual and dates back to Talmudic times when Rabbi Mar de-Rabina felt that his disciples had become too frivolous at the marriage of his son. Legend has it that he grabbed a costly glass and threw it to the floor. This had a **sobering** effect on his guests and gave the clear message that in celebration there should always be awe and "trembling," as well. Some believe that even in the height of their joy, the couple must pause in remembrance of the destruction of the Temple in Jerusalem. The shattered glass is a reminder to all in attendance that the world is replete with **imperfection** and it an imperative to all to **partake** in the mending of the world.

There are other rituals and traditions that are practiced at a Jewish wedding. Many depend on the level of observance of the couple. The ones discussed in this article should be considered "the basics."

Notes

Midianite: It is a member of an ancient desert people of northwest Arabia near the Gulf of Aqaba, believed to have descended from Midian.

For Fun

Books to Read
I. **Read** *the Bible*: Genesis 24:12–21; Genesis 12:16; Genesis 29:18; Genesis 34:12–31; Judges 14: 3; 1 Samuel 18:25

II. **Read the "Song of Songs" in** *the Bible*.

The protagonists of the *Song of Songs* are a woman and a man, and the poem suggests movement from courtship to consummation. For instance, the man proclaims: "As the lily among thorns, so is my love among the daughters." The woman answers: "As the apple tree among the trees of the wood, so is my beloved among the sons. I sat down under his shadow with great delight, and his fruit was sweet to my taste."

Movie to See

Jacob is a film based on *the Bible*'s "Book of Genesis"— Matthew Modine and Lara Flynn Boyle turn in heartfelt performances as Jacob and Rachel in this poignant romance. Jacob agrees to work for seven years in order to marry the woman he loves, only to be deceived by her father. Forced to start a family with another woman, Jacob agrees to continue his labor in order to win the love of his life...

Song to Enjoy

Here is part of the lyrics of "You'll Be in My Heart". Find the audio and enjoy the song. You can complete the lyrics while listening.

You'll Be in My Heart
by Phil Collins

Come, stop your crying, it will be all right Just take my hand, hold it tight
I will protect you from, all around you
I will be here, don't you cry
For one so small, you seem so strong
My arms will hold you, keep you safe and warm
This bond between us, can't be broken
I will be here, don't you cry
CAUSE you'll be in my heart
Yes, you'll be in my heart
From this day on
now and forever more
You'll be in my heart
No matter what they say
You'll be here in my heart
always
Why can't they understand the way we feel?
They just don't trust, what they can't explain
I know we're different but, deep inside us
We're not that different at all
And you'll be in my heart
Yes, you'll be in my heart
From this day on,
now and forever more
Don't listen to them
cause what do they know?
We need each other, to have to hold
They'll see in time
I know
When destiny calls you, you must be strong
I may not be with you, but you've got to hold on
They'll see in time
I know
we'll show them together
Cause you'll be in my heart
Believe me, you'll be in my heart
I'll be there From this day on
now and forever more
Oh,You'll be in my heart (You'll be here in my heart)
No matter what they say
I'll be with you be here in my heart
(I'll be there always)
Always
I'll be with you
I'll be there for you, always
Always and always
Just look over your shoulder
....

Unit 5
Women and *the Bible*

> She was the cornerstone of our family and a woman of extraordinary accomplishment, strength and humility. She was the person who encouraged and allowed us to take chances.
>
> —Barack Obama

Unit Goals

- To understand the life of women in *the Bible*.
- To develop a right attitude towards women in *the Bible*
- To get acquainted with some basic cultural concepts concerning women in *the Bible*
- To discover why Esther is considered a savior of the Jewish people
- To get to know Ruth, Naomi and Esther
- To learn useful words and expressions about women in *the Bible*
- To improve English language skills and western culture awareness

Before You Read

(1) Do you think there is still a male bias and a male priority present in both the private life and public life of women? If so, give some examples.
(2) What is your definition of women? Share your ideas with your partner.
(3) Form groups of three or four students. Try to find, on the Internet or in the library, more information about these women in the following pictures. Get ready for a 5-minute presentation in class.

Deborah   Judith   Jael   Rebekah

Start to Read

Text A Old Testament Post-creation Views

The status of woman in the *Old Testament* is not uniform. There is a male **bias** and a male priority generally present in both the private life and public life of women. However, it never becomes absolute. In the **Decalogue** (Ten Commandments) of Exodus 20, both male priority and gender balance can be seen. In the tenth commandment, a wife is depicted in the examples of a neighbor's property not to be **coveted**: house, *wife,* male or female slave, ox or donkey, or any other property. In this perspective, wife along with other properties belongs to the husband. On the other hand, the fourth commandment does not make any distinction between honor to be shown to parents: "father and your mother." This is **consistent** with the mutual respect shown for both parents throughout the *Old Testament*.

Double standard and male priority can also be seen in Moses' orders on what to do with the captured Midianites: "Kill every male among the little ones, and kill every woman who has known man intimately. But all the girls who have not known man **intimately**, spare for yourselves". The women of Israel were most honored and influential within the family. They gained considerable respect on the birth of her first child, especially if it was a male child. Even here, she was honored because of her function of providing a male heir, not because of her value as a person. On a positive note, Proverbs 1:8 tells a son not to reject his mother's teaching, and Proverbs 31:10-31 **eulogizes** the ideal wife, even though she is idealized for her hard labor for her family. The laws of inheritance favored the male. A male Hebrew slave was freed after six years of servitude, while a different set of rules covered female slaves. If a man rapes an **unbetrothed** virgin, he must pay her father 50 **shekels** of silver and then marry her. Judges 19 records a most degrading use of a daughter by her father. "The **gruesome** story of his using his concubine to protect himself defies imagination." **Infidelity** to God is portrayed as an "**adulteress**", not an "adulterer".

The Bible portrays Rebekah, Rahab, Deborah, Jael, Esther, and Judith and their contributions to the nation of Israel with faithfulness and extreme **candor**. These women are represented in the *Old Testament* as **multidimensional** human beings—self-reliant, resourceful, influential, and courageous—but at the same time capable of resorting to morally questionable means in order to accomplish their ends.

Distinctions were usually made between men and women during the Old Testament period. Only men were required to attend the annual festivals though women were permitted to attend if they chose to do so. The Mosaic Law recognized women's responsibilities at home as wives and mothers. However, this did not prohibit women from all religious service. Women served at the door of the **Tabernacle**. Both men and women contributed their valuables for use in the building of the Tabernacle. The Laver for ministry in the court of the tabernacle was made of brass from the mirrors of the women only.

Women as well as men were able to **consecrate** themselves with the vow of a Nazarite. Women shared in the sacred meals and great annual feasts. They

shared with the men in offering sacrifices. They also were **privileged** to experience **theophanies** (appearances of angels and other divine apparitions).

The *Old Testament* presents strong female role models, like the Judge Deborah, Judith and Queen Esther, who were depicted as saving the Hebrew people from disaster. In the book of Proverbs, the divine attribute of Holy Wisdom is presented as female.

Hebrew women attended worship services and provided a ministry in music. They sang and danced in worship and often celebrated before the Lord with singing, dancing, and **tambourines**. The "daughters of music" were singing women, but they were not included in the temple choir. Prophecy was also often sung as may be seen in the **Psalms** which were inspired words put to song. Miriam and Deborah composed the two oldest pieces of literature preserved in *the Bible*, which are regarded as literary masterpieces. Prophecy often included instruments. In Exodus15:19-21 Israel's first prophetess (Miriam) led the women in **timbrel**, dancing, and singing of the same song of Moses which is the most ancient praise song in the biblical record.

After You Read

Knowledge Focus
I. Pair Work
(1) What does the *Old Testament* say about the status of woman?
(2) What is the meaning of "You shall not covet" in the tenth commandment?
(3) What can women gain if they give birth to male heirs?
(4) Does the laws of inheritance favor female?
(5) What story is recorded in Judges 19? What can be reflected from the story?
(6) How were distinctions made between men and women during the Old Testament period?
(7) How is male bias presented in worship services?

II. Solo Work: Write T in the blank if the statement is true and F if it is false according to Text A.
(1) A woman's role in the church is the same as a man's. (　)
(2) A woman is never to open her mouth in church. (　)
(3) Women should be teachers because they can bear and feed their children. (　)
(4) A woman is obliged to listen to her husband, though she is free to reject his advice when she knows it is wrong. (　)
(5) A widow should be depressed and pray day and night. (　)

(9) In times of war, pretty women are to become the wives of conquering men who find them attractive. ( )

(10) You can't trust a woman's promise because women are deceitful. ( )

Language Focus

Build your vocabulary.

A. Write the correct word next to its definition.

| candor | gruesome | consecrate | covet |

(1) _____ to desire eagerly

(2) _____ the quality of being truthful and honest

(3) _____ to officially make something holy and able to be used for religious ceremonies

(4) _____ frightful and shocking

B. Use the proper forms of the words to complete the sentences.

(1) She always _____ power but never quite achieved it.

(2) An official policy of the government emphasizing _____ with regard to discussion of social problems and shortcomings.

(3) That _____ story was enough to turn one's blood cold.

(4) The men solemnly _____ their property and their lives to the liberation of their country.

Comprehensive Work

I. Group work: Form groups of three or four. First discuss with your group members the following qualities of choosing an ideal husband and a wife. Then talk about your criteria of choosing your spouse.

Here are the qualities that a Jewish man looked for in a wife:

(1) Jewish descent, because transmission of "Jewishness" was through the Jewish mother

(2) someone from a respectable family, since family characteristics could be transmitted to succeeding generations

(3) the daughter of a man who was learned and had studied

(4) a girl about the same age as the man or younger

(5) someone known for her good sense, good behavior and kindliness

(6) if possible, someone who was physically beautiful, but an intelligent mind and a cheerful personality were in the long run even more important.

A husband a Jewish woman looked for was:

(1) someone a few years older than herself, and of the same social standing

(2) a student of the Hebrew Scriptures, for scholarship meant that a man was intelligent, prepared to work, and able to reason and think

(3) someone possessing enough money and goods to be able to give her status, comfort and security

(4) someone whose family was reputable, with no scandal or bad blood associated with his family

(5) someone physically attractive, because Jews believed that a happy sex life was one of the greatest gifts God gave to a married couple

II. Pair Work: Work with your partner and consider the following questions.
(1) Have you detected any major differences between women in *the Bible* and women in modern society?
(2) Can you think of any cultural differences between the life of women in *the Bible* and the women in Israel today?
(3) What do you think is the right attitude towards women?

III. Essay Writing
The traditional thinking towards gender is best described in the ancient "Book of Songs" (1000-700 B.C.):

> *When a son is born,*
> *Let him sleep on the bed,*
> *Clothe him with fine clothes,*
> *And give him jade to play...*
> *When a daughter is born,*
> *Let her sleep on the ground,*
> *Wrap her in common wrappings,*
> *And give broken tiles to play...*

The loss of female births due to illegal prenatal sex determination and sex-selective abortions and female infanticide will affect the true sex ratio at birth and at young ages, creating an unbalanced population sex structure in the future and resulting in potentially serious social problems. The shortage of women is creating a "huge societal issue". Do you agree? Please write an essay of 300 words to view your point.

IV. Solo Work
1. Put in the missing words.
   Women in ancient Israel had their position in society defined in the Hebrew Scriptures and in the interpretation of those scriptures. Their status and freedoms were severely l_____ by Jewish law and custom in ancient Israel:
   ◆ Women were restricted to roles of little or no authority.
   ◆ Women were confined to the homes of their fathers or husbands.
   ◆ Women were to be inferior to men, under the direct authority of men, their fathers before m_____, or their husband after.
   ◆ Women were not a_____ to testify in court trials.
   ◆ Women could not a_____ in public venues.
   ◆ Women could not talk to s_____.
   ◆ Women were required to be doubly veiled when they ventured outside of their homes.

2. Proofreading and error correction.

    When we hear the name Delilah, we often think of a temptress—A woman who uses her feminine qualities to cheat and destroy a man. The name Delilah is actually a Semitic name meaning "devotee". She is thought to have been a Philistine, probably a temple prostitute.

    In *the Bible*, Delilah was the woman responsible for Samson's downfall. She valued money more than the love of this strong man. Philistine rulers visited her and offered to pay her a tremendous number of money if she would persuade Samson to tell her the secret of his strength.

    Three times, she teasingly asked Samson the secret of his strength and how he could be tied up and subdued. Three times Samson teased her by giving her wrong information. She continued nagging him day after day, pleading for him to tell her the secret of his strength. He finally succumbed to her question and told her the truth. When Samson's hair was shaved, his strength left him. He was taken captive while Delilah earned her money.

    We may never be faced with a choice such as was given to Delilah, but there will be choices that speak to our integrity. There may be many times when we choose between honoring a trust placed in us, or act for our own gain. These tests may come in many forms, both in professional and personal life. At each crossroad, we must judge our actions being sure that they weight in on the side of honor and love.

(1) _____
(2) _____
(3) _____
(4) _____
(5) _____

Read More

Text B   Daughters of Eve

    The women portrayed in this passage all played decisive roles during the thousands of years covered by the biblical narrative. What is particularly **intriguing** about them is that most of them **circumvent** male authority in a **patriarchal** society, and some even subvert it. Even more remarkable is the fact that these women, other than the ruthless Jezebel, are never punished for their unconventional conduct. On the contrary, the biblical scribes treat the women with deep sympathy and are sensitive to their plight. All of them, with the exception of Jezebel, are rewarded for their **boldness**.

    Most of the women defy male authority when it is unjust or fails to answer their needs or those of their family or people. They belong to a patriarchal society in which men hold all visible power, and their options are few and stark. Given these circumstances, the women challenge, **seduce**, and trick. They take risks, and some, such as Queen Esther and Judah's daughter-in-law Tamar, are prepared to stake their lives on the outcome. Both Tamar and Ruth are widows who would be doomed to a life of poverty and anonymity but for the initiative they take in devising careful plans of sexual seduction. Not only do the men respond, but the descendants of their acts of seduction become progenitors of the House of David generations later. Both women are rewarded for the risk they take to ensure the survival of the family.

We are drawn to their **vulnerabilities** as much as to their strengths. Like the timeless heroines of the *Hebrew Bible*, we too struggle to love, to parent, to succeed in relationships, and to make our way through the **labyrinth** of a dangerous world. In each of the stories, the women are the **protagonists** around whom the action revolves.

The young Eve speaks to us with her optimism as she leaves the Garden of Eden with her man to start adult life in the real and imperfect world. Our heart aches for Sarah, who, with the best of intentions, puts another woman into the bed of her husband, Abraham, to produce the son she cannot conceive. The illicit and passionate love affair between David and Bathsheba, although it matures into a long-term marriage, raises serious and troubling universal issues. These are but a few of the compelling stories of the women of *the Bible* whose lives resonate with us today.

Now that women have begun studying the biblical text in substantial numbers, feminist scholars and others have begun writing much about women in *the Bible*. Some of them feature fighters like **Deborah**, the biblical Joan of Arc, who leads the Israelites in battle, and the midwives Puah and Shifrah, who save Hebrew male babies despite Pharaoh's edict to drown them in the Nile. Another heroine is the prostitute **Rahab**, who risks her life to help Joshua's spies escape from Jericho. While *the Bible* recounts the actions for which these heroines are remembered, it tells us nothing about their interior lives and processes of decision and thus gives few clues how we can emulate them today.

Except for Delilah and Jezebel, these are women with whom many of us are able to identify and who interact with the men in their lives with surprising results. These intelligent, brave women dare to take the initiative. They are assertive, unwilling to be victims in the face of overwhelming circumstances. They are not looking for ways to raise their self-esteem, nor are their lives directed by a need to "feel comfortable". What keeps them going despite **adverse** circumstances is the power of a purpose-driven life and an all-embracing faith values that demand both a long-term view of history and a decisive, resourceful approach to the immediate present.

One is hard to find in them a hint of **alienation**, **cynicism**, or ennui. On the contrary, they convey a can-do approach to life as they prevail, overcome, and refuse to bow in the face of overwhelming odds. They make and execute their imperfect decisions to the best of their abilities, and they are willing to acknowledge and live with the consequences of their actions—the essential meaning of the responsibility and accountability that accompanies free will, God's greatest gift to humans.

Questions for discussion or reflection.
(1) Most of the women defy male authority when it is unjust or fails to answer their needs of those of their family or people. Take Tamar and Queen Esther as examples to illustrate this.
(2) How much do you know about Rahab? Find more about her.

Text C Stories of the Women

The legal status of biblical women is unequal to the status of men. Women are second-class citizens living under the authority of the head of their family, usually their fathers or husbands. And yet, surprisingly enough, the women are neither **downtrodden** nor crushed by stern, brutal patriarchs. Within the family, the women wield enormous power. When they see their family or their tribe in danger, and the men fail to act, women fill the vacuum, taking the risks and assuming responsibilities for the destiny of their people.

The narrative also suggests that women are a metaphor for all minorities struggling to make their voices heard. The women's situation is analogous to that of the Israelites, a tough, small people set among more powerful pagan cultures. In biblical times, polygamy was practiced widely. Yet each polygamous family portrayed in *the Bible* is unhappy. Whether the problem is the rivalry between **Rachel** and **Leah**, the two sisters married to Jacob, or between **Hannah** and Peninnah, both married to Elkanah, or the conflicting demands by David's many wives and their feuding children, the biblical authors subtly point out the disadvantages of a polygamous marriage.

In contrast, Sarah and Abraham form a distinctly **monogamous** marriage within a polygamous culture, as do Rebecca and Isaac. In the Garden of Eden, too, we have one woman and one man. The narrative makes clear that an intense relationship between husband and wife in a polygamous marriage is nearly impossible. The presence of multiple, contending wives dilutes all the relation-ships within the family unit. *The Bible* strongly implies that polygamy does not work, that **monogamy** is a preferable structure. The intensely committed personal and loving relationship between one male and one female parallels the intensely committed relationship between one human and God.

In the *Old Testament*, **sexuality** is by no means a secret, sinful, or forbidden subject. Instead, sex is discussed with remarkable openness and with no trace of prudishness. We are carried away by the beautifully written *Song of Songs*, as it celebrates in explicit terms the sensual love between **Shulamite** and her lover. *The Bible* regards sexuality as the Creator's gift, integral to all human life, a tool for strengthening the bonds of intimacy, trust, companionship, responsibility, and commitment.

On the other hand, sexuality can also be abusive and selfish. *The Bible*'s unvarnished realism does not spare us this aspect of human ambivalence. The Israelite hero Samson becomes addicted to Delilah's sexual favors. She hands him over to her people, Israel's enemies, who blind, torture, and imprison him. The worst example of sex as a destructive force is Amnon's **inexorable** plot to rape his virgin half-sister **Tamar**, King David's beautiful daughter. She **staggers** out of his house, her life forever ruined.

The Bible instructs even as it entertains. It does not whitewash any aspect of human psychology or conduct. It draws the reader in by exposing its protagonists' feet of clay. No one is spared critical comment or the depiction of unflattering weaknesses—and no one is above the law. The women, like their men, are responsible for their actions and the consequences. The women and the men are neither saints nor sinners, and, interestingly enough, their actions are treated with equal candor.

The stories of the women in *the Bible* offer us a prism through which to consider our own lives. After all, human nature has not changed one iota since the day Eve questioned the rules in the Garden of Eden in response to her God-given drive to acquire knowledge and create life. The outcome is the first exercise of free choice and the first lesson in personal responsibility and morality.

Questions for discussion or reflection.
(1) How do you understand polygamous and monogamous marriage in *the Bible*? Give some examples to explain these two different kinds of marriages.
(2) Do women possess power in their families according to *the Bible*?

Notes

(1) **Jezebel:** She is the Phoenician queen of ancient Israel. Her story is told in 1st and 2nd Kings.
(2) **Deborah:** She was a prophetess and the fourth, and the only female, Judge of pre-monarchic Israel in the Old Testament. Her story is told twice, in chapters 4 and 5 of Judges.
(3) **Rahab:** She is a Canaanite woman living in Jericho, is a prostitute and also a biblical heroine. According to the narrative in Joshua 2, before the conquest of Canaan, Joshua sends two men as spies to see the land. They come to Rahab's house for lodging, information. The king, hearing about the two men, demands that Rahab give them up. Like the midwives in Egypt, Rahab is faced with a "moment of truth." Like them, Rahab defies the ruler and rescues the Israelites. She tells the king's men that the two men have left and that the king's men should chase them. Meanwhile, she has hidden the men under the flax drying on her roof. (The life of Rahab can be found in Joshua 2, Joshua 6, Hebrews 11:31, Matthew1:5, James 2: 25)

For Fun

Books to Read
(1) Keats' 1819 poem "Ode to a Nightingale" describes the night bird's song as one of unbearable sweetness and sorrow, longing and loss. In this verse from the poem, Keats projects his own melancholy mood onto the figure of Ruth.

> Thou wast not born for death, immortal Bird!
> No hungry generations tread thee down;
> The voice I hear this passing night was heard
> In ancient days by emperor and clown:
> Perhaps the self-same song that found a path
> Through the sad heart of Ruth, when, sick for home,
> She stood in tears amid the alien corn.

(2) **The Song of Ruth:** A Love Story from the *Old Testament* (1954) A novel by Frank G Slaughter (1908—2001), American bestseller novelist and physician, whose books sold more than 60 million copies. Slaughter's novels drew on his own experience as a physician and reflected his interest in history and the Biblical world. He often introduced readers to exciting findings in medical research and new inventions in medical technology.

Movie to See

Enjoy the film ***The Story of Ruth.***

This Biblical epic stars Elana Eden as Ruth, who serves in the temple where the High Priestess (Viveca Lindfors) leads the worship of the Pagan idols of the people of Moab. When Ruth falls in love with Mahlon (Tom Tryon), a Hebrew, she must come to terms with his spiritual beliefs, but in time she embraces his faith and converts to Judaism when they marry. Ruth travels with Mahlon and his mother Naomi (Peggy Wood) to their homeland of Bethlehem. Ruth suffers hardship and religious persecution, and when Mahlon dies, Ruth's faith is severely tested. But her belief in God survives this trial by fire, and in time Ruth finds a new love with Boaz.

Song to Enjoy

Here is part of the lyrics of "The Song of Ruth". Find the audio and enjoy the song. You can complete the lyrics while listening.

The Song of Ruth
by Joel Chernoff

Wherever you go
There you will find me
Wherever you lodge
That is my home
Wherever you die
There I'll be buried
Your people are mine
Your God is my God

Do not ever urge me to go
Or desert your side and leave you
For may God to me
And more if anything
But death separate you from me
Dai dai dai - dai dai dai dai

Dai dai dai dai - dai dai dai
For may God to me
And more If anything
But death separate you from me
Do not ever urge me to go
Or desert your side and leave you
For may God to me
......

Unit 6

Shepherds and *the Bible*

> I'm a shepherd, not a sheep, and I've always prided myself on being a leader and not a follower.
> —Dustin Diamond

Unit Goals

- To gain a general knowledge of shepherds in *the Bible*
- To develop a right attitude towards shepherds in *the Bible*
- To get acquainted with some basic cultural concepts concerning shepherds in *the Bible*
- Get to know Jacob, David, Goliath, Moses, Jesus
- To learn useful words and expressions about shepherds in *the Bible*
- To improve English language skills and western culture awareness

Before You Read

(1) Look up your dictionary and define the meaning of "shepherd".
(2) Does "shepherd" in *the Bible* have any specific meanings?
(3) Figure out the good qualities of good leaders by referring to those of good shepherds.

	Good shepherds	Good leaders
1.	Know the condition of your flock	
2.	Discover the shape of your sheep	
3.	Help your sheep identify with you	
4.	Make your pasture a safe place	
5.	The staff of direction	
6.	The rod of correction	
7.	The heart of the shepherd	

(4) Form groups of three or four students. Try to find, on the Internet or in the library, more information about shepherds such as Abraham, Jacob, Moses and David. Get ready for a 5-minute presentation in class.

Start to Read

Text A Shepherds

The shepherd and his flock

One of the most common images in *the Bible* is that of the shepherd and his sheep because it is so commonly spoken of in *the Bible*.

We should remember that God's chosen people were shepherds. Abraham was a keeper of sheep. As a matter of fact, Abraham was so successful that he and Lot had to split up, because they could not sustain both of their herds in the same grazing areas. **Jacob**, too, was a shepherd, and this is how he became wealthy while working for Laban, caring for his flocks. When Jacob and his family went to join Joseph in Egypt, they were shepherds, which is part of the reason why the Egyptians avoided **intermarrying** with the Hebrews. If Judah married a **Canaanite** and allowed his sons to do likewise, it would not have been long until the tribe of Judah would have ceased to exist as a distinct tribe, due to their intermarriage with the **Canaanites**. Since the Egyptians loathed shepherds, they would not have considered intermarrying with the Hebrews.

The shepherd and his flock in *the Bible*: a model for leaders

Shepherding is an image that **pertains to** ruling, to a leader (or shepherd) exercising authority over a group of people (his flock). This is clearly indicated in both the *Old* and the *New Testaments*.

To be a shepherd over a flock is to be a leader over a group of people. David is perhaps the best-known shepherd of Bible History. David saw his relationship to God as that of a sheep to its shepherd. God's relationship to the nation Israel **was likened** to that of a shepherd and his flock; God was Israel's Shepherd, and the people were His flock.

The imagery of a shepherd and his flock thus provided a picture of the way God cared for His people, and thus this imagery also serves as a model for human leaders. God cares for His people as a shepherd cares for his flock. Human leaders are likewise to **rule over** men as a shepherd tends his flock. I believe we can safely infer that God prepared Moses to lead the Israelites by first having him serve as a shepherd in the wilderness for 40 years. God likewise prepared David for leadership by his experience as a shepherd in the days of his youth.

To be a good leader was to be a good shepherd. The same principles that guided David as the shepherd of a little flock prompted David to step forward in the face of Goliath's ranting. Just as David must have seen his little flock **terrorized** by a bear or a lion, so he saw the armies of Israel terrorized by the Philistines, and Goliath in particular. God had given David the strength to care for his flock, and God would surely give David the strength to care for this larger flock, by attacking the one who threatened them.

The shepherding model not only encouraged David to **stand up** against Goliath, it also served Nathan well when rebuking David for his abuse of power as Israel's king. When David **sinned against** God by taking Bathsheba and killing her husband, Uriah, God confronted him through the prophet Nathan. Nathan got David's attention by telling him a story that would have touched the heart of any good shepherd.

As you well know, through this story Nathan **got** the point **across**, and David repented of his sin.

The promise of the good shepherd

Israel's leaders were a great disappointment. The patriarchs were far from perfect. Even the best of Israel's leaders had **feet of clay.** Moses' failure as a leader kept him from entering the Promised Land. David abused his powers as king when he sinned by taking Bathsheba and killing Uriah. His leadership with his family was flawed, and his last days as king were not his finest. Eli and Samuel were great men, but their leadership, especially in regard to their families, was far from exemplary. Even the great prophet Elijah sought to resign from his ministry, and from life itself. Solomon's early years as king were awe inspiring, but his later life was in **shambles**. In the end, there was no perfect leader throughout the history of Israel.

Jesus—the good shepherd

The ultimate spiritual shepherd of course is Jesus Christ, as He clearly portrayed Himself—

"I am the good shepherd. The good shepherd lays down his life for the sheep. He who is a hireling and not a shepherd, whose own the sheep are not, sees the wolf coming and leaves the sheep and flees; and the wolf snatches them and scatters them. He flees because he is a hireling and cares nothing for the sheep."

The "Good Shepherd" cares for His sheep, so much so that He will **lay down His life** for them. He cares for the sheep because they are His sheep. And because they are His sheep, He knows them, and they know Him. They recognize His voice, and they follow Him. Ultimately, the Good Shepherd lays down His life for His sheep.

The Bible & Culture

After You Read

Knowledge Focus

I. Pair Work with your partner and consider the following questions.
  (1) What is the reason for Abraham and Lot to split up?
  (2) What is the relationship between Jacob and Laban?
  (3) Why did the Egyptians avoid intermarrying with the Hebrews?
  (4) What are the similarities between good shepherds and good leaders?
  (5) How did David prove himself to be a good shepherd?

II. Solo Work: Write T in the blank if the statement is true and F if it is false according to Text A.
  (1) The Egyptians fail to intermarry with the Hebrews only because they were shepherds.   ( )
  (2) Moses is the best known shepherd.   ( )
  (3) Serving as a shepherd is to prepare one for leadership.   ( )
  (4) The leadership of both David and Samuel with their families are exemplary.   ( )
  (5) Intermarrying with the Canaanites may cause the Hebrews to cease to exist as a distinct tribe.
      ( )

Language Focus

I. Building your vocabulary

  A. Match the phrases in Column A with their meanings in Column B.

Column A	Column B
1. get across	A. an underlying weakness or fault
2. stand up against	B. to lose one's life in order to help others
3. sin against	C. to be understood or accepted
4. feet of clay	D. to do wrong
5. lay down one's life	E. to be compared to
6. pertain to	F. to fight against
7. be likened to	G. to control
8. rule over	H. to have a connection

  B. Use the proper forms of the phrases to complete the sentences.

lay down one's life	get across	be likened to	rule over
stand up against	sin against	pertain to	feet of clay

  (1) Abraham Lincoln delivered Gettysburg Address in memory of those who _____ in the Civil War.
  (2) The comedian didn't seem to be able to _____ his jokes to his audience — they all fell flat.
  (3) Except for his obscure birth, Sir Robert _____ in many ways Sir Winston Churchill, whom he admired.
  (4) School children in Gaza, cricket fans in India and African church-goers have helped set a

Guinness world record for the largest number of people to _____ poverty.

(5) Almost all the men are liable to _____ propriety if they have not any training class.

(6) Any inquiries _____ the granting of planning permission should be addressed to the Town Hall.

(7) European powers no longer _____ great overseas dominions.

(8) In the preliminary competition for the World Gymnastics Championship, the former champion gave the appearance of having _____.

II. **Fill in the blanks with the proper forms of the words.**

(1) The aim must always be to create a _____ (sustain) peace, just as we aim to achieve _____ (sustain) development.

(2) A gang of young men with knives have been _____ (terror) local people.

(3) Sincere _____ (repent) is manifested when the same temptation to sin, under the same conditions, is ever after resolutely resisted

(4) The recent oil price rise _____ (exemplary) the difficulties which the motor industry is now facing.

(5) Many public figures deliver a _____ (resign) speech to explain the circumstances of their exit from office.

(6) The two tribes have been _____ (marry) for hundreds of years.

(7) They are scrapping the traditional method of correcting work because they consider it _____ (confront) and threatening.

(8) Kids of that age really shouldn't need _____ (prompt) to say thank you for things.

Comprehensive Work

I. **Form groups of three or four. First discuss with your group members the following questions.**

(1) Why were shepherds God's chosen people?

(2) Discuss with your group whether the following secrets derived from shepherds and their flocks can work in your daily life.

- Know your team.
- Meet your team. Regularly—daily, weekly or monthly, depending on your place and type of work.
- Train your team. Every team member should have at least two days training a year. Newer and more senior colleagues should have more.
- Grow your team. Through varied experience and regular training, you should be developing each team member to be more and more confident and more skilled.
- Set objectives for each team member. As far as possible, these objective such be **SMART**—**S**pecific **M**easurable **A**chievable **R**esourced **T**imed.

II. **Essay Writing**

The following is what a community wants to provide for its residents. Read it and write an essay based on them about how to build a harmonious community.

The community of the Good Shepherd respects the inherent dignity and basic human rights of the people we support. We provide quality care that enhances individuality and supports full community involvement.

We pledge:

- To afford individuals with developmental disabilities the opportunities to make progressive steps to grow spiritually, physically, emotionally, and mentally.
- To provide a fostering atmosphere that enables individuals to enjoy the liberties that are associated with living independently and interdependently.
- To strengthen and nurture each individual's ability to communicate their likes and dislikes. We respect their decisions to the fullest extent without compromising health and safety.
- To strive to enhance daily living skills and community involvement opportunities.
- To challenge ourselves to continually upgrade our abilities, knowledge, and awareness.
- To increase our sensitivity to our residents' diverse needs.
- To embrace persons of all faith and economic situations. This same spirit welcomes the families of our residents and persons from the community at large.

III. Solo Work

1. Put in the missing words.

In many societies shepherds were an important part of the economy. Unlike farmers, shepherds were often wage earners, being paid to w_____ the sheep of others. Shepherds also lived a_____ from society, being largely nomadic. It was mainly a job of solitary males without children, and new shepherds thus needed to be recruited externally. Shepherds were most often the younger sons of farming peasants who did not inherit any land. Still in other societies, each family would have a family m_____ to shepherd its flock, often a child, youth or an e_____ who couldn't help much with harder work; these shepherds were fully integrated in society.

Shepherds would normally work in g_____ either looking after one large flock, or each bringing their own and merging their responsibilities. They would live in small cabins, often shared with their sheep and would buy food from local communities. Less often shepherds lived in covered wagons that traveled with their flocks.

2. Proofreading and error correction.

Many remember David as the fair-haired shepherd boy who defeated a giant named Goliath. Others recall David as the wise Jewish ruler who brought the tribes of Israel together as a united country. The ancient texts also present David as a powerful warrior, cunning diplomat, and talent musician. However, with all these tremendous accolades, the foundation of David's fame and faith can be traced to a period of severe trial and doubting in his life. Indeed, David was a true philosopher.

(1) _____

(2) _____

Early in his journey, David was chosen to succeed Saul as the king of Judah. Although Saul was initially impressed by David's skills as a soldier, politician, and musician, Saul became wary of his successor, so he put out a contact on David's life. David was forced to live on the run, often spending weeks hiding in the network of caves surrounding the Dead Sea.

(3) _____

It is here that David really began asking the tough questions of life. Lonely in the dark or on the run through enemy territory, David opened-up and honestly shared his thoughts, struggles, and fears. David was frustrated with God's plan for his life, and he wrote about it in his prayer journals. Although Saul stopped at nothing to kill David, David never followed through on his opportunities to kill Saul.

(4) _____

When Saul finally died in an unrelated battle, David returned to Judah and claimed his position as king over Judah in 1009 BC. Seven years later, the north tribes of Israel accepted him as king and he became ruler of a United Jewish nation until his death in 969 BC. David wasn't a perfect leader or a perfect man, but he developed the soul of a legendary philosopher-king, and forged a legacy that endures to this day.

(5) _____

Read More

Text B Shepherd Leader

Shepherd leadership is whole-person leadership. It's not just a matter of thinking in a certain way or doing things in a certain way. It's a fully integrated life—a matter of head and hand and heart. We like to say that it's a way of thinking and doing and being.

First of all, shepherd leadership is a way of thinking. In the field, sheep are not famous for their strategic planning. As far as we know, animals do not have the capacity to visualize the future. The shepherd's first job in the field is to think and to think ahead. Although humans have this capacity, we know that not everybody uses it. For many people, the concerns of day-to-day survival often **override** any effort to plan for the future—despite good intentions to the contrary. This is where shepherd leadership enters the picture.

A shepherd leader is somewhat like a good travel guide. The dictionary tells us that a guide assists travel in unfamiliar territory or to an unfamiliar **destination** by accompanying the traveler. If you have ever enjoyed touring with a great guide, you know what a wonderful and enriching experience it can be. Somehow, without directly trying to control your every move, a good guide nevertheless empowers you to see more and learn more than would ever be possible on your own.

Shepherd leaders are characterized by mental **agility**. They have the ability to shift gears from deep reflection to quick thinking and decision making in a matter of moments. Most people would agree that good leaders are characterized by both kinds of thinking. Few understand how quickly actual leaders must shift between these two modes. The mind of a shepherd leader must always be out ahead, envisioning the next destination and the best way to get there. There are green fields and dangerous valleys, and the shepherd must anticipate both.

 Thinking is something a shepherd leader may often do alone. In contrast, when in the doing mode, the shepherd leader is often with others. In the field, the shepherd is out among the sheep taking care of their needs. Likewise, shepherd leaders are busy doing things for their followers. We see the shepherd leader of Psalm 23 doing something very important for his followers: cultivating abundance. If an ancient shepherd's sheep enjoyed a green pasture, it's because the shepherd had carved it out of the wilderness. Likewise when leaders provide an environment of contentment and abundance, there is far more growth and progress. Shepherd leaders are also out among their followers, assessing and meeting needs. They are managing conflict and removing **irritants** and obstacles. Wherever there's a shepherd, there's a life abundant.

 Finally, shepherd leadership is a way of being. In particular, it's a way of "being with" the follower. By "being with" we mean going beyond doing things for the follower or thinking about the follower. A hallmark of shepherd leadership is both the ability and the willingness to see life from the perspective of the follower. Psalm 23 is a powerful demonstration of David's ability to see life from the perspective of a follower.

 It would be shortsighted to think of the shepherd-sheep relationship as a one-sided deal for the shepherd. In reality, the shepherd and the sheep had a mutually beneficial relationship. The sheep enjoyed a longer, healthier life under the protection of the shepherd. Likewise, the shepherd enjoyed a longer, healthier life because of the sheep, which provided him with a ready source of warm clothing and relieved him of the obligation to hunt for all of his food. Historians contend that sheep would have long ago become extinct had it not been for their willingness to become domesticated in the care of shepherds. Many ancient civilizations revolved around the relationship between humans and sheep. In those days, sheep were not regarded as "dumb animals" but were held in very high esteem.

 Shepherd leaders are distinctive in that while thinking ahead, they are very much "with" the sheep. Shepherding is not a remote form of leadership; it is high touch. Shepherds do not issue a lot of **memos** and orders from the corner office; rather, they get out in the field to model and guide.

Questions for discussion or reflection.
(1) What are the qualities of shepherd leaders?
(2) Would you please explain that "Shepherd leadership is a way of being"?

Text C Shepherds' Implements

 We learn of some of the equipments and methods of the shepherds of the time in this article. David "chose him five smooth stones out of the brook, and put them in a shepherd's bag which he had, even in a scrip" The scrip is a bag made of dried skin, and typically this was used to carry food while the shepherd was out in the fields, such as bread, cheese, dried fruit or olives.

 A shepherd would also **normally** carry a rod. This rod would be used for protection and a weapon against wild animals. It would typically have been made of oak wood and be a couple of feet long, and one end was typically thicker—this was the hitting end—the one with more **inetia**. In addition to the thickened lump, spikes would be driven into it for a greater impact.

Ezekiel refers to the rod in Ezekiel 20,

> *Ezekiel 20:37: And I will cause you to pass under the rod, and I will bring you into the bond of the covenant:*

> *This refers to the practice of causing the sheep to pass under the rod for counting or inspecting. In the book of Leviticus, Moses wrote of the tithe of the herd,*

> *Leviticus 27:32: And concerning the tithe of the herd, or of the flock, even of whatsoever passeth under the rod, the tenth shall be holy unto the Lord.*

In order to do this, the flock was herded through a narrow opening. The shepherd would dip the end of the rod in some colouring material, and mark the head of every tenth sheep as it passed. In this way one tenth of the flock could be separated out without **partiality**.

The scepter, which was an implement of the kings of the time, had its origins in the shepherd's rod. As a king, they were the shepherd of the people, and the rod was a symbol of protection, power and authority.

David's weapon of choice against Goliath, however, was not the club, but his sling. The sling was also a very useful implement. Typically, it was made of a patch of leather to hold the stone, and two strings of sinew, rope or leather. By swinging the apparatus above his head, and letting go of one of the strings at the appropriate time, the stone could be made to travel quite some distance. As in the case of Goliath, this could be used as a weapon against **predators**, such as the lion or bear or even robbers.

The sling could also be useful as a herding implement. If a sheep was lagging or heading off in the wrong direction a stone could be directed either behind or ahead of the sheep, as appropriate, to redirect it. Contrast between the sling and scrip in 1 Samuel,

> *1 Samuel 25:29: Yet a man is risen to pursue thee, and to seek thy soul: but the soul of my lord shall be bound in the bundle of life with the LORD thy God; and the souls of thine enemies, them shall he sling out, as out of the middle of a sling.*

Another implement carried by shepherds, was their staff, mentioned, for example, in Psalm 23:4. This was a stick of about 1.5 metres long, and was used for sheep handling, a walking stick, and as another protection device.

1. After-reading exercise

How much do you know about implements carried by shepherds? Please fill in the blanks in the following chart based on Text C.

Implements	Functions
a scrip	
a sling	
a staff	
a scepter	
a rod	

Notes

Goliath: He is a giant, a person or object of larger-than-average stature. A *David-and-Goliath* situation is one in which an underdog takes up the challenge of an opponent against all odds.

For Fun

Book to Read

Read *the Bible*:

The Bible designates the 23rd Psalm as "A Psalm of David." King David started out as a shepherd. He traveled a dangerous path through many dark valleys. And he was anointed with oil to be the leader of the chosen people. Jesus also identified himself as the good shepherd who cares for the flock. Here is the poem:

The Lord is my shepherd, I shall not be in want.
He makes me lie down in green pastures, he leads me beside quiet waters, he restores my soul.

He guides me in paths of righteousness for his name's sake.
Even though I walk through the valley of the shadow of death
I will fear no evil, for you are with me;
your rod and your staff, they comfort me.

You prepare a table before me in the presence of my enemies.
You anoint my head with oil; my cup overflows.

Surely goodness and love will follow me all the days of my life,
and I will dwell in the house of the Lord forever.

Unit 6 Shepherds and the Bible

Movie to See
The Good Shepherd **in 2006.**

In the Second World War Edward becomes a member of the OSS, an Intelligence Service operating in London. When the Cold War begins the USA transform the OSS in the CIA for which Edward Wilson gives his services. As the Bay of Pigs debacle unfolds, Wilson, now head of CIA counterintelligence, begins searching for...

Song to Enjoy

Here is part of the lyrics of "One King". Find the audio and enjoy the song. You can complete the lyrics while listening.

One King
by David Phelps

In the beginning there was the Word
Pure love was spoken to reach every man
They stopped and listened but all that they heard
Was a language that they could not understand.
No joy, no peace, no hope inside

So He came with starlight and love in His eyes
No regal welcome for His infant cry
There have been many babies to become a king
But only one King became a baby

He left behind His throne of pure light
Gave up His crown that we might be free
He chose a manger that Bethlehem night

And reaching through time and space He saw me
No joy, no peace, no hope inside

So He came with starlight and love in His eyes,
No regal welcome for His infant cry
There have been many babies to become a king
But only one King became a baby

He could have chosen to break through the sky
With anthem and angel wing
But He knew we'd understand a baby's cry
And learn love from a servant king

So He came with starlight and love in His eyes,
No regal welcome for His infant cry
There have been so many babies to become a king
....

Unit 7

Prophets and *the Bible*

> Don't let the prophecies, ancient or modern, trap you in a box of fear and futility. Change the dance by becoming the light that you are, the light that continues through and beyond the box into the adventure of forever.
> —Ruth Ryden

Unit Goals

- To gain a general knowledge of prophets in *the Bible*
- To develop a right attitude towards prophets in *the Bible*
- To get acquainted with some basic cultural concepts concerning prophets in *the Bible*
- To learn useful words and expressions about prophets in *the Bible*
- To improve English language skills and western culture awareness

Before You Read

(1) What is a prophet? Are there prophets in our world today?
(2) Do you believe what is supposed to happen in 2012?

(3) Is it possible that the ancient Maya's prophecy highlights our modern crisis in consciousness and the process of our collective awakening?
(4) How can we prepare for 2012?
(5) Form groups of three or four students. Try to find, on the Internet or in the library, more information about Isaiah, Jeremiah and Ezekiel. Get ready for a 5-minute presentation in class.

Start to Read

Text A The Prophet Isaiah

During times of national **turmoil**, people look for ways to interpret events and find a sense of meaning. On our day, viewers watch CCTV, listen to Voice of China, or read newspapers, seeking the wisdom of commentators and **pundits** who try to put wars, disasters, and unrest into perspective. During the terrible national crises **leading up to** the first destruction of Jerusalem and afterwards in the exile, the prophets called the people of Israel to understand their sorrows **in light of** the Torah and covenant.

Although the people did not always listen, the prophets warned that **straying from** God's commandments would bring punishment, while returning to God would bring renewal and restoration. Three prophetic voices in particular—those of Isaiah, Jeremiah, and Ezekiel—provided the mixture of righteous social and religious criticism and hopeful vision that was required to **sustain** the people through difficulties, especially their captivity in Babylon.

Many ancient Near East societies had a tradition of prophecy. In Exodus, Moses conveys God's word to Aaron. Aaron is Moses' prophet, according to the text. Prophets in *the Bible* are to speak exactly what God says to them.

Isaiah and Jeremiah report that God called them even before they were born. Through powerful visions, God asked them to call to account not only common people but also the institutions of priesthood and monarchy. The biblical prophets had allegiance only to God, a position that both gave them uncompromised authority and left them isolated and vulnerable to the scorn of all their listeners for being the bearers of news no one wanted to hear. The prophets shared in the sufferings they predicted for the nation, yet seldom lived to see the hopeful side of the visions come into being. A prophet was, above all, a person of faith.

The prophecies themselves often follow a clear literary pattern:

Demands for reform
The people's refusal to reform
Predictions of disaster if the people do not mend their ways
The consequences
In the face of the consequences, a reminder of God's faithfulness and promises.

A paramount shaper of the prophetic vision was Isaiah. Isaiah was a witness to one of the most turbulent periods in Jerusalem's history, from both the political and the religious standpoint. His status enabled him to take an active part in events, and in some cases to guide them. His relations with the senior members of the royal house, as described in *the Bible*, and the fact that he had free access to the palace, together with the complex linguistic style of his prophecies, suggest that he belonged to the Jerusalem aristocracy. This, though, did not prevent him from being an outspoken mouthpiece of the common people, who were being victimized by the rampant corruption of the ruling class: "What need have I of all your sacrifices? Says the Lord... Put your evil doings away from my sight... Devote yourselves to justice... Uphold the rights of the orphan; defend the cause of the widow".

Isaiah was the most "political" of the prophets. In the face of Assyrian expansionism he counseled a passive political and military approach. He put his faith in divine salvation, which would certainly follow from a necessary change in the moral leadership and in the people's spiritual tenacity. Every "earthly" attempt to alter the course of events was foredoomed, since the mighty Assyria was no more than a "rod" in God's hands with which to punish the sins of Jerusalem: "Again the Lord spoke to me, thus: 'Because that people has spurned the gently flowing waters of Siloam assuredly, my Lord will bring up against them the mighty, massive waters of the Euphrates, the king of Assyria and all his multitude". When the comprehensive religious reforms introduced by King Hezekiah seemed, at first, to justify the hopes **held out** for him by Isaiah, the prophet supported him in the difficult moments of the Assyrian siege: "Assuredly, thus said the Lord concerning the king of Assyria: He shall not enter this city; he shall not shoot an arrow at it, or advance upon it with a shield, or pile up a siege mound against us. He shall go back by the way he came, he shall not enter this city declares the Lord".

However, Isaiah **took** an unwaveringly **dim view of** Hezekia's attempts to forge **alliances with** Egypt and with the envoys of the Babylonian king Merodach-baladan, as a wedge against Assyrian expansionism. Such efforts, he said, **attested to** insufficient faith in the Lord. Isaiah is also considered the most universal of the prophets: "In the days to come, the Mount of the Lord's House shall stand firm above the mountains... And the many peoples shall go and shall say: Come, let us go up to the Mount of the Lord ...". Christian theologians have drawn heavily on Isaiah's prophecies for exegetical purposes.

After You Read

Knowledge Focus

I. Pair Work: Work with your partner and consider the following questions.
   (1) What did the prophets call the people of Israel to understand during the national crises?
   (2) Did people listen to the prophets' warnings?
   (3) What if they stay away from the divine commands?
   (4) Aaron is Moses' prophet. What else do you know about him?
   (5) Would you please explain "Assyrian expansionism"?

II. Solo Work: Test your knowledge about prophets in *the Bible*. Write T if the statement is true and F if it is false.
   (1) The prophets usually live to see the hopeful side of the visions become reality.   (   )

(2) Isaiah was born of a family of upper class. ( )
(3) Isaiah was a spokesman of Jerusalem aristocracy. ( )
(4) Isaiah was the most nonpolitical of the prophets according to the text. ( )
(5) Jeremiah is considered the most universal of the prophets. ( )

Language Focus

I. Build your vocabulary.

A. Match the phrases in Column A with their meanings in Column B.

Column A | Column B
1. in light of | A. to think unfavorably of
2. stray from | B. able to be reached, used, visited, etc
3. alliance with | C. to demonstrate
4. lead up to | D. to wander away
5. access to | E. to happen
6. hold out | F. because of
7. take a dim view of | G. to offer
8. attest to | H. jointed or United with

B. Use the proper forms of the phrases to complete the sentences.

| stray from | alliance with | in light of | lead up to |
| access to | hold out | attest to | take a dim view of |

(1) _____ recent incidents, we are asking our customers to take particular care of their personal belongings.
(2) Young children should not be allowed to _____ their parents.
(3) Mary _____ her son's recent behaviour.
(4) They can each _____ my hard work ethic and persistence.
(5) Some of us feel that the union is in _____ management against us.
(6) The pilot had no recollection of the events _____ the crash.
(7) Doctors _____ little hope of her recovering.
(8) The system has been designed to give the user quick and easy _____ the required information.

II. Fill in the blanks with the proper forms of the words.

(1) He was convinced that he was being _____ (victim) for his energetic pursuit of penetration.
(2) For this reason, China _____ (waver) pursues a foreign policy of peace and independence. It resolutely protects its national independence and sovereignty and opposes
(3) If pride exists amongst any folks in our country, and _____ (assure) we have enough of it, there is no pride more deep-seated than that of two penny old gentle women on small towns.
(4) The trend is away from aggressive _____ (expansion) toward realistic survivalism.
(5) Since bigger firms were not prepared to give it their backing, the project was _____ (foredoom) to failure.

(6) Having heard of the news, he was in a constant, _____ (turbulence) riot.

(7) Shi Ming, by Liu Xi of Dong Han Dynasty, is one of the important _____ (exegetics) works in the history of Chinese language.

(8) A significant portion of the population is color-blind, so color alone is _____ (sufficient) to distinguish between selections.

(9) When the women's liberation movement appeared, at first only a few housewives gave it open _____ (allegiant).

(10) The government adopted a (an) _____ (compromise) posture on the issue of independence.

Comprehensive Work

I. Group Work

Select one passage from Isaiah, Jeremiah, or Ezekiel and illustrate what kind of people they are. You can use any art form you wish. Share what you have created.

II. Essay Writing

Pick one social ill or problem. Then write a "prophetic" message in the style of one of the three prophets to call attention to the situation. You can use an oracle, a vision, a parable, or even a rant. Try to use language and images that will communicate to an audience of your contemporaries.

III. Solo Work

1. Put in the missing words.

   Isaiah is a book that unveils the full dimensions of God's judgment and salvation. God is "the Holy One of Israel" who must punish his rebellious people but will afterward redeem them. Israel is a nation blind and d_____, a vineyard that will be trampled, a people devoid o_____ justice or righteousness. The awful judgment that will be unleashed upon Israel and all the nations that defy God is called "the day of the Lord." Although Israel h_____ a foretaste of that day, the nations bear its full power. It is a day associated in the NT with Christ's second coming and the accompanying judgment. Throughout the book, God's judgment is referred to as "fire". He is the "Sovereign Lord", far above all nations and rulers.

   Yet God will have compassion on his people and will r_____ them from both political and spiritual oppression. Their restoration is like a new exdus as God redeems them and saves them. Israel's mighty Creator will make streams spring u_____ in the desert as he graciously leads them home. The theme of a highway for the return of exiles is a prominent one in both major parts of the book. The Lord raises a banner to summon the nations to bring Israel home.

2. Proofreading and error correction

   Ezekiel had a vision of four living creatures, each of which had four faces. Chapter 1 verse 10 reads: "Their faces looked like this: Each of the four had the face of a man, and on the right side each had the face of a lion, and on the left the face of an ox; each also had the face of an eagle." What does all this mean?

   God chose four men to write about the life of Jesus, correspond to these   (1) _____

 four creatures. Matthew sees Jesus as the lion or king. (The lion is associated with the royal tribe of Judah to which King David and his descendants belonged.) Accordingly Matthew begins his gospel with the words "A record of the genealogy of Jesus Christ the son of David, the son of Abraham", and continues by tracing his linage all the way down.

Mark sees Jesus as the exact opposite, an ox or a servant. There is no genealogy, or even any kind of birth story. It wouldn't be appropriate for a servant. Either is there much teaching recorded. Mark is all about action. Jesus is serving his father.   (2) _____
(3) _____

Luke sees Jesus as the man. He gives us all the details about his birth, and then traces his ancestry right the way back up to Adam (whose name means man). It is Luke who gives us the more personal details of Jesus' life. Only he tells us how Jesus was thrown out of his own city of Nazareth and sweated droops of blood in Gethsemane.   (4) _____

John sees Jesus as the flying eagle, that soars up in the heaven realms.   (5) _____
This represents God. In John the birth story is very different from what Matthew and Luke give. John is the gospel of "I am". I am the bread of life, the light of the world, the door, the good shepherd, the resurrection, and the life, the way, the truth and the life, the true vine.

Read More

Text B The prophet Jeremiah

You've probably seen cartoon or movie depictions of the *Prophet of Doom*, a **shaggy-bearded** individual in ragged robes. These **caricatures** for the most part are based on the figure of Jeremiah, the original biblical prophet of doom. It was Jeremiah's destiny to be called to prophecy in a time of relative prosperity and peace for **Judah** just before the fall of Jerusalem and the destruction of the First Temple. It was a time when the people and their leaders were **smugly** comfortable in their mistreatment of the poor and their adoption of **pagan** religious practices.

The prophet Jeremiah was active in Jerusalem during the tragic period of the city's destruction by the **Babylonians**, a process that involved several stages. Jeremiah's prophecies of destruction spoke of an **ineluctable, unavertible** disaster: "Lo, I am bringing against you, O House of Israel, a nation from afar declares the Lord. It is an enduring nation... a nation whose language you do not know... Their quivers are like a yawning grave they are all mighty men. They will devour your harvest and food, they will devour your sons and daughters..." (Jeremiah 5:15-17). And again: "As for you, do not pray for this people, do not raise a cry of prayer on their behalf, do not plead with Me; for I will not listen to you" (7:16). The prophet, who launched his mission in his native village of Anathoth, lying northeast of Jerusalem, was rejected by his fellow villagers, as his doom-laden prophecies would later be rejected in Jerusalem: "**Assuredly**, thus said the Lord of Hosts concerning the men of **Anathoth** who seek your life and say, 'You must not prophesy any more in the name of the Lord, or you will die by our hand ...' I am going to deal with them: the young men shall die by the sword, their boys and girls shall die by famine" (11:21-22).

Jeremiah severely **castigated** the people for forsaking God and the Torah and turning to **idolatry.** Aware of the **inevitability** of a terrible punishment, he felt disgust with his life. Gradually he became the leading **exponent** of the approach which called for surrender to Babylonian might and not attempting a rebellion against its awesome strength under the **auspices** of Egypt. This was considered a **defeatist stance** and as such was rejected both by the people and by the various kings during whose reigns Jeremiah uttered his prophecies. The concept which had been successfully **enunciated** by the prophet Isaiah about a century earlier, holding that Jerusalem and the Temple possessed an almost magical **inviolability**, had become **distorted** by Jeremiah's time, and was no longer bound up with the moral leadership of the nation. The prophet railed against this approach: "Thus said the Lord of Hosts, the God of Israel: mend your ways and your actions, and I will let you dwell in this place. Don't put your trust in illusions and say, The Temple of the Lord, the Temple of the Lord, the Temple of the Lord are these [buildings]. ... therefore I will do to the House which bears My name, on which you rely... just what I did to Shiloh" (7:3-4, 14). Considered a traitor, Jeremiah was placed outside the law during the reign of Zedekiah and placed in **detention** until the destruction of the city by Nebuchadnezzar. He saw the shattering of the last hope for the survivors of the destruction in the murder of **Gedaliah**, whom the Babylonians had appointed to rule over Judah. Although Jeremiah was saliently a prophet of **apocalypse**, he emphasized the temporary nature of the destruction and the consolation to be found in the certainty of the nation's return to its land.

Questions for discussion or reflection.
(1) What was considered a defeatist stance?
(2) Why was Jeremiah thought to be a betrayer?

Text C Ezekiel the Prophet

Ezekiel was one of the most **dynamic** individuals in Hebrew Scriptures. Serving as a priest and prophet, Ezekiel's ideals for society were shaped by his duties to both offices. As a result, Ezekiel was a complex person.

Ezekiel was one of the prophets of Israel who communicated God's message in a variety of ways. Frequently, he would act out his prophecy. In Chapter 4, he used a tile and an iron pan to act out a scene of Jerusalem under siege. In Chapter 5, he burned his hair and beard to signify the coming destruction of the city. In a culture where there was limited written communication, such dramatic gestures made the prophet's messages more memorable.

Ezekiel's use of various means of prophetic expression gave dramatic force to his message. At the core of his message was the unfolding of God's saving purpose in the history of the world—

from God's **withdrawal** to the great redemption of God's people.

Ezekiel's mission was to encourage the people to remain faithful while in Babylon. Though exile had its sorrows, Ezekiel urged the people to prosper in their new circumstances, lending their expertise as craftspeople to the imperial building programs under way in **Nebuchadnezzar's** kingdom. Quickly, the memory of Jerusalem's devastation faded, and the exiles began to assimilate, intermarry, and take up the customs of those around them.

But it is his visions for which **Ezekiel** is best known. The "four living creatures" and "**wheels within wheels**" from Ezekiel's vision of God's chariot have made their way into Western art and the mystical traditions of Judaism and Christianity.

The familiar vision of "**dry bones**" in Ezekiel Chapter 37 is truly remarkable because it suggests that those who are dead may live again. The vision is a step-by-step reconstruction of a skeleton that eventually got flesh, and then God breathed into it so that it became a living being again. This vision expressed to Israel a sense of God's mercy and a vision of hope for the people in the depths of their demoralized troubles. It predicted that God would renew the vitality of the Israelites and that God would inspire them with strength and courage to return to Israel.

Ezekiel's prophecy **foreshadowed** things to come. The metaphor of the bones described the hopeless defeatism of his fellow Israelites as he saw in exile in Babylon. But the living breath of God, the very wind itself, would breathe new life into them and bring them home. Ezekiel, living just after the destruction of Jerusalem in exile in Babylon, looked forward to a time of return. This return did occur when Cyrus, the Persian king, conquered Babylon some forty-eight years after the exile began. Cyrus permitted the people of Israel to go home. This prophecy has also been applied to more recent times when many people have seen the words of the prophet as the initial acts of God's strategy to return the people of Israel to the Promised Land the establishment of the state of Israel in May 1948. Ezekie's vision of a rebuilt temple inspired those who returned to Jerusalem after the exile. And every child who ever sang "The leg bone's connected to knee bone" has, knowingly or unknowingly, celebrated Ezekiel's profound and hopeful vision, the reinvigoration of the "dry bones" of the House of Israel by the mighty wind of God's spirit.

The messages of Isaiah, Jeremiah, Ezekiel, and the other Biblical prophets have inspired countless people over the centuries to work for a better world, to challenge injustice, and to lift the human spirit.

Questions for discussion or reflection.
(1) What dramatic gestures did Ezekiel make to communicate God's message?
(2) Do you know "four living creatures and "wheels within wheels"?
(3) What does the vision of "dry bones" suggest?

Notes

(1) **Babylonian captivity:** Although the term Babylonian captivity, or Babylonian exile, typically refers to the deportation and exile of the Jews of the ancient Kingdom of Judah to Babylon by

Nebuchadnezzar II in 586 BC, in fact the exile started with the first deportation in 597 BC. The captivity and subsequent return to Israel and rebuilding of the Jerusalem Temple are pivotal events in the history of the Jews and Judaism, and had far-reaching impacts on the development of modern Jewish culture and practice.

(2) **Gedaliah**: According to the Hebrew Bible, Gedaliah—the son of Ahikam (who saved the life of the prophet Jeremiah—Jer. 26:24) and grandson of Shaphan (who was involved in the discovery of the scroll of Teaching that scholars identify as the core of the book of Deuteronomy —II Kings 22:8-10) served briefly as governor of Judah. After the destruction of Jerusalem, Nebuchadnezzar appointed Gedaliah as governor of Judah and left him to govern the country as a tribute to him (2 Kings 25:22; Jer. 40:5; 52:16).

Book to Read

The Prophetic Literature: An Introduction by David L. Petersen. Louisville

David Petersen, a professor of Old Testament at Iliff School of Theology and longtime student of ancient Israel's prophets, is eminently qualified to write this introduction. Beginning with a chapter that concisely but carefully defines the character of biblical prophetic literature, Petersen sets forth the issues central to its interpretation, including a helpful presentation of ancient Near Eastern prophecy. The primary audience for this volume, though not explicitly named, is clearly students who are reading or have read the *Old Testament* prophets and who wish to have a brief but solid overview of the nature of this literature.

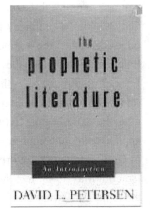

Movies to See

1. *2012*

The film briefly refers to Mayanism, the Mesoamerican Long Count calendar, and the *2012* phenomenon in its portrayal of cataclysmic events unfolding in the year 2012. Because of solar flare bombardment the Earth's core begins heating up at an unprecedented rate, eventually causing crustal displacement. This results in an onslaught of Doomsday event scenarios plunging the world into chaos. Ranging from Los Angeles falling into the Pacific Ocean, the eruption of the Yellowstone National Park caldera, cataclysmic earthquakes wreaking havoc around the globe, and Megatsunamis surging across the Earth, The film centers around an ensemble cast of characters as they narrowly escape multiple catastrophes in an effort to reach ships in the Himalayas, along with scientists and governments of the world who are attempting to save as many lives as they can before the disasters ensue.

2. Jeremiah

Jeremiah tells the tale of the prophet who abandons his family and the woman he loves in order to relay God's message of the impending demise of the Holy City. Although he's met with disbelief and eventually branded a traitor for delivering such atrocious news, he continues his task until his prophecy is fulfilled and Jerusalem is destroyed by the Babylonians.

Song to Enjoy

Here is part of the lyrics of "Time for Miracles". Find the audio and enjoy the song. You can complete the lyrics while listening.

Time for Miracles
by Adam Lambert

It's late at night and I can't sleep
Missing you just runs too deep
Oh I can't breathe thinking of your smile

Every kiss I can't forget
This aching heart ain't broken yet
Oh God I wish I could make you see
Cuz I know this flame isn't dying
So nothing can stop me from trying

Baby you know that
Maybe it's time for miracles

Cuz I ain't giving up on love
You know that
Maybe it's time for miracles
Cuz I ain't giving up on love
No I ain't giving up on us

I just wanna be with you
Cuz living is so hard to do
When all I know is trapped inside your eyes

The future I cannot forget
This aching heart ain't broken yet
Oh God I wish I could make you see

...

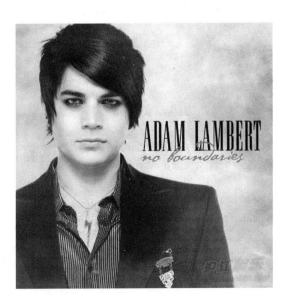

Unit 8
Slaves and *the Bible*

> Man is the only Slave. And he is the only animal who enslaves. He has always been a slave in one form or another, and has always held other slaves in bondage under him in one way or another.
> —Mark Twain

Unit Goals

- To get to know what *the Bible* says about slavery
- To develop a right attitude towards slavery in *the Bible*
- To discover the fate of Jacob's descendants in Egypt
- To learn useful words and expressions about slaves in *the Bible*
- To improve English language skills and western culture awareness

Before You Read

(1) Are there slaves in *the Bible*? How are they treated?
(2) Consider why accounts of a journey from bondage to freedom have such a strong appeal?
(3) Develop a creative presentation of the themes of liberation and deliverance expressed in the Exodus narrative. Feel free to choose poetry, song, painting, dance, or play as your medium. Make your creation as contemporary as you can.

Start to Read

Text A The General Picture of Slavery

Rules against mistreatment

The Bible prohibits the Hebrews from killing their slaves; since slaves were considered property, such a rule was not typical throughout history.

Hebrews are also forbidden to injure a slave, and an injured slave is allowed to go free. It is forbidden to force a slave to work through the Sabbath, to return an escaped slave, or to **slander** a slave. Slaves were to be treated as part of an extended family; they were allowed to celebrate the **Sukkot** festival, and

expected to honor Shabbat. Israelite slaves could not to be compelled to work with rigor, and debtors who sold themselves as slaves to their creditors had to be treated the same as a hired servant.

Named slaves

Biblical figures who kept slaves included the patriarchs Abraham and Isaac, Boaz (from the Ruth story) and King Solomon. Slaves mentioned in *the Bible* include Hagar, Sarah's handmaid who was used by her as a **surrogate** mother, and **Eliezer** of **Damascus**, who was in charge of Abraham's household and **charged with** finding a bride for Isaac. Also, **Bilhah** is described as Rachel's handmaid and **Zilpah** as Leah's handmaid, both of whom are given to Jacob as concubines and whose children with him **rank** equally with those of Rachael and Leah, **on the basis** that they were acting as surrogates of their mistress.

There is also the story of the sale of Joseph by his brothers for twenty pieces of silver and the enslavement of the Hebrews in Egypt and their liberation by the hand of God in the Exodus, led by Moses, who was himself born a slave.

Most of these biblical references to slave ownership predate the handing down of the Mosaic Law at Mount Sinai following the Exodus.

Enslavement

In the Ancient Near East, captives obtained through warfare were often compelled to become slaves, and this was seen by the law code of Deuteronomy as a legitimate form of enslavement, as long as Israelites were not among the victims; the **Deuteronomic Code** institutes the death penalty for the crime of kidnapping Israelites in order to enslave them.

Yet the Israelites did not **get involved in** distant or large scale wars, and apparently capture was not a significant source of slaves. The **Holiness Code** of **Leviticus** explicitly allows participation in the slave trade, adding that non-Israelite residents who had been sold into slavery should be regarded as property, and could be inherited. Foreign residents were included in this permission, and were allowed to own Israelite slaves.

It was also possible to **be born into** slavery. Indeed, if a male Israelite slave was freed, then his wife and any children they had had together would still remain the property of his former owner, according to the Covenant Code, unless the slave had been married to the wife before his enslavement began. However, although the text doesn't actually mention the wife's nationality, Adam Clarke, an 18th century methodist theologian, argued that this should be interpreted to only refer to marriage to a Canaanite woman; in Clarke's opinion, there was an Israelite law instructing that if an Israelite slave had children by a Canannitish woman, those children must be considered as Canaanitish only, and might be sold and bought, and serve for ever.

Debt slavery

Like that of the Ancient Near East, the legal systems of the Israelites divided "slaves" into different categories "in determining who should benefit from their intervention, the legal systems **drew** two important **distinctions:** between debt and **chattel** slaves, and between native and foreign slaves. The authorities intervened **first and foremost** to protect the former category of each—citizens who had fallen on hard times and had been forced into slavery by debt or famine".

Poverty, and more general lack of economic security, compelled some people to enter debt bondage. Furthermore, in the ancient Near East, wives and (non-adult) children were often viewed as property, and were sometimes sold into slavery by the husband/father for financial reasons. Evidence of this viewpoint is found in the Code of Hammurabi, which permits debtors to sell their wives and

children into temporary slavery, lasting a maximum of three years; the Holiness Code also exhibits this, allowing foreign residents to sell their own children and families to Israelites, although no limitation is placed on the duration of such slavery.

The earlier Covenant Code instructs that if a thief is caught after sunrise, and is unable to **make restitution** for the theft, then the thief should be enslaved. The Book of Kings instructs that the children of a deceased debtor may be forced into slavery to **pay off** outstanding debts; similarly it is evident from the Book of Isaiah that, in the Kingdom of Judah, (living) debtors could be forced to sell their children into slavery in order to pay the creditors.

After You Read

Knowledge Focus

I. Pair Work: Work with your partner and consider the following questions.

(1) How much do you know about "surrogate mother" in *the Bible* and in modern society?
(2) Would you please tell the story of the sale of Joseph by his brothers?
(3) What are the sources of slaves?
(4) What kind of people can become debt slaves?
(5) Under what kind of condition can a thief be enslaved?

II. Solo Work: According to the knowledge mentioned above, write T if the statement is true and F if it is false.

(1) Sarah's slave Hagar was badly treated in *the Bible*. ( )
(2) Moses was born to be a slave. ( )
(3) It is illegal for the Hebrews to get involved in slave trade. ( )
(4) Foreign residents could own and inherit Israelite slaves. ( )
(5) Neither male nor female slaves can be freed even if he and she get married before his enslavement.
( )
(6) The Code of Hammurabi permits debtors to sell their wives and children into permanent slavery.
( )

Language Focus

Build your vocabulary.

A. Match the phrases in Column A with their meanings in Column B.

Column A	Column B
1. pay off	A. to make a difference to
2. draw distinctions	B. to cause to become connected
3. pull rank (on)	C. to be successful
4. on the basis of	D. to make use of one's superior rank to gain an advantage over (someone)
5. get involved in	E. to give as a duty or responsibility
6. make restitution	F. to return something lost

7. first and foremost   G. on account of
8. charge with   H. the most important

B. Use the proper forms of the phrases to complete the sentences.

| pay off | draw distinctions | on the basis of | first and foremost |
| pull rank | get involved in | charge with | make restitution |

(1) Is it safe to predict the result _____ one opinion poll?
(2) All her hard work _____ in the end, and she finally passed the exam.
(3) Is it so easy to _____ between the enjoyment of a sandwich and the enjoyment of the surrounding landscape, which we call poetry?
(4) When my assistant became obstinate I had to _____ and insist that he obey.
(5) In spite of being elected to office, she remains _____ a writer.
(6) Sometimes _____ an activity can take your mind off your problems.
(7) He was sentenced to time served, probation, community service, and ordered to _____ and undergo counseling.
(8) He _____ getting this message to the commissioners.

Comprehensive Work

I. Group Work

Slavery then and now: a debate

Topic: That wage slavery in the modern world is the same as slavery in past ages.

(1) Divide into two sides.
(2) Decide which side will support the proposal and which will oppose it.
(3) In small groups on each side, draw up a list of at least three points to support your argument.
(4) Share the points between groups, and decide which points should be argued most strongly.
(5) Nominate the people who will speak, and a chairperson.
(6) Team members meet and prepare their arguments.
(7) Go over the rules for a debate, what may or may not be said and done.
(8) Conduct the debate.
(9) Hold a debriefing/discussion.

II. Essay Writing

    In our day he is always some man's slave for wage, and does that man's work; and this slave has other slaves under him for minor wages, and they do his work. The higher animals are the only ones who exclusively do their own work and provide their own living.

    Mark Twain's "The Lowest Animal"

    High housing prices have rendered the post-80's generation in China to be mortgage slave. They become "mortgage slaves" (可以指"房奴"、"车奴"及"孩奴"等) to their apartments and cars, even to the newly born children. ***Dwelling Narrowness,*** (蜗居) a hit TV series, reflects the public sentiment on house slaves.

    Please write an essay on: "**Who enslaved you?**"

III. Solo Work

1. Put in the missing words.

Thomas Jefferson, James Madison, and George Washington were slaveholders. So, too, were Benjamin Franklin and the theologian Jonathan Edwards. John Newton, the composer of "Amazing Grace," captained a slave ship early in his life. Robinson Crusoe, the fictional c_____ in Daniel Defoe's famous novel, was engaged in the slave t_____ when he was shipwrecked.

Slavery has often been treated as a marginal aspect of history, confined to courses on southern or African American h_____. In fact, slavery played a crucial role in the making of the modern world. Slavery provided the labor f_____ for the Slavery played an indispensable role in the settlement and development of the New World.

Slavery dates to prehistoric times and could be found in ancient Babylon, classical Greece and Rome, China, India, and Africa as w_____ as in the New World.

2. Proofreading and error correction.

If there is anything in *the Bible* that makes modern people nervous, it is its treatment of slavery. Slavery is humanely regulated in the legal portions of the *Old Testament*, and in the *New Testament* slaveholders are exhorted to show kindness to slaves, but somewhere in *the Bible* is there anything which can be interpreted as a disapproval of the institution as such. People of our generation, Christians including, tend to have a very hard time with this because it seems to amount to a tacit approval of the institution, and we balk at the idea that God did not consider the institution itself to be immoral.

(1) _____

(2) _____

Part of the problem is that we have false ideas about what slavery was really like. The life of a slave was not easy, but we get an exaggerated idea of the hardship of slavery from watching movies or reading historic material that is written on a popular level. Here the purpose is usually to dramatize the plight of slaves or to make some point about the evils of slavery in general, but the historical reality was less dramatic. In most case the life of a slave was much different from the life of any lower-class worker. Those who have been in the military have experienced something like it — being legally bound to an employer and to a job that one cannot simply "quit" at will, not free to leave without permission, subject to discipline if one disobeys or is grossly negligent — al l of this is familiar enough to those of us who have served in the military. And yet we know that the daily life of a good soldier is not especially hard. This is what it was like to be a slave.

(3) _____
(4) _____

(5) _____

Read More

Text B Treatment of Slaves

Except for murder, slavery has got to be one of the most immoral things a person can do. Yet slavery is **rampant** throughout *the Bible* in both the *Old* and *New Testaments*. *The Bible* clearly approves of slavery in many passages, and it goes so far as to tell how to obtain slaves, how hard you can beat them, and when you can have sex with the female slaves.

Many Jews and Christians will try to ignore the moral problems of slavery by saying that these slaves were actually servants or indentured servants. Many translations of *the Bible* use the word "servant", "**bondservant**", or "manservant" instead of "slave" to make *the Bible* seem less immoral than it really is. While many slaves may have worked as household servants, that doesn't mean that they were not slaves who were bought, sold, and treated worse than livestock.

The following passage shows that slaves are clearly property to be bought and sold like livestock.

However, you may purchase male or female slaves from the foreigners who live among you. You may also purchase the children of such resident foreigners, including those who have been born in your land. You may treat them as your property, passing them on to your children as a permanent inheritance. You may treat your slaves like this, but the people of Israel, your relatives, must never be treated this way. (Leviticus 25:44–46 NLT)

The following passage describes how the Hebrew slaves are to be treated.

If you buy a Hebrew slave, he is to serve for only six years. Set him free in the seventh year, and he will owe you nothing for his freedom. If he was single when he became your slave and then married afterward, only he will go free in the seventh year. But if he was married before he became a slave, then his wife will be freed with him. If his master gave him a wife while he was a slave, and they had sons or daughters, then the man will be free in the seventh year, but his wife and children will still belong to his master. But the slave may plainly declare, 'I love my master, my wife, and my children. I would rather not go free.' If he does this, his master must present him before God. Then his master must take him to the door and publicly pierce his ear with an awl. After that, the slave will belong to his master forever. (Exodus 21:2–6 NLT)

Notice how they can get a male Hebrew slave to become a permanent slave by keeping his wife and children **hostage** until he says he wants to become a permanent slave. What kind of family values are these?

The following passage describes the sickening practice of sex slavery. How can anyone think it is moral to sell your own daughter as a sex slave?

When a man sells his daughter as a slave, she will not be freed at the end of six years as the men are. If she does not please the man who bought her, he may allow her to be bought back again. But he is not allowed to sell her to foreigners, since he is the one who broke the contract with her. And if the slave girl's owner arranges for her to marry his son, he may no longer treat her as a slave girl, but he must treat her as his daughter. If he himself marries her and then takes another wife, he may not reduce her food or clothing or fail to sleep with her as his wife. If he fails in any of these three ways, she may leave as a free woman without making any payment. (Exodus 21:7–11 NLT)

So these are the Bible family values! A man can buy as many sex slaves as he wants as long as he feeds them, clothes them, and screws them!

What does *the Bible* say about beating slaves? It says you can beat both male and female slaves with a rod so hard that as long as they don't die right away you are cleared of any wrong doing.

When a man strikes his male or female slave with a rod so hard that the slave dies under his hand, he shall be punished. If, however, the slave survives for a day or two, he is not to be punished, since the slave is his own property. (Exodus 21:20–21 NAB)

You would think that Jesus and the *New Testament* would have a different view of slavery, but slavery is still approved of in the *New Testament*, as the following passages show.

Slaves, obey your earthly masters with deep respect and fear. Serve them sincerely as you would serve Christ. (Ephesians 6:5 NLT)

Christians who are slaves should give their masters full respect so that the name of God and his teaching will not be shamed. If your master is a Christian, that is no excuse for being disrespectful. You should work all the harder because you are helping another believer by your efforts. Teach these truths, Timothy, and encourage everyone to obey them. (1 Timothy 6:1–2 NLT)

In the following parable, Jesus clearly approves of beating slaves even if they didn't know they were doing anything wrong.

The servant will be severely punished, for though he knew his duty, he refused to do it. "But people who are not aware that they are doing wrong will be punished only lightly. Much is required from those to whom much is given, and much more is required from those to whom much more is given." (Luke 12: 47–48 NLT)

Questions for discussion or reflection.
(1) Why is slavery unrestrained throughout *the Bible* in both the *Old* and *New Testaments*?
(2) How are the Hebrew slaves treated according to *the Bible*?
(3) What does *the Bible* say about beating slaves?

Unit 8 Slaves and the Bible

Text C Slavery and the Bible

Slavery is **condoned** by the Torah, which occasionally compels it. Besides the **mainstay** of the slave trade, it was seen as legitimate to enslave captives obtained through warfare, but it was also a capital crime to kidnap Israelites and non-Israelites for the purpose of enslaving them. It was also possible to be born into slavery, if the child's mother wasn't married to the father prior to the father's enslavement.

However, like other **Semitic** cultures of the time, *the Bible* does set minimum rules for the conditions under which slaves were to be kept; many of these rules resemble earlier regulations from the region, such as the Hittite Laws and the Code of **Hammurabi**. Slaves were to be treated as part of an extended family; they were allowed to celebrate the Sukkot festival, expected to honour Shabbat, and, if Israelite, could not to be compelled to work with rigour. This is not to say that slaves were never biblically regarded purely as property; if a slave was **gored** by an ox, the ox owner was fined 30 shekels, the fine going to the slave's master, rather than the slave.

The Bible uses the Hebrew term *ebed* to refer to slavery; however, *ebed* has a much wider meaning than the English term slavery, and in several circumstances it is more accurately translated into English as servant. As a figurative reference, *ebed* can also refer to forms of devotion, including both religious piety and being a courtier. Like the rest of the Ancient Near East, the legal systems of the Israelites also made a distinction between Israelite and non-Israelite slaves, and distinguished slavery-with-marriage from the other forms of slavery.

Foreign residents were permitted to sell their children into debt bondage, and in the kingdom of Judah debtors could be compelled to do so; the kingdom of Israel sold children off to balance the debts of the dead debtors. If a beautiful woman was captured by military activity, she could be enslaved with the intent of betrothing her later, but if she was subsequently rejected she had to be freed, and she could never be sold.

Slaves in debt bondage, and Israelite slaves owned by foreign residents, were automatically freed at the next national Jubilee (occurring either every 49 or every 50 years, depending on interpretation), if they hadn't already purchased their freedom; male Israelite slaves were automatically **manumitted** after they have worked for six years, as were female Israelite slaves, or not. Non-Israelite slaves were to be enslaved forever, and treated as **inheritable** property, but if slaves

of any nationality ran away they were to be allowed to **roam** freely, and returning them to their masters was forbidden.

The Slave trade

The fear of **apostasy** was behind most of the classical **rabbis'** regulation of the slave trade. Despite *the Bible* allowing Israelite slaves to be owned by non-Israelite residents, the **Talmud** prohibited sale of Jewish slaves to non-Jews. Although the **Samaritans** believed themselves to be the original Israelites, the rabbis counted them as non-Jews in regard to this regulation. Nevertheless, short temporary loans of slaves were potentially permitted. The Talmud argued that the sale of Jewish slaves to a convert or to a non-Jew, even to a non-Jewish temple, was to be **upheld**, but all Jews would then be required to buy the slave's freedom, whatever the price. Trade with **Tyre**, which had formally been significant, was now to be restricted to the slave trade, and only then for the purpose of removing slaves from non-Jewish religion.

Other types of trade were also discouraged, including men selling themselves to women. The Talmud instructed that treating slaves as security for a loan, while not itself forbidden, must immediately result in the **manumission** of the slave in question. Religious racism by the classical rabbis meant that they completely forbade the sale or transfer of **Canaanite** slaves out from Palestine to elsewhere.

Female slaves

The biblical ability for fathers to sell their daughters into slavery was restricted by the classical sources, to extend only to pre-pubescent daughters, and only then as a last resort before the father has to sell himself. The sale was only regarded as complete when payment is received, or when a deed is written in the name of the daughter's father. Although the biblical text clearly differentiates between selling daughters with the intention of their marriage, and other forms of slavery, the Talmud argued that when a pre-**pubescent** girl was sold into slavery, their master must marry her, or marry her to his son, when she starts **puberty**. If the master failed to marry the girl, or marry her to his son, she was to be freed.

The classical rabbis instructed that masters could never marry female slaves—they would have to be manumitted first. Similarly, they ruled that male slaves could not be allowed to marry Jewish women. By contrast, masters were given the right to the services of the wives of any of their slaves, if the enslaved husband had been sold into slavery by a court of law. Unlike the biblical instruction to sell thieves into slavery (if they were caught during daylight, and couldn't repay the theft), the rabbis ordered that female Israelites could never be sold into slavery for this reason.

Questions for discussion or reflection.
(1) What rules does *the Bible* set to keep slaves?
(2) What does the Hebrew term "ebed" mean?
(3) What types of slave trade are forbidden according to *the Bible*?

Notes

(1) **Deuteronomic Code:** The Deuteronomic Code forms several mitzvah, approximately one third of the mitzvot in the Torah, and is therefore a major constituent of Jewish Law. While several of the laws are repetitions of those present elsewhere in the Torah, many have notable variations, and there are additionally many further laws which are unique to the code.
(2) **The Holiness Code:** It is a term used in biblical criticism to refer to Leviticus 17-26, and is so called due to its highly repeated use of the word Holy. It has no special traditional religious significance and traditional Jews and Christians do not regard it as having any distinction from any other part of the Book of Leviticus. Biblical scholars have regarded it as a distinct unit and

have noted that the style is noticeably different from the main body of Leviticus: unlike the remainder of Leviticus, many laws of the Holiness Code are expressed very closely packed together, and very briefly. According to the documentary hypothesis, the Holiness Code represents an earlier text that was edited and incorporated into the priestly source and the Torah as a whole.

For Fun

Book to read

Uncle Tom's Cabin by Harriet Beecher Stowe was the best-selling novel of the 19th century, and the second best-selling book of that century, following *the Bible*. It is credited with helping fuel the abolitionist cause in the 1850s. In the first year after it was published, 300,000 copies of the book were sold in the United States alone. The book's impact was so great that when Abraham Lincoln met Stowe at the start of the Civil War, Lincoln is often quoted as having declared, "So this is the little lady who made this big war."

Movie to See:

Uncle Tom's Cabin (1987): For years, the name "Uncle Tom" and the title *Uncle Tom's Cabin* have been synonymous with the most egregious form of racial condescension. John Gay's script for the 1987 film version of Harriet Beecher Stowe's *Uncle Tom's Cabin* hoped to "set the record straight" and restored the reputation of the 1852 abolitionist novel—mostly by returning to the source. Eliminating such theatrical "improvements" as Eliza's crossing the ice, this adaptation of Cabin depicts Uncle Tom (Avery Brooks) as an intelligent, non-submissive slave (there is only the slightest hint of "revisionism").

Song to Enjoy:

Here is part of the lyrics of "Uncle Tom's Cabin". Find the audio and enjoy the song. You can complete the lyrics while listening.

Uncle Tom's Cabin
by Artist (Band):Warrant

Just for the record let's get the story straight
Me and Uncle Tom were fishing it was getting pretty late
Out on a cypress limb above the wishin' well
Where they say it got no bottom, say it take you down to hell!

Over in the bushes and off to the right
Come two men talkin' in the pale moon light

Sheriff John Brady and Deputy Hedge
haulin' two limp bodies down to the water's edge

I know a secret down at Uncle Tom's Cabin, oh yeah
I know a secret that I just can't tell

They didn't see me and Tom in the trees
Neither one believing what the other could see
Tossed in the bodies, let 'em sink on down
To the bottom of the well where they'd never be found

I know a secret down at Uncle Tom's Cabin, oh yeah
I know a secret that I just can't tell
I know a secret down at Uncle Tom's Cabin
I know a secret that I just can't tell
I know a secret down at Uncle Tom's Cabin
Know who put the bodies in the wishing well!

Soon as they were gone me and Tom got down
Prayin' real hard that we wouldn't make a sound

Running through the woods back to Uncle Tom's shack
Where the full moon shines through the roof tile cracks

Oh my God, Tom, who are we gonna tell?
The Sheriff he belongs in a prison cell
Keep your mouth shut that's what we're gonna do
Unless you wanna wind up in the "Wishin' Well" too?

……

Unit 9

Weapons and Warfare and *the Bible*

> A sword is never a killer, it is a tool in the killer's hands.
> —Seneca

Unit Goals

- To gain a general knowledge of types of weapons in *the Bible*
- To get acquainted with the size and organization of armies
- To discover the heroic qualities found in the leaders during the early years in Canaan.
- To get to know Jael, Gideon, Samson, Deliah, Jephthah, Samuel
- To learn useful words and expressions about weapons and warfare in *the Bible*
- To improve English language skills and western culture awareness

Before You Read

(1) Do you know the following weapons, which can be traced back to the Bible time? What are their English names? Where can you see them now?

(2) The picture in the middle of the following is a military weapon used in the Bible time. What is its name? Which of the animals around could have been used to pull it in war?

(3) Form groups of three or four students. Try to find, on the Internet or in the library, more information about weapons used in *the Bible*. Get ready for a 5-minute presentation in class.

《圣经》与文化
The Bible & Culture

Start to Read

Text A Weapons

The book of Judges describes the period when the Israelites were settling into the Promised Land following the Exodus from Egypt. Because the conquest was not complete, warfare was frequent, and **resulted in** the hero stories preserved in **Judges**. These heroes were known as "judges", meaning, not people who decided court cases, but military leaders who delivered Israel from her enemies. What weapons did these heroes use, and what was their strategy in defeating their enemies?

Offensive weapons

Offensive weapons in use at this time can be divided into three categories according to their range. Short-range weapons were used in hand-to-hand combat and included the sword or **dagger** and the spear. Medium-range weapons were designed to be thrown at enemies a short distance away. Occasionally spears were light enough to be thrown, but the shorter and lighter javelin was better suited for throwing. Long-range weapons could be thrown or fired at an enemy further away. Examples of long-range weapons include the sling, used to hurl stones, and the bow, for propelling arrows.

The Israelites used mostly "primitive" weapons, such as farm implements and household articles, and had few metal weapons. By contrast, their enemies possessed metal weapons, particularly iron weapons. Iron was much harder and more durable than bronze or copper, and its manufacture took greater technological skill than the Israelites possessed. The Iron Age commenced in Israel during the days of the judges. The Philistines already had something of a monopoly of iron **metallurgy**. As long as the Philistines maintained this monopoly, Israel could not hope to **dislodge** them **from** the plain. On those occasions when the Israelites did **prevail against** their enemies, it **was credited to** divine help; some of their success must also have been the result of better strategies or tactics.

Iron chariots

The men of the tribe of Judah could not drive out the inhabitants of the plain because they had iron chariots. Pulled by two horses, the chariot was in **effect** a moving platform for two or three soldiers. It was most valuable in making rapid **flanking** movements where the land was fairly flat and open. The coastal area of Palestine was relatively level, while the hill-country inland featured steep slopes and deep valleys. In ancient times the hills were heavily

forested and Israelite **guerilla** tactics proved successful in this territory. However, in the coastal plain the Canaanite and Philistine iron chariots proved to be the tanks of their period, racing across the flat country. But chariots were ineffective on wooded hills.

Since the Iron Age had just begun in Canaan, iron chariots would have been the latest and best military weapon. Some scholars believe the iron would have been used to make part of the wheels and fittings of the chariot, while others think there was an iron plate to **reinforce** the wooden body of the chariot. In either case, the iron would have **been superior to** bronze, and would have made the chariot more durable.

Since Israel did not obtain chariots until the time of the monarchy, they simply could not dislodge the people of the coastal plain. But in one **instance** there was a strikingly different result. Jabin and Sisera, from the stronghold of Hazor, had a massive force of 900 iron chariots. But Deborah and Barak, the Israelite leaders, were successful against this superior force because God routed the enemy. There is also the implication that there was a late spring storm which turned the river Kishon into a raging torrent and **rendered** the iron chariots useless in the battle.

Apart from the chariots, the only other enemy weapon mentioned in Judges is the sword. The Midianites possessed them, but in their panic to flee from Gideon, killed one another.

The assassination of Eglon

The Israelites also used some traditional weapons. The story of Ehud, who plotted a daring one-man assassination attack on King Eglon of Moab, is told in Judges 3:12-30. The standard sword of this period was curved, with one sharp edge used for **slicing** and **slashing.** It is sometimes called a sickle sword, and is the basis of the expression "smite the enemy with the edge of the sword". This type of weapon would not have served Ehud's need, since it could not easily have been concealed from the palace guards, nor could it be used to thrust or **stab to death**. So the text explains: "Ehud had made a double-edged sword about a foot and a half long, which he strapped to his right thigh under his clothing". Such metal weapons were still very rare in Israel.

In another incident the judge Gideon told his son, **Jether**, to kill **Zebah** and **Zalmunna** with a sword. However, Jether was afraid because of his youth, and Gideon did it himself. This is one of the rare instances recorded in the book of Judges of an Israelite using a sword.

After Gideon's son **Abimelech** had been severely wounded, he asked his armor-bearer to kill him. The armor-bearer took the sword and killed Abimelech, as commanded. This was apparently one of the accepted functions of the armor-bearer in these times; later King Saul made a similar request of his own armor-bearer.

There is no record in Judges of other individual Israelites using the sword, and the only other conventional weapon mentioned is the sling. We are told that 700 left-handed slingers from the tribe of Benjamin could sling a stone at a hair and not miss.

After You Read

Knowledge Focus

I. Pair Work: Work with your partner and consider the following questions.

(1) What is the meaning of "judge" in *the Bible*?
(2) What weapons did judges use to defeat their enemies?
(3) How many kinds of offensive weapons are divided into according to the text?
(4) What primitive weapons did the Israelites use?
(5) What is the best military weapon according to the text?

II. Solo Work: Fill in the blanks according to Text A.

Offensive weapons in use at this time can be divided into three categories according to their range. Short-range weapons were used in hand-to-hand _____ and included the _____ or _____ and the _____. Medium-range weapons were designed to be thrown at enemies a short distance away. Occasionally spears were _____ enough to be thrown, but the shorter and lighter _____ was better suited for throwing. Long-range weapons could be thrown or _____ at an enemy further away. Examples of long-range weapons include the _____, used to hurl _____, and the bow, for propelling_____.

Language Focus

I. Build your vocabulary.

A. Match the words and phrases in Column A with their meanings in Column B.

Column A   Column B
1. prevail   A. to remove something or someone, especially by force, from a fixed position
2. be credited to   B. to gain control or victory
3. in effect   C. in fact, or in practice
4. dislodge from   D. to cause
5. stab to death   E. to injure someone with a sharp pointed object such as a knife
6. be superior to   F. as a consequence of
7. at the instance of G. be better than average
8. result in   H. add to an account

B. Use the proper forms of the words and phrases to complete the sentences.

| prevail against | be credited to | in effect | dislodge from |
| stab to death | be superior to | result in | at the instance of |

(1) _____ the government have lowered taxes for the rich and raised them for the poor.
(2) The earthquake _____ stones the walls and the roof.
(3) Parents of autistic child _____ school board.

(4) He was jailed for fifteen years for _____ his wife.
(5) For all babies, breastfeeding _____ far bottle feeding.
(6) The profit of $ 480 will _____ his margin account.
(7) Robert applied for the scholarship _____ his professor.
(8) Icy road conditions in Tibet _____ two roads being closed.

II. Fill in the blanks with the proper forms of the words.
(1) The town is kept cool by the _____ (prevail) westerly winds.
(2) David completely _____ (monopoly) the conversation last night; Bill and Sally couldn't get a word in edgeways.
(3) Since the other side had taken _____ (offend) action, we had no choice but to defend ourselves.
(4) The air-conditioner was _____ (effect) in such a crowded room.
(5) Her latest novel is _____ (strike) different from her earlier work.
(6) The attack on him descended to a level of personal character _____ (assassinate).
(7) Small actions add up and a track record of high character is _____ (value) in any relationship.
(8) They had approached each other obliquely and addressed each other by _____ (imply).
(9) More likely than not, recognition is the most available and effective form of ongoing positive _____ (reinforce).
(10) Most products were tested mainly for their safety, performance, convenience, _____ (durable) and environmental impact.

Comprehensive Work
I. Group Work
Discuss the following questions within a group of three or four members.
(1) What heroic character traits did the judges have?
(2) Are these traits still needed in today's society, for example in case of some disasters?
(3) What other traits are needed in today's society? Why?

II. Pair Work
Discuss the following questions with your partner.
(1) What is the book of Judges about?
(2) Why couldn't the men of the tribe of Judah drive out the inhabitants of the plain, although they had great tactics?
(3) What does the expression "smite the enemy with the edge of the sword" mean? Do you know its biblical reference?

III. Essay Writing
Surf the Internet for any information about one or two of the weapons mostly used in today's war. Write an essay to compare it with one of the weapons you have learned in Text A.

IV. Solo Work

1. Put in the missing words.

Hot pursuit, battle cries, secret plans, and chariots experience the intensity of Bible battles from the front lines! Ride with those who led the battles. Stand b_____ the soldiers who fought them. Learn about tons of ancient armor and equipment. This book *Bible Wars & Weapons* puts you in the midst of *the Bible*'s most famous conflicts and reveals what all the fighting was about, its action and adventure straight from *the Bible*! Part of the 252 collection-based on Luke 2: 52-*Bible Wars & Weapons* will make your heart p_____ and help you become smarter, stronger, deeper, and cooler.

What excites boys more than action, adventure, and cool weapons? In *Bible Wars & Weapons* boys ages 8 to 12 can read all about the action and adventure of battle in Bible times. They can experience the thrill and intensity of battle from the frontlines—with those who led the battles and the soldiers who f_____ them. Filled with cool maps that show sites of battle and illustrations of army u_____, boys learn about tons of cool equipment and the armor used during that time. This is action and adventure at its best—straight from the pages of *the Bible*. As part of the 2:52 Soul Gear collection, these high-energy, fast-moving stories will encourage boys in their quest to be smarter, stronger, deeper, and cooler as they d_____ into young men of God.

2. Proofreading and error correction.

Barak was not eager to fight, and when you look at the odds he faced, it's hardly surprising. His enemy was much larger in numbers, well equipped, and with excellent morale. Their technology was far superior to his—the controlled metal-making, so their weaponry was far superior to everything he could give his soldiers to fight with. His enemy, Sisera, had well-disciplined and seasoned troops. As far as Barak could see, facing them would be tantamount to suicide.

(1) _____

(2) _____

He was eventually persuaded to fight by one of the most forceful women in *the Bible*, Deborah. She convinced him that won a battle was not just a question of equipment and training, but of strategy as well—and she had a plan.

(3) _____

They stage the battle near a large swampy area that slowed down the formidable iron-wheeled chariots of the enemy—once these had had a brake put on them, so to speak, they would not be nearly as maneuverable or effective.

(4) _____

At this stage, God stepped in and sent a rainstorm, which not only slowed the chariots but brought them to a standstill. The archers who would

(5) _____

normally had shot from the back of the chariots now had wet bowstrings and limited visibility. Barak's Israelite militia were able to vanquish their enemy totally. Mud was their ally, and the day was won.

Read More

Text B Alternative Weapons

Many objects served as weapons when nothing better was available. We are told that Shamgar struck down 600 Philistines with an ox **goad**, in a **tantalizingly** brief reference. Perhaps he was ploughing with his oxen when the Philistines appeared over the hill. The ox goad was a farm implement, about two or three meters (eight or ten feet) in length, with one end pointed, and sometimes metal-tipped, to **prod** the ox to plough. The other end was fashioned with a scraper to dislodge the clods that became **entangled** in the plough. Shamgar's heroic feat fits the pattern in the book of Judges of gaining victory with inferior weapons.

In Judges 4 and 5, we learn how Sisera fled the battlefield to avoid being killed or captured. He came to the tent of **Jael**, who seemed to offer him safety. However, while he was sleeping off his fatigue, she took a hammer and **tent-peg** and **pounded** the peg through his temple. The hammer she used was probably made of stone and the tent-peg a wooden object.

Gideon's surprise attack

Gideon was faced with the task of fighting the **Midianites.** They had large **encampments,** with women, children, cattle, camels and tents, which meant their greatest weakness was that they could easily be panicked by a surprise attack. This was exactly the strategy that **Gideon** chose to employ, which explains why he used such a small force of only 300 men. The smaller the force, the less chance there was of detection in a surprise attack. Gideon divided his troops into three companies and positioned one company on each of three sides of the Midianite camp. He probably left open the east side, where the terrain was most **problematic**, so that any survivors would have had a difficult time if they fled.

Gideon waited until the Midianites were all sleeping soundly, and until the new **sentries**, unaccustomed to the darkness and to night conditions, came on duty. Since co-ordination is absolutely essential in a surprise attack, he himself was to signal the attack, to ensure that nobody made a false start. At his signal, everyone smashed his jar, blew his **trumpet** and shouted. The noise panicked the Midianites; when they looked out of their tents they saw the flickering torches, which could easily have been used to set the tents alight, and so increase the panic. Fearing that they were surrounded by a huge enemy

force, the Midianites rushed to escape, falling on each other with their swords in the confusion. The surprise attack had succeeded to perfection, and Gideon won the battle with ease.

Another unusual weapon was used by a woman against Abimelech. When he attacked **Thebez**, all the people fled to the city's tower. Safe in the tower, the woman waited till Abimelech was close to the entrance, then dropped a millstone on his head, mortally wounding him. A millstone was normally about five to eight centimetres (two or three inches) thick and 50 centimetres (eighteen inches) in diameter.

Samson's weapons

Samson did not use **orthodox** weapons either. When he was met by a roaring lion, he had no weapons at all; using his bare hands and brute strength, he tore the lion apart as if it had been a tender young goat. On another occasion, he was weaponless because he had just been handed over to the Philistines. He picked up the fresh **jawbone** of a donkey (this must have been heavier and moister than an old, dried-out jawbone) and killed 1000 Philistines with it, **wielding** it like a club.

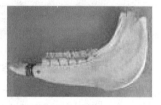

On another occasion, Samson went to Gaza, in Philistine territory, to visit a prostitute. Since it was night, the Philistines closed the city gate on him. (The city would have had a thick wall surrounding it, and only one exit.) When the hero went to leave, he found the gate **barred** shut. Undeterred, he pulled up the gate-posts and the gate itself, and walked free from the city. Since a city would have taken great pride in its **fortifications**, his action would have been a great humiliation to the citizens, and left the place temporarily defenseless. Finally, at the end of his life, Samson used his hands and arms to **topple** the columns of the Philistine temple and thus kill himself and 3000 Philistines with him.

Questions for discussion or reflection.
(1) What unusual weapon did Samson use to kill exactly one thousand Philistines?
(2) What implement did Jael use as a weapon to "secure" victory over the Canaanites?

Text C War

War was part of life in ancient Israel, though the way it was waged changed **drastically** in the time between 1300-586BC. At first the soldiers were voluntary militia, then later an organized and disciplined army. Finally they were a desperate, defensive force against the Roman invaders.

The army

In the early part of Israel's history, each tribe provided a **militia** from its able-bodied men. This group was willing and able to fight, and had received some training. They were not a regular army as we understand the term, not full-time soldiers, but men who were called

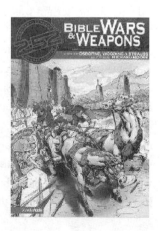

on to defend their clan whenever there was a need—somewhat like the men who fought for Scotland in the Battle of Culloden.

The advantage of militia is that the men will fight passionately for their homes and families. The disadvantage is that they cannot be held for long-term wars or fighting. At harvest time, for example, men often simply downed their weapons and returned home to bring in the harvest.

Despite their undoubted courage, the tribal militias were not really successful. Their enemies, for example the Philistines, were well-organized—1 Samuel 4:2 tells us that the Philistines were drawn up in lines when they attacked Israel, which suggests a disciplined, well-trained enemy. As well, the Israelites were poorly equipped, with little or no armor.

When King Saul, and then King David and his son King Solomon took the throne, there was a dramatic change. These kings began to copy the strategies of their enemies. They formed regular armies with full-time trained soldiers. They used new strategies and tactics, things that worked well for their enemies—for example, laying siege to a city. But they also held onto the **tactics** that had worked for them before: surprise attacks, psychological warfare and **propaganda**.

Very little is known about the organization of the army under the Israelite kings. When *the Bible* speaks of soldiers in "thousands", it does not mean **numerically** thousands, but is instead a term describing a Unit of soldiers.

Battles

There were no great set-piece battles like those of Alexander or Napoleon—of at least if there were, *the Bible* does not describe them. Very little is known about the deployment of troops during any particular battle—*the Bible* describes the reasons for the battle, who was involved, and what the result was, but it tells us virtually nothing of the strategies used by the opposing generals.

Before the reign of David, fighting took the form of skirmishes or raids. In this early period, the Israelites were experts at guerilla fighting. They relied on surprise attacks that panicked their enemies.

Weapons

There were four branches in the army: spearmen, swordsmen, archers, and **slingers.** Weapons used by these groups can be divided into two groups: those the soldier held and wielded at close quarters with the enemy, and those he projected, either with his arm or with the help of some other **centrifugal** force, for example the sling.

There are few references to weapons in the period of the Judges, or in the battles that were fought then—no Israelite spears, bows, shields, **javelins**, axes or maces—or the protective body armor. Their enemies, on the other hand, were well armed—Goliath had a full suit of armor.

After the introduction of monarchy by Saul, David and Solomon, weapons became much more common. The **standing** army was equipped with effective weapons, and when the Philistine control over the manufacture of metal was broken, the weapons industry of Israel came under the control of the king.

Hand held weapons included the sword, the mace or club, and spears and javelins. Projectile weapons using centrifugal force included the bow and arrow, and the sling. The slingers were probably more accurate at hitting their target than the archers.

Engineering

Siege warfare was the method Joshua frequently used in the story of the infiltration of Canaan, since he lacked the numbers to face an enemy in an open battle. Siege warfare was practiced by Jephthah in Ammon.

It was expensive and time-consuming, but it was also effective. The great empires of the ancient Near East perfected this type of warfare. The Assyrians developed specialized storm troops who were able to take advantage of any breaches in the wall. Trained sappers built zigzag trenches allowing their own soldiers to get closer to the walls of the **besieged** city, without being hit by missiles coming from the city. Their engineers developed new siege weapons such as covered battering rams and mining tools.

The attackers would seal off the city under attack by encircling it with their army. The soldiers would settle down to work, but it was a busy time for the engineers, who would begin building siege works. An earthen wall might be built to encircle the city; it would have guard towers at regular intervals, to keep watch for breakouts. Siege ramps made of earth and wood would be built as soon as the battering rams were ready for use.

Unless relief came from outside, the inhabitants of the city were trapped. All they could look forward to was starvation, surrender, slavery or death—and probably a horrible death at that. Jeremiah describes some of the terrible things that happened during a siege: "I will make them eat the flesh of their sons and their daughters, and everyone shall eat the flesh of his neighbor in the siege". And Isaiah comments that "their corpses were as refuse in the midst of the streets".

Questions for discussion or reflection.
(1) What are the advantages and disadvantages of militia?
(2) What are four branches in the army? Give some examples.

Notes

Shamgar: Son of Anath, is the name of one or possibly two individuals named in the "Book of Judges". The name occurs twice; at the first mention Shamgar is identified as a Biblical Judge, who repelled Philistine incursions into Israelite regions, and slaughtered 600 of the invaders with an ox goad (a formidable weapon sometimes ten feet long); the other mention is within the Song of Deborah, where Shamgar is described as having been one of the prior rulers, in whose days roads were abandoned, with travelers taking winding paths, and village life collapsing.

For Fun

Book to read

The First Vampire by Alicia Benson

Some journeys take more than one lifetime, and three thousand years after he was betrayed, captured, blinded and turned into a vampire, Samson is still holding a grudge. In fact, ever since Delilah used a devilish brew from Lilith to turn him into a vampire and then turned him over to the Philistines, Samson has been plotting revenge against his former lover and arch nemesis.

When he finally catches up to the reincarnate Delilah in modern day New York City, it seems as though he has all the time in the world to see that the last chapter of their sordid saga is finally written. But much like old enemies, old passions die hard, and Samson is forced to make a surprisingly hard choice. Does he want her dead more than he wants her back in his bed?

Intelligent, disquieting and deeply erotic, ***The First Vampire*** cleverly weaves the past into the present in a captivating tapestry of suspense, intrigue and betrayal.

Movie to See

Enjoy the film ***Samson and Delilah***

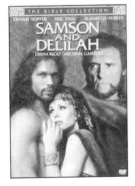

Samson was born to aged parents. He was a Nazirite set apart for God's service and therefore did not cut his hair or drink alcohol. His exploits included tearing a lion apart with his bare hands, killing a company of the men of Ashdod, setting fire to their fields and orchards, and slaughtering a thousand men with the jawbone of an ass. After a Philistine woman named Delilah enticed Samson to reveal the secret of his great strength, she cut off his hair, and the Philistines gouged out his eyes, bound him with strong fetters, and set him to grind at the mill in the prison. But Samson's hair, the secret of his strength, began to grow again. The day came when the Philistine lords sent for the blind Samson to laugh at him. Samson felt for the pillars on which the house rested, pulled them down, and died along with many Philistines. Pay attention to the weapons used in the film.

Song to Enjoy

Here is part of the lyrics of "Samson". Find the audio and enjoy the song. You can complete the lyrics while listening.

Samson
by Regina Spektor (2006)

You are my sweetest downfall
I loved you first, I loved you first
Beneath the sheets of paper lies my truth
I have to go, I have to go
Your hair was long when we first met

Samson went back to bed
Not much hair left on his head
He ate a slice of wonder bread and went right back to bed
And history books forgot about us and *the Bible* didn't mention us
The Bible didn't mention us, not even once

You are my sweetest downfall

I loved you first, I loved you first
Beneath the stars came falling on our heads
But they're just old light
They're just old light
Your hair was long when we first met

Samson came to my bed
Told me that my hair was red
Told me I was beautiful and came into my bed
I cut his hair myself one night
A pair of dull scissors and the yellow light
He told me that I'd done alright
and kissed me till the morning light the morning light
and he kissed me till the morning light

....

Unit 10

City and *the Bible*

> A man cannot govern a nation if he cannot govern a City; he cannot govern a city if he cannot govern a family; he cannot govern a family unless he can govern himself; and he cannot govern himself unless his passions are subject to reason.
>
> —Hugo Grotius

Unit Goals

- To gain a general knowledge of the cities in *the Bible*
- To get acquainted with some basic cultural concepts concerning city in *the Bible*
- To learn useful words and expressions about cities in *the Bible*
- To improve English language skills and western culture awareness

Before You Read

(1) Do you know what story the picture on the right shows? In *the Bible*, _____ and Abel are the first and second sons of Adam and _____. Cain is a crop farmer and his younger brother Abel is a shepherd. _____ is portrayed as sinful, committing the first _____ by killing his brother, after God has rejected his offerings of produce but accepted the animal sacrifices brought by Abel.

(2) Form groups of three or four students. Try to find, on the Internet or in the library, more information about cities in *the Bible*. Get ready for a 5-minute presentation in class.

Start to Read

Text A Cities

The function of cities is to enable humans to better achieve peace, harmony, prosperity, and happiness. How those functions should be handled depends upon what kind of city is involved. For this we may turn to *the Bible* for insight and guidance.

According to *the Bible*, Cain, the first murderer, is also the founder of the first city. That city does **put an end to** his wandering and provides him with protection against those who would seek to punish him further for his deed.

The city is a product of necessity. It is also the mother of invention since it is the Cain family which **accounts for** most of the world's inventions, from military **weaponry** to musical instruments, clearly conveying the understanding that it is precisely the same impulses that bring humans to murder and engage in similar **undesirable** behavior that also bring them to the achievements that make civilization possible.

It cannot be **accidental** that Cain, the first murderer, also founds the first city. In some respects, this can be seen simply as the **linkage** between **urbanization** and violence upon which many have commented. But the Biblical story is more subtle than that. Cain murders out of passion. He simply cannot control his passions at a particular moment or in a particular situation. **Significantly** enough, cities are places where density and the pressures related to them lead people into uncontrollable acts of passion, acts which are often violent in character, far more so than rural areas. That is one dimension of the Biblical account. Another is that people who commit violence need to protect themselves against **retribution**. The earliest cities in *the Bible* are primarily places of protection. Historians of the ancient Near East generally agree that cities originally **came into existence** for defensive purposes, as places where the inhabitants of a region could come together to collectively defend themselves.

The Bible describes four city archetypes. *The Bible* actually suggests a **paradigm** of urbanism in relation to biblical morality, through those four archetypical cities: **Sodom** is the utterly corrupt city in which sexual perversion is rampant and the milk of human kindness entirely absent. It deserves heavenly punishment because it does not even have ten righteous men within it. Babylon is the **metropolis** and **polyglot** city, in which everything can be found—good, bad, and indifferent. **It is doomed to** destruction if it cannot cleanse itself. **Nineveh** is the metropolis that does repent and is welcomed back into the community of the righteous accordingly. Jerusalem is the city founded on righteousness, designed to be the spiritual center of the world once Israel repents and the nations recognize God's **sovereignty**.

Thus *the Bible* model **distinguishes between** the possibilities inherent in homogeneous and heterogeneous cities. To be frank, *the Bible* does so, contrary to the modern spirit which has made pluralism a good in and of itself, not merely a necessity in **heterogeneous** societies. *The Bible* seems to prefer the right kind of homogeneous city and, indeed, fears for the consequences of the **cosmopolis** which is constantly **prone to lapsing into** random violence, the source of the destruction of civilizations, according to *the Bible*.

The Bible also provides for repentance or return, in Hebrew, *teshuva*. The biblical-Jewish concept of *teshuva* suggests how, contrary to simple-minded modern thinking that progress as inevitably **unfolding**, the possibility of *teshuva* enables humans to cope with the tragic flaws built into them.

In this sense, Nineveh is a very special biblical model of a city. It is a city in which the whole population returns, does *teshuva*, to the annoyance of Jonah, the Hebrew prophet who had very reluctantly accepted God's mission to bring the city the message of its sinfulness.

For much of the world today, the problem is how to **strive for** Jerusalem while living in

Babylon. The Babylonian heterogeneity of our cities is real enough. So, too, for many of us, is the striving for Jerusalem.

The Bible makes clear provision for the legitimate existence of different peoples and cultures. In that sense *the Bible* is truly pluralistic and multi-cultural. *The Bible* does not see all humans becoming part of one world state, like ancient Rome, or one world church. What *the Bible* sees for the proper future is not the **abolition** of differences but retaining their differences.

After You Read

Knowledge Focus

I. Pair Work: Work with your partner and consider the following questions.
  (1) What are the functions of cities?
  (2) How many kinds of city archetypes does *the Bible* describe?
  (3) Why does Sodom deserve heavenly punishment?
  (4) How much do you know about Nineveh and Jonah?
  (5) How do you understand "*The Bible* is truly pluralistic and multi-cultural"?

II. Solo Work: Fill in the blanks according to Text A.

Sodom is the utterly _____ city in which _____ perversion is rampant and the milk of human kindness entirely _____, it deserves heavenly _____ because it does not even have ten _____ men within it. Babylon is the _____ and polyglot city, in which everything can be found—good, bad, and _____. It is doomed to _____ if it cannot cleanse itself. Nineveh is the metropolis that does _____ and is welcomed back into the commUnity of the righteous accordingly. Jerusalem is the city founded on righteousness, designed to be the _____ center of the world once Israel repents and the nations recognize God's sovereignty.

Language Focus

I. Build your vocabulary.
  A. Match the phrases in Column A with their meanings in Column B.

Column A	Column B
1. prone to	A. to gradually get into a worse state
2. lapse into	B. to notice or understand the difference between two things
3. strive for	C. tending to show a particular negative characteristic
4. be doomed to	D. to try very hard to do something, especially for a long time
5. as a consequence of	E. to cause to suffer something unavoidable
6. contrary to	F. as a result of
7. distinguish between	G. to make something stop happening
8. put an end to sth.	H. be completely different

B. Use the proper forms of the phrases to complete the sentences.

| prone to | be doomed to | put an end to sth. | distinguish between |
| strive for | lapse into | as a consequence of | contrary to |

(1) He was _____ depressions even as a teenager.
(2) If you start thinking of yourself as a victim or allow yourself to _____ prolonged negativity, you won't be hurting anyone except yourself.
(3) The next objective for the Chinese people to _____ is to reach the well-to-do level by the end of this century.
(4) The plan _____ fail by their refusal to give it any financial support.
(5) Scientists think it unlikely that any species will actually become extinct _____ the oil spill.
(6) The rain was heavy but, _____ our fears, our fields were not flooded.
(7) He's colour-blind and can't _____ red and green easily.
(8) The government is determined to _____ terrorism.

II. Fill in the blanks with the proper forms of the words.

(1) A narrow-minded person can tolerant nothing _____ (desire).
(2) The _____ (plural) teachers not only can direct the study of professional knowledge, but also play an important role in culturing moral character.
(3) A _____ (retribution) system must punish severe crime more harshly than minor crime.
(4) The specifications have told you all the circumstances, so you must act _____ (accord).
(5) The most important thing to realize about human _____ (sin) is that forgiveness is available.
(6) The _____ (abolish) of slavery had been exercised in many countries.
(7) Her ideas have been shamelessly _____ (perversion) to serve the president's propaganda campaign.
(8) Our budget will only be _____ (significant) affected by these new cuts.
(9) I believe that in spite of its _____ (heterogeneous), Asians who live in Northeast Asia and Southeast Asia, do share certain personal and societal values.
(10) She's a wild _____ (control) girl, but that new school should knock some sense into her.

Comprehensive Work

I. Group Work: Form groups of three or four members and complete the following table.

Do you agree that people in cities, just like Cain, are more likely to have uncontrollable acts of passion than those in rural areas?		
Member	Agree ?	Reasons
A:		
B:		
C:		
D:		

II. Pair Work: Discuss the following questions with your partner.

(1) Give a brief introduction to your hometown. Is it similar to Sodom, Babylon, Nineveh or Jerusalem? Why or why not?

(2) In Text A, you can read such a sentence: "For much of the world today, the problem is how to strive for Jerusalem while living in Babylonian." What does it mean? Do you agree with this statement?

III. Essay Writing

The Bible makes clear provision for the legitimate existence of different peoples and cultures. Would you like to live in a world with different peoples and cultures? Write an essay at least 200 words to discuss its advantages and disadvantages.

IV. Solo Work

1. Put in the missing words.

The story of Babel is there to explain to a primitive society how we get from Noah to Abraham with so many different l_____ having developed in so short a time. What could be the cause of this impediment to human cooperation and understanding?

The choice of the name "Babel" is not an accident. The reference to Babylon reflects the way that Babylon was abhorred by Hebrew society. Babylon represented everything that was w_____ with humanity. As a city, Babylon was both envied and loathed. The city was beautiful and graced with streets and palaces. The hanging gardens of Babylon are one of the seven wonders of the a_____ world. Writing and science were developing there. In the meantime, the Hebrews were a nomadic society concerned with day to day survival. Babylon represented oppression, cruelty and violence by which it remained powerful.

So Babel (Babylon) is portrayed as a society where everyone speaks with the same language and through human cooperation attempt to climb to h_____ on a tower. This is not a God centered society but a fellowship of men dedicated to elevating man to his proper p_____ as God of this world. This is a theme often repeated in *the Bible*. The ziggurats stand as evidence against them. So Babylon gets the blame for confusion because they try to get up to God's level. The disdain that ancient Israel felt for Babylon is reflected in the Tower story.

2. Proofreading and error correction.

Nineveh was located in the eastern bank of the Tigris River in (1) _____
northeastern Mesopotamia (Iraq). It flourished from about 800 to 610 B.C. as

the capital of the Assyrian empire. It is first mentioned in the Bible back in Genesis as being founded by Nimrod (Genesis 10: 9-12).

During its time of power, the Assyrian empire conquered the northern Israelite kingdom of Israel, with their capital at

Samaria, and transported them away into captivity. Like the southern Israelite kingdom of Judah, with their capital at Jerusalem Fact File, they never returned, and became known as the "Lost Ten Tribes" of Israel. The Assyrians themselves eventually were lost, although some identify their descendants as being in central Europe today.

(2) _____

Nineveh was the city that the reluctant prophet Jonah was sent to God. Jonah did not want to go, so he ran. However, after a famous adventure with a whale at sea he accepted what he was to do—get the people of Nineveh to repent of their evil. He went, and was successful.

(3) _____
(4) _____

Jonah however still was not happy because he did not like the Assyrians very much because of all of the harms that they had inflicted upon Israel. He was hoping that they would refuse to repent so that God would destroy them. He may well have been the only prophet in history that hoped that his ministry would fail!

(5) _____

Eventually, the Assyrian empire declined and fell. It was overtaken by the Persian and Babylonian empires who were themselves just then on the rise. Today, Nineveh is just a vast stretch of ancient ruins.

Read More

Text B A Biblical Theology of the City

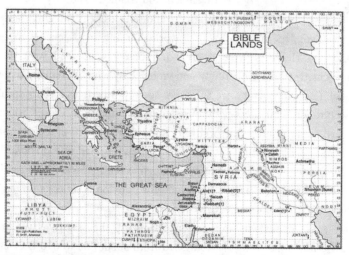

As more and more people become city-dwellers, it is **imperative** that the church understands how to reach out to the expanding cities of the 21st century. Here Tim Keller shares some biblical insights.

God designed the city with the power to draw out the resources of creation (of the natural order and the human soul) and thus to build civilization.

When we look at the New Jerusalem, we discover something strange. In the midst of the city is a crystal river, and on each side of the river is the Tree of Life, bearing fruit and leaves which heal the nations of all their wounds and the effects of the divine covenant curse. This city is the Garden of Eden, remade. The city is the fulfillment of the purposes of the Eden of God. We began in a garden but will end in a city.

The city is not to be regarded as an evil invention of ungodly fallen man. The ultimate goal set before humanity at the very beginning was that human-culture should take city-form. There should be an urban structuring of human historical existence. The cultural **mandate** given at creation was a **mandate** to build the city. Now, after the fall, the city is still a benefit, serving humankind as refuge from the howling wilderness condition into which the fallen human race, exiled from paradise, has been driven. The common grace city has remedial benefits even in a fallen world. It becomes the drawing together of resources, strength and talent.

There is no absolute way to define a "city". A human settlement becomes more "urban" as it becomes more a) dense and b) diverse in its population. The city is made to be a developmental tool, a form of cultural "gardening", designed to draw out the riches he put into the earth, nature and the human soul at creation.

First, the city (as the Garden) is a place of refuge and safety. People, who are too weak to live in other places, choose to live in the city. In the earliest days, cities provided refuge from wild animals and **marauding** tribes and criminals. When Israel moved into the Promised Land, the first cities were built as "cities of refuge", where the accused person could flee for safety and civil justice. Even today, people like the homeless, or new immigrants, or the poor, or people with "**deviant**" lifestyles, must live in the city. The city is always a more merciful place for minorities of all kinds. Cain built his cities for self-protection and the vengeance of others. So the refuge of the city can be misused, as when people with sinful lifestyles find refuge in the city from the disapproval of the broader culture.

Second, the city as a cultural mining/development centre.

Even the description of the wicked city of Babylon shows the power of the city to draw out the resources of creation—of the physical world and the human soul. In Revelation 18, we see that the city is a place of 1) music and the arts, 2) crafts and works of all arts and manufacturing, 3) trade and retailing, 4) technological advance, 5) family building.

Third, the city as the place to meet God.

Ancient cities were religious institutions. They were usually built around a "**ziggurat**"—the original skyscrapers! They were temples where a particular god was thought to "come down". The cities were seen to be the royal residences of the god, and the city was dedicated to him/her. The city was where the **cultus** for that god was centred, and where you went if you wanted to serve him or her. All of this was probably a twisted "memory trace" of the original design of God, that the **Edenic** city, the new Jerusalem, would be the place where people would meet him, where his temple/presence would be.

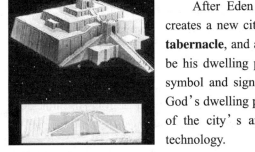

After Eden was lost to people (temporarily) through sin, God creates a new city in the desert, by dwelling among his people in the **tabernacle**, and around his Tent is a city of tents. The city of God will be his dwelling place. Later, the earthly city of Jerusalem becomes a symbol and sign to the future city of God. In the earthly Jerusalem, God's dwelling place, the temple stands as the central integrating point of the city's architecture and as apex of its art and science and technology.

Tell whether the following statements are True or False according to Text B.

In Tim Keller's opinion,

1. The city is just a sociological phenomenon or invention of humankind. ( )
2. The fallen human race exiled from paradise into the howling wilderness condition, but the city serves humankind as a refuge. ( )
3. Cain built his cities for self-protection, and that's the purpose of God inventing cities. ( )
4. Ancient cities were built around temples where a particular god was thought to "come down". ( )

Text C Bible Archaeology: Sodom and Gomorrah

Archaeologists have found strong evidence that the story of Sodom and Gomorrah's destruction is true. Stones and bricks are fire-blackened, wood is charred, and ashes cover all that's left.

The remains of Bab edh-Dhra (Sodom) are in poor condition, **eroded** and having few artifacts left, but those of the next ruin to the south, Numeira (Gomorrah), have yielded a lot of information. Each place that the archaeologists have dug at this site they've encountered a thick layer of destruction debris, including charred timbers and ash layers. Beneath this destruction debris are well-preserved remains. It's obvious that the destruction was sudden and unexpected, since there are human bone fragments in some rooms, together with **mortars** and pestles with barley still in them, and cooking implements with food residue still contained in them.

The huge cemetery at Babed-Dhra yielded a surprise. Three styles of burials were found. One showed the use of "charnel houses." One that was well **excavated** was about 25×45 feet, made of mud bricks and having wooden roof beams topped with reed matting and mud. Many pottery objects and piles of human remains were found. The interesting thing is that the roof beams had been burned from the top, and had collapsed inward. If this destruction had been done by an enemy, why would they have burned a charnel house? This seems to be good evidence of the truth of *the Bible*'s statements about "fire and **brimstone** from above."

It is well-known that this area is a "rift valley", **prone** to earthquakes and volcanic activities. The rift extends from north of the Sea of Galilee, down the Jordan River, through the Dead Sea, down through the Gulf of Aqaba into the Red Sea, then into the continental regions of Africa, where it is known as the "Great Rift Valley." There are vast deposits of **asphalt** (Genesis 14:10 calls them

"slime pits") in the southern Dead Sea portion. There are also underground deposits of petroleum and **methane**. A combination of earthquake and lightning could certainly set off a fiery explosion that would rain fire and brimstone on Sodom and Gomorrah, as described in Genesis 19.

There are many times that God uses natural means to achieve supernatural results. Many answers to our prayers are handled this way. But this does not detract from His miraculous **interventions**. At Sodom, God sent angels to warn people; He led Lot to safety, and when people disobeyed, then He destroyed the cities just as He had said He would. He may have used natural processes, but His timing was miraculous.

Please match the underlined words or phrases in the passage with their possible meaning.

1. yield	A. something left after other parts have been taken away
2. debris	B. to give or supply
3. residue	C. the remains of something that has been destroyed
4. excavate	D. having a tendency to
5. prone to	E. to diminish, take away
6. set off	F. to find by digging the ground
7. detract	G. to cause to burst with a violent release of energy

Notes

Sodom and Gomorrah: They have been used as metaphors for vice and sexual deviation. The story has therefore given rise to words in several languages, including the English word "sodomy," a term used today predominantly in law (derived from traditional Christian usage) to describe non-vaginal intercourse, as well as bestiality.

For Fun

Film to See
O Jerusalem (2006)

The film is an epic drama re-creating the historic struggle surrounding the creation of the State of Israel in 1948. At the center of these events are two young, American friends—one Jewish, the other Arab. The film is told from the alternating viewpoints of the Jews, Arabs and Brits, all of whom collide in their fight for the control of Jerusalem, while bringing to the forefront themes of courage, terrorism, deprivation, politics and a strong sense of morality. Their involvement takes them from the streets of New York to The Holy Land, where they risk their lives—making incredible sacrifices along the way—to fight for what they believe in, as the city of their dreams teeters on the brink of destruction.

Song to Enjoy

Here is part of the lyrics of "Jerusalem". Find the audio and enjoy the song. You can complete the lyrics while listening.

Jerusalem
by Matisyahu

[Chorus]

Jerusalem, if I forget you,
fire not gonna come from me tongue.
Jerusalem, if I forget you,
let my right hand forget what it's supposed to do.

In the ancient days, we will return with no delay
Picking up the bounty and the spoils on our way
We've been traveling from state to state
And them don't understand what they say
3,000 years with no place to be
And they want me to give up my milk and honey
Don't you see, it's not about the land or the sea
Not the country but the dwelling of his majesty

[chorus]

Rebuild the temple and the crown of glory
Years gone by, about sixty
Burn in the oven in this century
And the gas tried to choke, but it couldn't choke me
I will not lie down, I will not fall asleep
They come overseas, yes they're trying to be free
Erase the demons out of our memory
Change your name and your identity
Afraid of the truth and our dark history
Why is everybody always chasing we
Cut off the roots of your family tree
Don't you know that's not the way to be

[chorus]

Caught up in these ways, and the worlds gone craze
Don't you know it's just a phase
Case of the Simon says
If I forget the truth then my words won't penetrate
Babylon burning in the place, can't see through the haze
Chop down all of them dirty ways,
That's the price that you pay for selling lies to the youth
No way, not ok, oh no way, not ok, hey
....

Unit 11

Holidays and *the Bible*

> Working hours are never long enough. Each day is a holiday, and holidays are grudged as enforced interruptions in an absorbing vocation.
> —Winston Churchill

Unit Goals

- To gain a general knowledge of holidays in *the Bible*
- To develop a right attitude towards holidays in *the Bible*
- To get acquainted with some basic cultural concepts concerning holidays in *the Bible*
- Learn the historical, agricultural, spiritual, and prophetic purposes of each holiday
- To learn useful words and expressions about holidays in *the Bible*
- To improve English language skills and western culture awareness

Before You Read

(1) What can you see in the following pictures? Actually they are about two Jewish holidays. Do you know what they are, how they are celebrated, and why?

(2) According to the following pictures, what are forbidden on Yom Kippur (Day of Atonement)?

(3) Form groups of three or four students. Try to find, on the internet or in the library, more information about Tabernacles, Trumpets and Day of Atonement. Get ready for a 5-minute presentation in class.

Start to Read

Text A Jewish Holidays

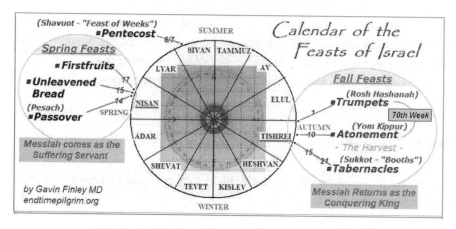

Fall Holidays

Most Christians don't know about the Fall Holidays of ancient Israel: **Trumpets** (Rosh Hashanah), Day of **Atonement** (Yom Kippur), and **Tabernacles** (Sukkoth). If the spring festivals so clearly **prophesied** the first coming of Messiah, it **stands to reason** that the fall festivals are also prophetic of His second coming. The way these holidays are celebrated reveals specific information of the way they will be **prophetically fulfilled**.

Preparations for the Fall Holidays begin a full month **in advance**. On the Jewish calendar is a forty-day season called Teshuvah (return or repentance). It begins on Elul 1 and ends on the Day of Atonement. This forty-day season is a time for one to annually examine his life and restore relationships between God and man. The first thirty days of this season are the thirty days of the month of Elul. The last ten days of this forty-day season are the Feast of Trumpets and Day of Atonement, or the ten High Holy Days.

The Jews start the celebration of the Fall Holidays thirty days prior to the Feast of Trumpets, which falls on the first day of the seventh month. For thirty days the **shofar** is blown every morning in the Synagogue to remind the people that the holy days are approaching, and that they should prepare themselves. Their preparation **consists of** confessing their sins and seeking forgiveness, and going back to fix mistakes made during the year. The ten days between the Feast of Trumpets and the Day of Atonement (Yom Kippur) are called the Days of Awe.

The long period between the Feast of Weeks and the Feast of Trumpets is symbolic of the long period between the formation of the church at the Feast of Weeks and the regathering of Israel to the trumpet blast calling all born again believers.

 Feast of Trumpets / Rosh Hashana

The Feast of Trumpets (Rosh Hashanah) is the Jewish New Year, and begins the high Holy Days in the seventh month (**corresponding** to September or October). It is a celebration of the spiritual birthday of the world or creation, and is celebrated with blowing of the trumpets. The Feast of Trumpets is a powerful prophetic look at the final days and **Messiah's** return. Jewish **eschatology** teaches that on the Day of Atonement after six thousand years are complete, the Day of the Lord will come. On that day the shofar will sound and the righteous will be resurrected.

 The Day of Atonement / Yom Kipper

The holiest day in the Jewish year (a fast day not a feast day), the Day of Atonement (Yom Kippur), is spent in fasting, prayer, and confession. This was one gracious day a year given by God that each individual could receive forgiveness. The high priest enters the holy of holies to make **atonement for** the nation by sacrificing an animal. Jesus has provided our atonement, "for all have sinned and **fall short of** the glory of God..." and are **justified** freely by his grace through the **redemption** that came by Him.

 Feast of Tabernacles / Sukkoth

Feast of Tabernacles (Sukkoth or Booths) is celebrated Tishri 15 as outlined in Leviticus 23:33-43. This seven-day harvest festival, during which the Jewish people are told to live in "booths," or temporary shelters, is a reminder to future generations of how the Israelites had also lived in booths when God delivered them out of Egypt. A number of Christians believe this is the date of Christ's birth when He came to "tabernacle among us." We should look forward expectantly to the Feast of Tabernacles, just as we look forward to the coming of the Messiah to bring His government, His Kingdom, and His laws.

After You Read

Knowledge Focus

I. Pair Work: Work with your partner and fill in the blanks in the following chart.

Name	Time	Meaning	Activities
Trumpets			
Day of Atonement			
Tabernacles			

II. Solo Work: According to the knowledge mentioned above, write T if the statement is true and F if it is false.

(1) Fall festivals are prophetic of the first coming of Messiah. ( )
(2) Teshuvah begins on Elul 1 and ends on the Day of Atonement. ( )
(3) The Feast of Trumpets begins in September or October. ( )
(4) Yom Kippur is spent in confessing their sins and seeking forgiveness. ( )
(5) Feast of Tabernacles is a seven-day harvest festival. ( )

Language Focus

I. Build your vocabulary.

A. Match the words and phrases in Column A with their meanings in Column B.

Column A	Column B
1. stand to reason	A. to give a good reason for what one has done
2. fall short of	B. to be made of or formed from
3. confess to	C. to seem to be equal
4. justify oneself	D. to seem likely to be true
5. correspond to	E. to fail to satisfy
6. atone for	F. to make amends for an error
7. consist of	G. before it is due
8. in advance	H. to admit having done something

B. Use the proper forms of the phrases to complete the sentences.

stand to reason	fall short of	justify oneself	consist of
correspond to	confess to	in advance	atone for

(1) It was the only thing that I could do — I don't have to _____ to anyone.

(2) The working of this machine _____ that of the human brain.
(3) It's a simple dish to prepare, _____ mainly rice and vegetables.
(4) If 20% of the Earth's population has 80% of its resources, then it _____ that 80% of the population has only 20% of the resources.
(5) August car sales _____ the industry's expectations due to the US subprime mortgage crisis.
(6) The country's leader has expressed a wish to _____ his actions in the past.
(7) She _____ her husband that she had sold her wedding ring.
(8) US broadcast TV networks purposely have sold less advertising _____ of the new season, wagering that an economic recovery will drive up ad prices.

II. Fill in the blanks with the proper forms of the words.
(1) Considering the injuries he's had, there can be little _____ (expect) of him winning the race.
(2) The healing and _____ (redeem) power of experience lies in its ability to help us access and give birth to the deepest part of ourselves.
(3) It can be said, with some _____ (justify), that she is one of the greatest actresses on the English stage today.
(4) The cost of living in the city is more expensive, but salaries are supposed to be _____ (correspond) higher.
(5) His wife divorced him after the _____ (reveal) that he was having an affair.
(6) The statue is a lasting _____ (remind) of Churchill's greatness.
(7) The _____ (right) penny corrupts the righteous pound.
(8) They've won a few matches this season but they lack _____ (consist).
(9) Graham's always very _____ (approach). Why don't you talk the problem over with him?
(10) I wouldn't like to _____ (prophecy) what will happen to that marriage!

Comprehensive Work
I. Group Work
1. Complete the following table after discussion within a group of three or four members.

Holiday	Spring Festival		Rosh Hashanah
Date		Dec. 25	
Origin			
Celebration			

2. Create a sitcom to show how Jewish people celebrate the other holiday.

II. Pair Work: Work with your partner. Describe one of the Jewish holidays to each other without mentioning its name and ask your partner to guess it.

The Bible & Culture

III. **Essay Writing**: Describe one of the major Jewish festivals. Include the following in your description.
- The origin of the festival
- How the Hebrew Scriptures are used
- When it is celebrated
- What family traditions are associated with it

IV. **Solo Work**

1. Put in the missing words.

Passover is the most popular Jewish holiday. The dinner celebration is called a Seder. The Passover Seder is a meal with special foods, practices, and Scripture readings that commemorate the liberation from Egyptian slavery, in accordance w_____ God's instructions.

Seder means "order". The Seder invites each family to recount its own version of the great story of Passover with each family member actively involved. The meal induces the experience of going from s_____ to liberty through the food experiences and story as the meal turns into an elaborate feast.

The Seder is usually a family d_____ but can also be held with your family or with a church group. During the Seder, the narrative of the exodus is related and prayers of thanksgiving are offered up to God for his loving protection. The dinner table is beautifully set with fancy dishes and candles. There is a special pillow on the c_____ for the leader of the Seder to lean on to symbolize the comfort of a free person reclining. Orthodox Jewish tradition directs that, during Passover, meals be prepared and s_____ using sets of utensils and dishes reserved strictly for that festival.

The staff have held Seders since the Clinton administration of the late 1990s. On April 7, 2009 President Obama added a second-night Seder to his official schedule, to be observed April 9, 2009. This is the first time that a sitting president is known to have hosted and observed a Seder at the White House.

2. Proofreading and error correction.

Hanukkah is celebrated for eight days beginning on the 25th of Kislev (mid- to late-December). It's also called "Feast of Lights" (along with "Feast of Dedication" and "Feast of the Maccabees").

The only essential ritual of Hanukkah is the light of candles. One candle is lit on the first night   (1) _____
of Hanukkah, two are lit on the second, and so on, until all eight are lit on the eighth night. In addition to the lighting of the candles, any other Hanukkah traditions have developed over the years. One favorite is   (2) _____
eating fried foods in recognition of the miraculous oil. Another popular Hanukkah tradition is the game of "spin the dreidel". A dreidel is a four-sided spinning top

with the Hebrew letters drawn on each side. These letters mean "A great miracle happened there," and they also represent the rules of the game.

Each player begins with an equal amount of nuts, pennies, M&Ms, or other small pieces, then the players take turn spinning the dreidel. Before each spin, each person puts one piece into the pot. If the spin lands on nun, nothing happens. If it lands on gimel ("gimme!"), the player gathers all the pieces and everyone antes up again. A result of hay means the player takes half the pieces in the pot, and shin requires the player to put one more piece in the pot.

(3) _____

(4) _____

A more recent tradition associated with Hanukkah is gift-giving, which by all accounts derives directly from Hanukkah's proximity to Christmas. Many Jewish families have adapted the tradition of giving small gifts to their children to alleviate jealousy of non-Jewish friends who celebrate Christmas. Gifts are not exchanged with anyone else, however, and Hanukkah gifts generally tend to be smaller than their Christmas counterparts.

(5) _____

Read More

Text B Purim in Bible Times

To **commemorate** the miraculous turn of events recorded in Esther, **Purim** is celebrated with feasts, sending gifts of food to friends and the needy, and with the reading of Esther, the story of Purim. The earliest descriptions of Purim celebrations, from the Second Temple, offer no indication of the partying that is associated with the festival today. The emphasis was on the formal reading of the Scroll of **Esther**, which was to be conducted with great care and seriousness. Later customs originated in late fifteenth century Italy, such as donning masks, drinking, parody, and costumes. Purim is a joyous day celebrated by the entire family.

The following are main traditions of Purim:
1. Listening to the Megillah reading in the evening and again in the morning.
2. Sending at least two ready to eat foods to at least one friend.
3. Giving charity to at least two poor people.
4. Eating a festive meal during the day of Purim in honor of the holiday.
5. Reciting "Al Hanisim" in prayer and in grace after meal.

Fasting

To commemorate the day of prayer and fasting that the Jews held before their victory, Jews fast on the day before Purim from approximately three hours before sunrise until forty minutes after sunset.

Charity
It is a tradition to give to charity to commemorate the half-shekel given by each Jew in the time of the Holy Temple.

Prayers
Special prayers are said for evening, morning and afternoon, as well as in the grace after meals. The morning of Purim, there is a special reading from the Torah Scroll in the synagogue.

Purim Play
One of the most entertaining customs of the Purim holiday is the children dressing up as the characters found in the story of Esther. The Megillah (the Scroll of Esther) is read aloud as it is acted out in a play or acted out with puppets. The custom of donning masks and costumes on Purim probably originated in late fifteenth century Italy as an imitation of Christian carnivals. It was tied to the idea of God's "hiding his face" as found in the **Talmud**!

Noisemakers
Groggers are the noisemakers used during the reading of the Megillah. Every time the name of **Haman** is mentioned, everyone boos, hisses, stamps their feet, and twirls their **groggers**. Any type of noisemaker can be used. In medieval Europe, children would write Haman's name on stones or wood blocks, and bang them until the name was erased. When the name **Mordecai** is mentioned, the people cheer.

Food

Family and friends gather together to rejoice in the Purim spirit by having a special festive meal. As with other holidays, there is a traditional food. During Purim, **Hamantaschens** are served. Hamantaschen means "Haman's pockets." These are triangle-shaped cookies that supposedly look like the hat Haman wore. The cookies are sweet, filled with a fruit (usually prune) or poppy seed mixture.

Work
Work is permitted as usual on Purim unless, of course, it falls on a Saturday.

Questions for discussion or reflection.
(1) How many traditions do you know about Purim?
(2) What is the relationship between Esther and Purim?

Text C Holiday Customs

All Jewish holidays begin the evening before the date specified on most calendars. This is because a Jewish "day" begins and ends at sunset, rather than at midnight. If you read the story of creation in *Genesis*, you will notice that it says, "And there was evening, and there was morning, one day." From this, people infer that a day begins with evening, that is, sunset. Holidays end at nightfall of the date specified on most calendars, that is, at the time when it becomes dark out, about an hour after sunset.

Work on Holidays

Work is not permitted on Rosh Hashanah, on Yom Kippur, on the first and second days of Sukkot, on Shemini Atzeret, on Simchat Torah, on Shavu'ot, and the first, second, seventh and eighth days of **Passover**. The "work" prohibited on those holidays is the same as that prohibited on **Shabbat**, except that cooking, baking, **transferring** fire and carrying, all of which are forbidden on Shabbat, are permitted on holidays. When a holiday occurs on Shabbat, the full Shabbat restrictions are observed.

For observant Jews who work in the secular gentile world, this can be problematic in some years: if all of the non-working holidays fall on weekdays (as they sometimes do), an observant Jew would need to take 13 days off of work just to observe holidays. This is more vacation time that some people have available.

Extra Day of Holidays

You may notice that the number of days of some holidays do not accord with what *the Bible* specifies. In most cases, people celebrate one more day than *the Bible* requires. There is an interesting reason for this additional day.

The Jewish calendar is lunar, with each month beginning on the new moon. The new months used to be determined by observation. When the new moon was observed, the **Sanhedrin** declared the beginning of a new month and sent out messengers to tell people when the month began. People in distant communities could not always be **notified** of the new moon (and therefore, of the first day of the month), so they did not know the correct day to celebrate. They knew that the old month would be either 29 or 30 days, so if they didn't get notice of the new moon, they celebrated holidays on both possible days.

This practice of celebrating an extra day was maintained as a custom even after people adopted a precise mathematical calendar, because it was the custom of their ancestors. This extra day is not celebrated by Israelis, regardless of whether they are in Israel at the time of the holiday, because it is not the custom of their ancestors, but it is celebrated by everybody else, even if they are visiting Israel at the time of the holiday.

After-reading exercise.

Tell whether the following statements are True or False based on Text C.

1. Jewish holidays begin at sunset. ( )
2. Jewish holidays end at sunset. ( )
3. Cooking, baking and transferring fire are not permitted on Rosh Hashanah. ( )
4. All of the non-working holidays fall on weekdays. ( )
5. Jews used to celebrate one more day on holidays than *the Bible* requires. ( )

Notes

(1) **His second coming:** The Second Coming is when Jesus Christ will return to earth in fulfillment of His promises and to fulfill the prophecies made about Him. Jesus Himself promised, "At that time the sign of the Son of Man will appear in the sky, and all the nations of the earth will mourn. They will see the Son of Man coming on the clouds of the sky, with power and great glory" (Matthew 24:30). Revelation 19:11-12 proclaims this about the Second Coming, "I saw heaven standing open and there before me was a white horse, whose rider is called Faithful and True. With justice he judges and makes war. His eyes are like blazing fire, and on his head are many crowns. He has a name written on him that no one knows but he himself."

(2) **Shofar:** It is mentioned frequently in the Hebrew Bible, the Talmud and rabbinic literature. The blast of a shofar emanating from the thick cloud on Mount Sinai made the Israelites tremble in awe.

The shofar was used to announce holidays, and the Jubilee year. The first day of the seventh month is termed "a memorial of blowing", or "a day of blowing", the shofar. It was also employed in processions, as a musical accompaniment and to signify the start of a war.

For Fun

Movie to See:

You can view *the Bible* story film *One Night with the King* (2006)

The story of *the Bible*'s Queen Esther is filled with intrigue, romance, bravery, and honor. It is the story of a queen who became the savior of her people through a curious mix of fate and charm. It is also a story of remarkable love and devotion. This is Purim.

The story's setting is when Israel was in captivity to Babylon. The ruler of the Persian Empire is called Ahasuerus in *the Bible* and is historically known as Xerxes (486–465 B.C.) Ahasuerus divorced his Queen Vashti and began searching for a new queen to take her place at his side.

This movie is amazing for so many reasons, the cast, the scenery, the story-line and that it parallels what we see happening in the world today. The historical truth about an ancient Persian queen is exactly the same battle happening in Israel today. It's not often that you see a movie that can relate directly with current world affairs and still maintain truth and purity. This movie achieves all this and more. I highly recommend this movie to anyone who enjoys history, wholesome entertainment, a great love story or compulsive movie goers. What's great about this movie is that it can appeal to a wide variety of age groups and provides a much needed heroine/role model for young people today. This movie will inspire you and leave you cheering at the end! A must see!!

Song to Enjoy

Here is part of the lyrics of "My Queen Esther". Find the audio and enjoy the song. You can complete the lyrics while listening.

My Queen Esther
by Guardian

Esther called me today
She's a bona fide star
Said I spoke to a friend
Who wants to know how you are
With a shake in her voice
She said, "I'm doing ok."
With a shake in her voice
She said, "I can't live this way."
She doesn't know why
She wants to laugh but still she cries
Still she cries
Spoke to Esther today
She said it's hard to play queen
Though she fought it at first
This pain's become her routine
And she wants to believe

But the image won't play
And she wants to believe
But that's a long time away
Kingdoms collide
As she tries to rule the world inside
She starts to cry

Take that crown off my Queen Esther
It's too much for anyone to bear
Don't hide your face Queen Esther
My King says he'll meet you anywhere

He says it's ok
He knows your pain
He says it's ok
He'll show you the way
He'll take your pain
He'll show you the way
....

Unit 12

Education and *the Bible*

> The aim of education should be to teach us rather how to think, than what to think — rather to improve our minds, so as to enable us to think for ourselves, than to load the memory with thoughts of other men.
> —Bill Beattie

Unit Goals

- To become familiar with education in Old Testament times and New Testament times
- To get acquainted with the influence of *the Bible* on American education
- To learn useful words and expressions about education in *the Bible*
- To improve English language skills and western culture awareness

Before You Read

(1) What colleges are the following seals about? Do you think they have something in common, cspccially at the top center?

(2) Do you know the following significant Founding Fathers of America? Can you match the pictures with their names and also the universities offering courses in Hebrew that they attended?

Thomas Jefferson   James Madison   Alexander Hamilton

(3) What do you think is the purpose of education?
(4) Form groups of three or four students. Try to find, on the Internet or in the library, more information about education in the *Old Testament* and the *New Testament*. Get ready for a 5-minute presentation in class.

Start to Read

Text A Christianity's Influence on Education

While we stress the importance of the Hebrew Bible to the early American settlers, it is important to note that, of course, the *New Testament* was **revered** as well. However, the Hebrew Bible was seen as the original and pure source of Christian values, and also as a **legalistic** and **ritualistic** guide, something which the *New Testament* was not.

In addition, there was a political **agenda** involved in this special focus in the *Old* over the *New Testament*. Many New Englanders viewed the *New Testament* as an instrument of justification, used by powers-that-be in Europe, to preserve the existing order. Had not Paul written in his letter to the Romans (13:1-2):

> *Every person must **submit to** the authorities in power, for all authority comes from God, and the existing authorities are instituted by Him. It follows that anyone who **rebels against** authority is resisting a divine institution, and those who resist have themselves to thank for the punishment they receive.*

That sure **smacked** of the divine right of kings and **condemnation** of the rebels of the Puritan revolution. No wonder that the Hebrew Bible, with its message of obedience to God alone, of personal responsibility, and of freedom from tyranny, was far more **in tune with** the **mindset** of these Protestant **splinter** sects of America.

Focusing even further on the issue of individual responsibility, the **Massachusetts Bay Colony enacted** legislation requiring parents to teach their children to read and understand the basic principles of religion and capital laws. All towns in New England with a minimum of 50 households were required by law to establish schools and appoint teachers.

In 1670, British **commissioners** making a survey of conditions in the American colonies reported that in **Connecticut** fully one-quarter of the annual revenues were **set aside** for free public education. Universities were established (the first being Harvard University founded in 1636 as training school for Puritan ministers), and many printing presses were imported for the printing and dissemination of books.

Insisting on education for all, the Puritans were following Jewish law. Education for all thus became a **hallmark** of early America and not just New England. In addition to Harvard, many other colleges and universities were established under the auspices of various Protestant sects: Yale, William and Mary, Rutgers, Princeton, Brown, Kings College (later to be known as Columbia), Johns Hopkins, Dartmouth etc. *The Bible* played a central role in the curriculum of all of these institutions of higher learning with both Hebrew and Bible studies offered as required courses.

Many of these colleges even adopted some Hebrew words or phrase as part of their official **emblem** or seal. Beneath the banner containing the Latin Lux et Veritas, the Yale seal shows an open book with the Hebrew Urim Vtumim, which was a part of the ceremonial **breastplate** of the High Priest in the days of the Temple. The Columbia seal has the Hebrew name for God at the top center, with the Hebrew name for one of the angels on a banner toward the middle. Dartmouth uses the Hebrew words meaning "God Almighty" in a triangle in the upper center of its seal.

So popular was the Hebrew Language in the late 16th and early 17th centuries that several students at Yale delivered their commencement orations in Hebrew. Harvard, Yale, Columbia, Brown, Princeton, Johns Hopkins, and the University of Pennsylvania taught courses in Hebrew — all the more remarkable because no university in England at the time offered it.

Many of the population, including a significant number of the Founding Fathers of America, were products of these American universities — for example, Thomas Jefferson attended William and Mary, James Madison Princeton, Alexander Hamilton King's College (i.e. Columbia). Thus, we can be sure that a majority of these political leaders **were** not only well **acquainted with** the contents of both the *New* and *Old Testaments* but also had some working knowledge of Hebrew. Notes Abraham Katsh in *The Biblical Heritage of American Democracy* (p. 70):

> At the time of the American Revolution, the interest in the knowledge of Hebrew was só widespread as to allow the circulation of the story that "certain members of Congress proposed that the use of English be formally prohibited in the United States, and Hebrew substituted for it."

Their Biblical education colored the American founders' attitude toward not only religion and ethics, but also most significantly, politics. We see them adopting the biblical motifs of the Puritans for political reasons. For example, the struggle of the ancient Hebrews against the wicked Pharaoh came to embody the struggle of the colonists against English tyranny.

After You Read

Knowledge Focus

I. Pair Work: Work with your partner and consider the following questions.
(1) What is the relationship between the Hebrew Bible and Christian values?
(2) How did New Englanders view the New Testament?
(3) What did Massachusetts Bay Colony require parents to do?
(4) Why did education become a distinctive characteristic of early America?
(5) How popular was the Hebrew language in the late 16th and early 17th centuries?

Unit 12 Education and the Bible

II. Solo Work: Please sum up the Christianity's influence on university education.

Influence	Examples
The establishment of universities	
Curriculum	
Official emblem or seal	
Language	

Language Focus

I. Build your vocabulary.

Use the proper forms of the words to complete the sentences.

(1) It might be true that, on purely _____ (legal) terms, the factory is not accountable for the skin disease.

(2) Granny made it imperative, however, that I attend certain all-night _____ (ritual) prayer meetings.

(3) Its only _____ (justify) would be the painting of imperishable masterpieces.

(4) The college maintained a close connection with the _____ (disseminate) of agricultural knowledge to the farmers.

(5) A deep voice announced the _____ (commence) of the wedding rites, and the music began.

(6) The police _____ (commission) is furious because the suspect hasn't been found.

(7) I'm pleased that you've made such an _____ (auspice) start to the new term.

(8) His total disregard for the feelings of others was his _____ (condemn).

II. Fill in the blanks with the proper forms of the words.

| submit to | set aside | rebel against |
| in tune with | be acquainted with | |

(1) Adolescents, who are apt to _____ authority, hate being ordered about.

(2) I support the campaign because I'm _____ its aims.

(3) How could you _____ all the objections and cling to your own course?

(4) To _____ you is so beautiful. To be parted from you is so painful. Your figure is my most unforgettable memory.

(5) Such was his fortune, and he was obliged to _____ it.

Comprehensive Work

I. Group Work

    The Bible informed nearly every aspect of early American education, including the principles upon which schools were founded, their curricula, their financing, and the lives of leading educators. Which book influenced Chinese education most?

II. Pair Work

The following are two ways to teach alphabets. Discuss with your partner how their teaching contents are different in early America (1) and modern America (2).

(1) The curricula of schools in early America were permeated by biblical concepts. The New England Primer, for instance, presented the alphabet this way:

A — "In **A**dam's fall, we sinned all."

B — "My **B**ook and heart, shall never part."

C — "**C**hrist crucified, for sinners died."

F — "The idle **f**ool, is whipped at school."

(2) The following is a learning Alphabet cartoon.

Based on this cartoon, teachers can teach students the related topics: fish, fishing, fisherman, fishermen, boats, fishing rod, giant fish and etc.

III. Solo Work

1. Put in the missing words.

The Bible informed nearly every aspect of early American education, including the principles upon which schools were founded, their curricula, their financing, and the lives of leading educators. Armed with a living faith and a love for their children, our forefathers set to w_____ almost immediately building Christian schools. Eventually, eight colonial colleges were f_____ along with hundreds of Christian elementary and s_____ schools. Harvard was the first college, founded just six years after the Puritans landed in New England. There was no doubt as to Harvard's purpose. An early "student handbook" reads: "Let every student be plainly instructed and earnestly pressed to consider well, the main end of his life and studies is, to know God and Jesus Christ which is eternal life and therefore lay Christ in the bottom, as the only foundation of sound knowledge and learning." The College of William and Mary, Yale, Princeton, Columbia, Brown, Rutgers, and Dartmouth were founded by various denominations — Congregationalists, Anglicans, Baptists, Dutch Reformed, and so forth—to t_____ ministers, Christian teachers, and missionaries. The only college to have nonsectarian beginnings was the University of Pennsylvania, but it soon came u_____ Anglican control. Four of the colleges — Princeton, Brown, Rutgers, and Dartmouth — were founded directly as a result of the religious revival known as the Great Awakening. Later, the Second Great Awakening seems to have begun on the campus of Yale, under the leadership of the godly Timothy Dwight.

2. Proofreading and error correction.

The financing of education also reflected the influence of Christianity. Instead of having their programs underwritten by the state—which always meant state control—or by handful of wealthy benefactors, Christian schools were supported by thousands of people of average or more than average means. The principle of the tithe was more widely accepted, which freed more money for Christian work. Still, there were more worthy ideas than there was money to finance them. Harvard College in the early years was supported by "College Corn" donated by local farmers. Princeton was supported partially by gifts from interesting friends in Scotland. Henry Dunster helped to build Harvard's first buildings with his own hands, while John Witherspoon, president of Princeton during the American Revolution, donated his books to the Princeton library and grew foods for the college kitchen in his garden.

Later, opponents of Christian schools—men alike Horace Mann, a unitarian— would use public financing of education to gain a foot in the door of American education.

Colleges, schools, textbooks, and money are all necessary components for Christian education. But the most important ingredient is men and women of God to breathe life onto the dry bones of buildings, programs, and texts. Providentially, early America had a goodly number of such men and women.

(1) _____

(2) _____

(3) _____

(4) _____

(5) _____

Read More

Text B Education in Old Testament Times

While the word "school" occurs in *the Bible* only once (Acts 19:9), there are numerous references to teachers and teaching in both Testaments. There are many references in the *Old Testament* to the importance of religious training but there is no Mosaic legislation requiring the establishment of schools for formal religious instruction.

The primary purpose of education among the Jews was the learning of and obedience to the law of God, the Torah. Whereas the word torah can be used to refer to all Jewish beliefs, it generally refers to the Pentateuch, the first five books of *the Bible*: *Genesis, Exodus, Leviticus, Numbers* and *Deuteronomy*.

The secondary purpose in education was to teach about the practical aspects of everyday life: a trade for the boy and the care of the house, application of **dietary** laws and how to be a good wife for the girl.

The home was considered the first and most effective agency in the education process, and parents were considered the first and most effective teachers of their children. This responsibility is expressed in Genesis 18:19 where God states his expectation that Abraham will train his children and his household to walk in the ways of the Lord. Proverbs 22:6 is another familiar exhortation for

parents to teach their children according to the way of the Lord.

> *Deuteronomy 6:7 gives an interesting insight into how parents were to teach their children about God: "And you shall teach them diligently unto your children, and shall talk of them when you sit in your house, and when you walk by the way, and when you lie down, and when you rise up." The parent was to use the various ordinary activities of life as avenues to teach about God. All of life was **permeated** by religious meaning and teaching about God should flow naturally from its activities.*

Primary ways of imparting religious knowledge to children were examples, imitation, conversation and stories. Parents could **utilize** the interest aroused in their children by actual life observances such as Sabbath or Passover to teach about God.

Training in the Torah began very early. The father had an obligation to teach his children the Law by words and examples. A child could observe his father binding the **phylacteries** on his arm and head. The natural question, "What are you doing?" could be used to teach the child that it was everyone's duty to "Love the Lord your God with all your heart, and with all your soul, and with all your might" (Deuteronomy 6:5).

When the son reached the age of twelve, the Jews believed his education in the Torah was complete enough to help him know the Law and keep it. He was then known as a "son of the Law." As a symbol of this attainment, the father would fasten the phylacteries upon the arm and forehead of his son. The box placed on the forehead indicated that the laws must be memorized. The other box was placed on the left arm so that it would press against the heart when the arms were folded or the hands were clasped in prayer. The box pressed against the heart would symbolize that the laws were to be loved and obeyed.

Girls received their education at home. A girl's mother taught her what she needed to know to be a good wife and mother.

She learned about such things as dietary laws which had to do with the family's devotion to God. Girls learned the practical side of the laws the boys studied.

A girl learned how to make the home ready for special holidays and Sabbath. In such preparation she learned the manning of the customs and history behind the events. This heritage she would be able to pass on to her own children in their very early years.

The girl would learn a variety of skills such as weaving, spinning, and treating illnesses. She might also learn to sing and dance and play a musical instrument such as a flute or harp.

The Jewish people had opportunity to receive religious education from priests and **Levites** (Leviticus 10:10-11). The priests and Levites were to be supported by the offerings of the people and were to be the religious teachers of the nation. Apparently the educational function of their work was not well maintained. During the **revival** under King **Jehoshaphat**, the teaching function of Priests and Levites was resumed and the people were taught the ordinances of the Law. (2 Chronicles 17:7-9).

The **ineffective** work of the priests was **supplemented** by the teaching of the prophets. The first of these prophets, Samuel, attempted to make his reform permanent by instituting a school of the prophets in Ramah (1 Samuel 19:19-20). Later other schools of the prophets were begun at other places. The main study at these centers was the Law and its interpretation. Not all of the students of these schools had predictive gifts nor were all the prophets students in such schools. Amos is a notable example of a prophet who was not educated in one of these schools (Amos 7:14-15).

Questions for discussion or reflection.
(1) What are the purposes of education according to the Bible?
(2) How do boys receive their education? How about girls?
(3) Where do children receive their education?
(4) Who are the teachers?
(5) What are the methods of education?

Text C Education in New Testament Times

The synagogue apparently came into existence during the **Babylonian captivity** when the Jews were deprived of the services of the Temple. During captivity they began meeting in small groups for prayer and Scripture reading. When they returned to Israel the synagogue spread rapidly and developed into an important educational institution. Synagogue services made an important educational contribution to the religious life of the community. The elementary school system among the Jews developed in connection with the synagogue. Even before the days of Jesus, schools for the young were located in practically every important Jewish community.

The teacher was generally the synagogue "attendant." An assistant was provided if there were more than twenty-five students. The primary aim of education at the synagogue school was religious. The *Old Testament* was the subject matter for this instruction. Reading, writing and **arithmetic** were also taught. **Memorization**, drill and review were used as approaches to teaching.

Boys usually began formal schooling at the "house of the book" at age five. He would spend at least a half day, six days a week for about five years, studying at the synagogue. Parents brought their son at daybreak and came for him at midday. While not at school the boy was usually learning a trade, such as farming or **carpentry**.

If a boy wanted training beyond that given in a synagogue, he would go to a scholarly scribe. Saul of Tarsus received such advanced **theological** training "at the feet of **Gamaliel**" in Jerusalem.

No formal educational approach is described in the *New Testament*. However, Jesus is pictured as teaching large crowds. While Jesus was much more than a teacher, he was recognized as a teacher by his contemporaries. He was a God-sent teacher who taught with an authority and challenge which held his audiences captive.

Jesus was also a trainer of teachers. He selected the twelve and taught them how to teach others.

As risen Lord, Jesus commissioned his followers to carry their **evangelism** and teaching ministry into the world. As seen in Acts 2:42, Acts 4:1-2; Acts 5:21, Acts 5:28, teaching became an important work in the early church in Jerusalem.

The *New Testament* places importance on the teaching function of the church. Teaching is regarded as a primary function of the **pastor**. Volunteer teachers are also important to the work of the church.

In *New Testament* times churches met in the homes of members and Christian teaching was done there.

While the synagogue school still existed, the home was still considered a primary place of education for children. Timothy is a notable example of a child who had been educated in the Scriptures in the home.

A Christian education is one that...

(a) A Christian education trains a child along in each academic discipline, building upon skills learned and mastered ... "precept upon precept; line upon line".

(b) A Christian education aides the **covenant** child to understand the relationship between what they are learning in academics, the "real"world, and their duties as Christians.

(c) A Christian education trains up warriors for the Faith preparing them to take dominion as we have been commanded in all areas of life; e.g., history, math, science, language arts, civics, business, economics, etc. This learning and training prepares covenant children to transmit the power of the Christian worldview into a lifetime of practical Christian action (faith without works is dead). Each covenant child has a mission to fulfill.

(d) A Christian education is vital in the continuity of transferring God's covenant from generation to generation. Christian parents rear their children with the knowledge and expectation that they will hold fast to what they have been taught and continue to work for God's **covenantal** people for His glory.

(e) A Christian education provides a covenant witness for parents, raising up a new generation with knowledge of and a commitment to God's Law-Word.

(f) A Christian education helps parents to fulfill their covenantal duty to their children as they are commanded to teach the Word of God in formal and informal settings with the goal of relating all knowledge to God's authority — all spheres of thought are under God's authority.

(g) A Christian education operates under God's covenantal sanctions. God's commands concerning the training of our covenantal children are not idle suggestions.

Questions for discussion or reflection.

(1) What educational contributions did synagogue make to the religious life of the community?
(2) What are the functions of Christian education?

Notes

(1) **Massachusetts Bay Colony:**

The Massachusetts Colony (sometimes called the Massachusetts Company, for the institution that founded it) was an English settlement on the east coast of North America in the 17th century, in New England, centered around the present-day cities of Salem and Boston. The area is now in the

Commonwealth of Massachusetts, one of the 50 United States of America.

(2) **Babylonian captivity:**

Although the term Babylonian captivity, or Babylonian exile, typically refers to the deportation and exile of the Jews of the ancient Kingdom of Judah to Babylon by Nebuchadnezzar II in 586 BC, in fact the exile started with the first deportation in 597 BC. It is also worth mentioning that Daniel is taken into exile during an even earlier date of 605 BC. The captivity and subsequent return to Israel and rebuilding of the Jerusalem Temple are pivotal events in the history of the Jews and Judaism, and had far-reaching impacts on the development of modern Jewish culture and practice.

Book to Read
Testament: 2005 comic book by Douglas Rushkoff. The binding of Isaac is directly paralleled by a father refusing to implant an RFID chip into his adolescent son and putting it into the family dog instead.

Movie to See
Abraham and Isaac: 2009 short film directed by Mitchell and Webb. After a night of serious partying, God and his pal Satan decide to prank Abraham by instructing him to sacrifice his son Isaac, but get too "caught up in the moment" and forget to send the angel down in time.

Song to Enjoy
"We Can Work It Out" is the first promotional single by Sweetbox from the album *The Next Generation*, featuring Jamie Pineda as the new frontwoman. The song samples "Spring" from *The Four Seasons* by Vivaldi.

We Can Work It Out
by Sweetbox

I can't see why everybody has to fight
Cos two wrongs don't make a right
A fall in life is justified
That is what they say
Life's too short
There must be another way
We can work it out

(Together we can change it)
We can work it out
(Together we can make it)
And if we just forgive
In this world we live
And share some love
We can work it out
We should live to the fullest each and everyday
Cos there's no stop in time
And yesterday's past mistakes

Shouldn't bring us down
Life's too short
There's no need to be afraid
We can work it out
(Together we can change it)
We can work it out
(Together we can make it)
And if we just forgive
Within this world we live
And share some love
We can work it out
We can work it out
Yes, we can
We can work it out
(Together we can change it)
Together we can change it

Maybe we can make it
And if we just forgive
Within this world we live
If we life is too short
We can work it out
If we come together we can change it
We can work it
And together we can make it
And if we just believe in love
Within this world we live to love
(Just miracle) Just miracle
(Just very short)
We can work it out
Da la da
Da la da la da...

Unit 13

The Power of Dreams and *the Bible*

> Dreams pass into the reality of action. From the actions stems the dream again; and this interdependence produces the highest form of living.
>
> —Anais Nin

Unit Goals

- To gain a general knowledge of different dreams in *the Bible*
- To develop a right attitude towards American dream in *the Bible*
- To get acquainted with some basic cultural concepts concerning dreams in *the Bible*
- To learn useful words and expressions about dreams in *the Bible*
- To improve English language skills and western culture awareness

Before You Read

I. Answer the following questions.

(1) Do you dream? How often?
(2) What causes dreams?
(3) Do you believe in the power of dreams?
(4) How much do you remember your dreams?
(5) Do you dream in black and white or in color?
(6) Have your dreams ever predicted the future?

II. Form groups of three or four students. Try to find, on the Internet or in the library, more information about dreams in the *Old Testament* and the *New Testament*. Get ready for a 5-minute presentation in class.

Start to Read

Text A Four Main Dreams in *the Bible*

The ancient world and the biblical tradition knew about dreams. The ancients understood that the **unbidden** communication in the night opens sleepers to a world different from the one they manage during the day. The ancients dared to imagine, moreover, that this unbidden communication is one **venue** in which the holy purposes of God, **perplexing** and unreasonable as they might be, come to us. They knew too that this communication is not obvious. It requires interpretation.

Here are four familiar examples from *the Bible* in which the Holy Other addresses people in the **vulnerability** of the night:

The first occurs after Jacob has **duped** his older brother and is fleeing for his life. He is alone, running to his mother's relatives. But he must stop to sleep. In this condition, he is a good candidate for an intrusion from beyond. He dreams of angels coming and going, messengers and promise-makers. He hears God's voice of promise. The God rooted in his family promises land. This odd holy voice of the night also promises to be with this **fugitive** and to bring him safely home.

The dream requires a total redescription of Jacob's life defined by God's promise. The place of his sleep is converted, by vision and by utterance, into a place of promissory **companionship**.

That disclosure requires a response. Jacob pledges to be allied with the God of promise, a pledge that **entails** accepting himself as a carrier of the promise.

A dream also invades the troubled sleep of the mighty Pharaoh. Who would have thought that this manager of the daytime world would be so vulnerable? His dream involves a confusing **scenario** featuring cows and shocks of grain. He has no clue to the meaning of the dream. After Pharaoh's magicians and wise men, his "intelligence community," fail him, he summons an outsider, an Israelite, someone **uncredentialed**. Joseph tells Pharaoh the meaning of his dream: there will soon come a time when the empire will be **destabilized**. Truth in the night is spoken to the one who has power in the daylight. This dream, so the narrative reports, will cause settled power to become more **aggressively** acquisitive.

In this reading of the nighttime reality, Pharaoh is invited into an alternative world of need, trouble and deprivation. This reality, which comes to dominate the larger narrative about Joseph, was not even on the horizon of Pharaoh with all of his technical apparatus, his economic and military power and his intelligence community.

Too bad that Joseph ceases to be an interpreter and becomes a manager for Pharaoh! By his "**Egyptianization**," he signs on to the task of stabilizing the regime that the dream had worked to destabilize.

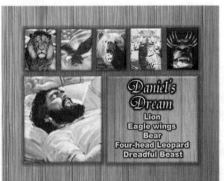

Paralleling the story of Joseph at the beginning of the *Old Testament* is the story of Daniel at the end of the *Old Testament*. It concerns a dream that **assails** power. Like Pharaoh, **Nebuchadnezzar** represents a settled life of exploitative power that expects not to be **disrupted**. Dreams are dangerous for such a ruler. They come in the night and declare God's intentions. The dream **dispatches** the king to a condition he did not intend—into a grass-eating beast.

The dream and the narrative about the dream deconstruct the idea in his power. He had come to think of himself as autonomous and did not acknowledge that sovereignty belongs to whomever God may give it. The dream asserts that Nebuchadnezzar had misunderstood his status in the world by **disregarding** the **ultimacy** of the holy God.

Daniel, the Jewish dream interpreter—gifted, surely, because of his rootage in faith—counsels Nebuchadnezzar to practice mercy and justice. The dream is given because of Nebuchadnezzar's "insanity". The narrative goes beyond the dream to tell of a return to sanity: Nebuchadnezzar offers a **doxology** to God and accepts his own **penultimacy** in the world of power.

Perhaps the best-known biblical dream appears at the conclusion of the visit by the **Magi**: "And having been warned in a dream not to return to Herod, they left for their own country by another road". The Christ child is threatened by power. In order to secure a future for the child, the voice of the holy intervenes in the night when the royal menace is at rest.

In all four cases, the course of public history, with its determined **configurations** of power, is disrupted by a hidden truth designed to create new possibilities. In the cases of Jacob and the wise men, the dream opens a way of wellbeing. In the cases of Pharaoh and Nebuchadnezzar, the functions of royal power are decisively shaped—in Pharaoh's case by a **resultant** program of acquisitiveness, in Nebuchadnezzar's case by madness that results from the absolute practice of power.

After You Read

Knowledge Focus

I. Pair Work: Work with your partner and consider the following questions.
   (1) What happened in Jacob's dream?
   (2) How do you interpret Jacob's dream?
   (3) What troubled Pharaoh in his dream?
   (4) Why did Nebuchadnezzar dream?
   (5) What is the best-known biblical dream according to the text?

II. Solo Work: According to the knowledge mentioned above, write T if the statement is true and F if it is false.
   (1) Pharaoh's wise men and magicians interpreted his dream.   (   )
   (2) The story of Daniel is in the middle of the *Old Testament*.   (   )
   (3) Nebuchadnezzar's dream is to tell him to return from insanity to sanity.   (   )
   (4) Jacob fled to Laban, his mother's brother, for life.   (   )
   (5) Jacob's dream opens a way of welfare.   (   )

The Bible & Culture

Language Focus

I. Build your vocabulary.

A. Write the correct word next to its definition.

| unbidden | venue | configure | entail |
| disrupt | resultant | fugitive | assail |

(1) _____ to make something necessary, or to involve something
(2) _____ to attack someone violently or criticize someone strongly
(3) _____ to prevent something, especially a system, process or event, from continuing as usual or as expected
(4) _____ someone who flees from an uncongenial situation
(5) _____ following as a result or consequence
(6) _____ the place where a public event or meeting happens
(7) _____ not invited or wanted
(8) _____ to arrange something or change the controls on a computer or other device so that it can be used in a particular way

B. Use the proper forms of the words to complete the sentences.

(1) The victim had been _____ with repeated blows to the head and body.
(2) A heavy fall of snow _____ the city's transport system.
(3) The drivers all sounded their horns and the _____ noise was unbearable.
(4) The stadium has been specifically designed as a _____ for European Cup matches.
(5) Some software can _____ to prevent children from giving out their phone numbers on the Internet.
(6) He is a _____ from justice trying to avoid being caught by the police.
(7) At night images would come _____ into her mind.
(8) Decorating the house will _____ spending a lot of money.

II. Fill in the blanks with the proper forms of the words.

(1) The accident on the main road through town is causing widespread _____ (disrupt) for motorists.
(2) _____ (acquisitive) describes the greed to increase one's possessions, to acquire, hoard and save.
(3) There were food shortages and other _____ (deprive) during the Great Depression.
(4) Mary didn't want to get involved in any _____ (perplex) relationship with a married man.
(5) A rational society should draw a line between legitimate profit-making and _____ (exploit) profiteering.
(6) Governments must ensure their health and education programmes were "targeted" and implemented in a way which did not _____ (stabilize) the overall economy.
(7) It seems _____ (reason) to expect one person to do both jobs.
(8) Some teenagers often behave _____ (aggressive) when their parents are nagging all day long.

(9) My sense of accomplishment at overcoming my fear and _____ (vulnerable) had left me feeling free, not abandoned.

(10) These questions are an _____ (intrude) upon people's privacy.

Comprehensive Work

I. Group Work

American culture really inherited much from *the Bible*. The American dream is one of them. It is often a topic for essays or debates. Please discuss with your group members the following questions:

(1) What does American dream mean?
(2) Is the American dream still working?
(3) Is the American dream still worth pursuing?
(4) What do you think of Obama's American dream?
(5) If we say that everyone can become rich if they work hard enough, does that mean that the poor are only too lazy? (Or do we have to take other factors into account?)

II. Essay Writing

Please write an essay about "What are the advantages/ disadvantages if people only try to pursue their very own dreams?"

III. Solo Work

1. Put in the missing words.

In trying to understand the way dreams were interpreted by the people of *the Bible*, it must be remembered that these early tribal people did not emerge from a vacuum. They inherited views and concepts about all aspects of life, including dreams, from previous c_____ . They also lived within a particular view of the world and a system of beliefs that coloured their dreams, what they expected of them, and their manner of reporting them. Therefore it is w_____ looking at this background to biblical dreams.

The first written account of a dream is in the Babylonian story of Gilgamesh. This dates from many hundreds of years BC. The very latest written version of the story has been dated at 600 BC. In the story, Gilgamesh, king of Uruk, dreams a meteor f_____ from the sky, and his mother tells him it foretells his meeting with a character who will p_____ an important part in his life. This character is Enkidu. Gilgamesh is pondering on his mortality, and sets out with Enkidu to seek eternal life. The story therefore links dreams with prophecy and also the search for the m_____ of life and immortality. The story is also the earliest recorded literature.

2. Proofreading and error correction.

Like other religions of the world, Christianity gives significant importance to biblical dreams. There are mainly two types of dreams—Prophetic dreams and Warning dreams.

The prophetic dreams concern about the things of direct relevance to the dreamer. *The Bible* says anyone could have a prophetic dream from God. The meanings of a prophetic dream are not clear and would require an interpretation. *The Bible* calls the prophetic dreams "dark sayings" and these dreams belong to God.

(1) _____

Christians around the world believe God helps people to interpret their dreams and this is most evident in one of the biblical stories. King Nebuchadnezzar has a dream concern the future of his country and he forgets about it. Later, he asks his wise men to tell him about the dream and it's meaning. Remember, the only other person who knows about the dream is the God. Later, it is the God who reveals it to one of the wise men—Daniel.

(2) _____
(3) _____
(4) _____

Warning Dreams: Christianity interprets warning dreams as the ones which warns the dreamer. It is believed these dreams are God-sent and implies what would happen in the nearly future. For instance, the Angel of the Lord appeared in the dream of Joseph (father of Jesus Christ) and asked him to take the young child and his mother to flee into Egypt and later to return to Israel.

(5) _____

Read More

Text B What does *the Bible* Say about Dreams?

Dreams are believed as being the **manifestations** of the mind's process of working on your worries and fears. At times, your efforts during your awakened state do not bear fruit. You fail in solving certain problems. You struggle to get rid of mental stress, only to find yourself still in trouble. It is during your sleep, when your conscious mind is not awake, that your brain tries to find solutions to your problems. Some of you must have experienced having found an answer to a seemingly difficult question after a night's sleep. You might have experienced the phenomenon of your problems getting solved through your dreams.

What does *the Bible* say about dreams? Dreams are the reflections of the stress in your life. Some believe that Satan could be sending you **intimidating** messages in the form of dreams. But there is little evidence in *the Bible* **scriptures** that the Satan can do so. *The Bible* tells you to trust in God, submit yourself to Him and rest assured that He will solve all the problems in your life. You should pray to God before going to

sleep and request him to take away your worries. *The Bible* **proclaims** that belief in God and a total loyalty towards Him is a definite way to overcome your difficulties.

It was believed that God talks to people through dreams. During the ancient times, people believed that God communicated with men of God and prophets through dreams. *The Bible* has a verse that talks about God warning people through dreams. *The Bible* states that God may encourage you through dreams. It is believed that it is your subconscious self that speaks to you through your dreams. Dreams can be the means by which your mind tells you that you need a change in life.

A verse in Bible, that says, "For a dream cometh through the multitude of business; and a fool's voice is known by **multitude** of words" discusses the causes of dreams. According to *the Bible*, multitude of physical or mental business causes dreams. *The Bible* believes in the idea that while you are physically asleep, your mind and brain are at work. Many a time, you wake up with a certain state of mind that appears to have developed as a result of your dreams. At times you wake up sad, at times scared while at other times, you wake up with an unexplained happiness. Soon you realize that all of it was a part of your dream. What appears real is actually not. *The Bible* talks about this phenomenon in Isaiah 29:8 that says, "It shall even be as when a hungry man dreams that he is eating; but he awakens, and his hunger remains: as when a thirsty man dreams that he is drinking; but he awakens faint, with his thirst **unquenched**".

The Bible makes it clear that there is a difference between messages from God and those from the Satan or demons. Only those with a "band of truth" are fortunate to interpret the messages they receive through dreams. It is also not correct to interpret every dream as messages from God. The sources of dreams or **premonitions** that you experience are not always clear. The reasons behind them cannot be easily understood. In case of bad dreams casing fear or illness, it is best to seek God's help. **Almighty** is the true healer.

Questions for discussion or reflection.
(1) What do you think are the reasons of dreams?
(2) It is said that dreams are the reflections of the stress in your life. Do you agree? Why or why not?
(3) What does *the Bible* say about dreams?

Text C Dream Interpretation

Freud treated dreams as "the royal road to the unconscious", a thesis that served his general conviction that consciousness, the reasoned control of life, **constitutes** only the surface part of the energies that **propel** or **immobilize** persons. This "master of suspicion" understood the unconscious as an urgent **dissenter** from the "enlightened" nature of humanity.

Freud, of course, did not link dreams to the holy, which he regarded as an illusion. He worked to put dream interpretation on a scientific footing, **transposing** the religious dimension of dreams into a psychological reality. Dreams were taken to be **disclosure** of the denied part of the self particularly the self's repressed desires.

Though he transposed dreams from religious to psychological realities, Freud nonetheless utilized a **rabbinic-midrashic** interpretive method, which involved a patient probing of multi-layered meanings and the inscrutable, **enigmatic** dimensions of life. Dreams, like ancient texts, require imaginative

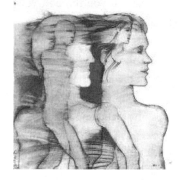

interpretation in order for us to receive what they disclose.

For all the modernity of Freud's approach, it has important points of continuity with the perspective of the ancient texts. Dreams are recognized as disclosures of otherness, an otherness that may indeed open us to authentic reality and to a truth that lies beyond reason. For Freud, as with Joseph and Daniel, everything depends upon the blessed gift of interpretation. Dreamers like Pharaoh and Nebuchadnezzar often lack the imaginative powers needed for receiving disclosures about the hidden self and its repressed desires.

Freud invites us to the work of "archaeology" of uncovering the origins of the self in the unconscious. But Freud's interpretation of dreams is also, as Paul Ricoeur understood, a practice of "teleology" of anticipating what the self may become. The teleological or, perhaps better, the **eschatological** dimension of a dream may lead to wise choices, like that of the wise men in Matthew, or to the choosing of an alternative future, as in the case of Jacob.

Another kind of dreamer, perhaps the greatest dreamer of the mid-20th century, is Martin Luther King Jr. His "I Have a Dream" speech of August 1963 represented a defiant political stance couched in religious rhetoric. It is important that the address was presented as a dream:

I still have a dream. It is a dream deeply rooted in the American dream. I have a dream that one day this nation will rise up and live out the true meaning of its creed: "We hold these truths to be self-evident: that all men are created equal." I have a dream that one day on the red hills of Georgia the sons of former slaves and the sons of former slave owners will be able to sit down together at the table of brotherhood ... I have a dream that my four little children will one day live in a nation where they will not be judged by the color of their skin but by the content of their character. I have a dream today! ... I have a dream that one day every valley shall be exalted, and every hill and mountain shall be made low, the rough places will be made plain, and the crooked places will be made straight, and the glory of the Lord shall be revealed and all flesh shall see it together.

Surely there is something in this speech that cannot be captured by political **pragmatism** or dismissed as a political **stratagem**. King's dream was a gift of imagination from beyond the realm of political realism. And if we say "from beyond", then clearly it is something like a dream that carries a message from the holy. The substance of the dream is a world other than the one near at hand. There is indeed an otherness to the dream, for King is able to imagine a world that is radically **discontinuous** with the one we see around us. It is this imagined otherness to which the vulnerable and the oppressed appeal, an otherness to which the rulers of this age have no access and which they characteristically seek to critique or censor.

King's dream, like every dream, is not simply the sign of a wish or projection but is the intrusion of God into a settled world. It has a holy intensity that reaches back into generations of suffering; it is a holy intrusion that reaches forward in sanity, continuing to generate a restless uneasiness with the way things are until the dream comes to fruition and a new world is enacted. The dream connects political possibility and religious authority in such a way as to be beyond critical argument or political control. That dream continues to **reverberate** and be **generative** among us because its **cadences** are not those of reasoned discourse but of an **elusive** piety, perhaps the favorite dialect of the biblical God.

Dream interpretation, so Jewish in its imaginative attentiveness, pertains to **psychological** matters and the reality of repression. But it is not limited to those concerns. Dreams concern larger realities and possible futures. There are many voices in the night, not all of them noble. Among them, however, is the voice of the holy God, who "plucks up and tears down" what we have trusted, who "**plants** and builds" what we cannot even imagine.

We do not **forgo** the use of reason; but we know in our own troubled context that our best reason has around it—in, with and under it—gifts of the "otherness" that make for newness. Our technological achievements require and permit us to learn again what the community of faith has known—and trusted—from the **outset**: there is something outside our controlled management of reality which must be heeded. Sometimes that something turns out to be a miracle of new life.

Questions for discussion or reflection.
(1) How does Freud interpret dreams?
(2) What new understanding of Martin Luther King's dream do you get from this text?

Book to Read
The Great Gatsby

The Great Gatsby is a novel by the American author F. Scott Fitzgerald. First published on April 10, 1925, it is set on Long Island's North Shore and in New York City during the summer of 1922 and is a critique of the American Dream.

The novel chronicles the chaos of World War I. American society enjoyed unprecedented levels of prosperity during the "roaring" 1920s as the economy soared. At the same time, Prohibition, the ban on the manufacture and sale of alcohol as mandated by the Eighteenth Amendment, made millionaires out of bootleggers and led to an increase in organized crime, for example the Jewish mafia. Although Fitzgerald, like Nick Carraway in his novel, idolized the riches and glamor of the age, he was uncomfortable with the unrestrained materialism and the lack of morality that went with it, a kind of decadence.

Movie to See
Daniel and the King's Dreams (2008)

King Nebuchadnezzar is having disturbing dreams and doesn't know what they mean. Only a young Jewish boy named Daniel is able to interpret the meaning of the King's dreams. Many years pass and, as happened in a dream, the King has a golden idol built in his image. Nebuchadnezzar demands that everyone worship the idol. However, three Jewish Ministers refuse to worship the idol so the king has them thrown into a fiery furnace. God protects them and they emerge from the flames unharmed. Nebuchadnezzar acknowledges the power of God and has the golden idol destroyed.

Song to Enjoy

The song "The Power of the Dream", composed by Kenneth "Babyface" Edmonds and David Foster, with words by Linda Thompson was performed in the opening ceremony by Céline Dion accompanied by Foster and the Atlanta Symphony Orchestra and Centennial Choir.

The Power of Dream
by Celine Dion

Deep within each heart
There lies a magic spark
That lights the fire of our imagination
And since the dawn of man
The strength of just "I can"
Has brought together people of all nations
There's nothing ordinary
In the living of each day
There's a special part
Every one of us will play
Feel the flame forever burn
Teaching lessons we must learn
To bring us closer to the power of the dream
As the world gives us its best
To stand apart from all the rest
It is the power of the dream that brings us here
Your mind will take you far
The rest is just pure heart
You'll find your fate is all your own creation

Every boy and girl
As they come into this world
They bring the gift of hope and inspiration
Feel the flame forever burn
Teaching lessons we must learn
To bring us closer to the power of the dream
The world Unites in hope and peace
We pray that it will always be
It is the power of the dream that brings us here
There's so much strength in all of us
Every woman child and man
It's the moment that you think you can't
You'll discover that you can
....
The power of the dream
The faith in things unseen
The courage to embrace your fear
No matter where you are
To reach for your own star
To realize the power of the dream
To realize the power of the dream

Unit 14
Jewish Values

> The timeless mission of the Jews is to make the world better by making people better.
> Jewish tradition teaches that kindness is what life requires of you.

Unit Goals
- To gain a general knowledge of Jewish value in America
- To be familiar with the Jewish symbolism in America
- To learn the history of early American Jews
- To learn useful words and expressions about Jewish values in *the Bible*
- To improve English language skills and western culture awareness

Before You Read

I. Can you answer the following questions about the early history of America?
   (1) Where is New England?
   (2) Why is it called New England?
   (3) Who were the earliest pilgrims that settled in New England?
   (4) How did they go to New England?
   (5) Why did they settle there?
   (6) What do you think they brought to New England?

II. Form groups of three or four students. Try to find, on the Internet or in the library, more information about Jewish values. Get ready for a 5-minute presentation in class.

Start to Read

Text A Jewish Impact on the Civilization of America

The creation of the United States of America represented a unique event in world history. Unlike other countries where democracy evolved over a period of hundreds of years, the United States was the first country to be created, from its **inception**, as a democracy. And *the Bible* —and Jewish values—played a major role in this process.

Many of the earliest "pilgrims" who settled the "New England" of America in early 17th

century were Puritan refugees escaping from religious **persecutions** in Europe.

Over the next century, America continued to be not only the land of opportunity for many people seeking a better life but also the land of religious tolerance. By the middle 1700's, the east coast of America was settled by a virtual "Who's Who" of Christian **splinter** sects from all over Europe. Among them were: the Puritans, the Quakers, Calvinists, the Huguenots, the Moravians, the Mennonites and the Amish.

These were just some of the numerous groups who arrived in America in search of religious freedom.

The majority of the earliest settlers were, of course, Puritans. Beginning with the Mayflower, over the next twenty years, 16,000 Puritans **migrated** to the Massachusetts Bay Colony, and many more settled in Connecticut and Rhode Island. Like their cousins back in England, these American Puritans strongly **identified with** both the historical traditions and customs of the ancient Hebrews of the *Old Testament*. Gabriel Sivan, in *The Bible and Civilization*, (p. 236) observes:

> No Christian community in history identified more with the People of the Book than did the early settlers of the Massachusetts Bay Colony, who believed their own lives to be a literal **reenactment** of the Biblical drama of the Hebrew nation. They themselves were the children of Israel; America was their Promised Land; the Atlantic Ocean their Red Sea; the Kings of England were the Egyptian pharaohs; the American Indians the Canaanites (or the Lost Ten Tribes of Israel); the pact of the Plymouth Rock was God's holy Covenant; and the **ordinances** by which they lived were the Divine Law. Like the Huguenots and other Protestant victims of Old World oppression, these émigré Puritans **dramatized** their own situation as the righteous remnant of the Church corrupted by the "Babylonian woe", and saw themselves as instruments of Divine Providence, a people chosen to build their new commonwealth on the Covenant entered into at Mount Sinai.

In England, the Puritan identification with *the Bible* was so strong that some Puritan extremists sought to replace English common law with Biblical laws of the *Old Testament*, but were prevented from doing so. In America, however, there was far more freedom to experiment with the use of Biblical law in the legal codes of the colonies, and this was exactly what these early colonist set out to do.

The earliest legislation of the colonies of New England was all determined by *Scripture*. At the first assembly of New Haven in 1639, John Davenport clearly stated the **primacy** of *the Bible* as the legal and moral foundation of the colony:

> Scriptures do hold forth a perfect rule for the direction and government of all men in all duties which they are to perform to God and men as well as in the government of families and commonwealth as in matters of the Church ... the Word of God shall be the only rule to be attended unto in organizing the affairs of government in this plantation. (See Abraham I Katsch, The Biblical Heritage of American Democracy, p. 97)

Subsequently, the New Haven legislators adopted a legal code—the Code of 1655—which contained some 79 statutes, half of which contained Biblical references, **virtually** all from *the*

Hebrew Bible. The Plymouth Colony had a similar law code as did the Massachusetts assembly, which, in 1641—after an **exhortation** by Reverend John Cotton who presented the legislators with a copy of Moses, His Judicials—adopted the so-called "Capital Laws of New England" based almost entirely on Mosaic law. A very significant political evolution was taking place in the New World. Unlike the Puritans in England who, of necessity, lived under English common law and were ruled by a King and Parliament, the Puritans of America had no central authority or national governing body. Yet, they did not **lapse into** anarchy. Instead, they created communities governed by elected councils of elders similar to the "presbyters" of England. Their communities were both stable and prosperous, with **mandatory** school systems modeled after the Jewish ones.

This unique political evolution goes a long way toward explaining the strong sense of independence shared by the colonies and the early success of democracy in America. The Puritans felt that God was watching them, and fear of heaven was a thousand times stronger than fear of the crown.

It almost seems as if these early settlers had recreated the Biblical period of the "Judges" when, following the conquest of Jericho and settlement of Canaan, Israel had no king or central authority and "every man did what was right in his own eyes".

What was right in Puritan eyes, of course, was what *the Bible* said. But what did it say exactly? So much of it could be subject to interpretation of the reader.

Without the Jewish Oral Law, which helped the Jews understand *the Bible,* the Puritans were left to their own devices and tended toward a literal interpretation. This sometimes led to a stricter, more fundamentalist observance than Judaism had ever seen. For example, the Jewish Sabbath is a day of **refraining from** work as *the Bible* **mandates**. However, "work"—in Hebrew melacha—is defined by Jewish Oral Law as **cessation** of all creative activity that was in progress when the Tabernacle was being built and which, *the Bible* states, ceased on the Sabbath. But the Puritans took the commandment to cease work as unconditional. And their prohibitions were actually more restrictive than what the Jews had themselves practiced. Even household chores such as sweeping floors, making beds, or feeding animals were not allowed for the twenty-four hours of the day of rest. **Adherence** was enforced by fines and public **floggings**.

After You Read

I. Pair Work: How did settlers of the Massachusetts Bay Colony identify themselves with the People of the Book? Work with your partner and finish the following chart.

Settlers of the Massachusetts Bay Colony	People of the Book
Themselves	Children of Israel
The Atlantic Ocean	
The kings of England	
American Indians	Canaanites
The pact of the Plymouth Rock	
The ordinances	The Divine Law

II. Solo Work: According to the knowledge mentioned above, write T if the statement is true and F if it is false.

(1) Puritans extremists in England successfully replaced English common law with Biblical laws of the *Old Testament*. ( )
(2) The Code of 1655 contained about 40 Biblical references. ( )
(3) The adoption of "Capital Laws of New England" based on Mosaic law signified the political evolution in the New World. ( )
(4) The communities governed by elected councils of presbyters were stable and prosperous. ( )
(5) Household chores are strictly prohibited on the Jewish Sabbath according to the Puritans. ( )

Language Focus
I. Build your vocabulary.
  A. Write the correct word next to its definition.

| primacy | inception | splinter | lapse |
| anarchy | mandate | cessation | flog |

(1) _____ the beginning of an organization or official activity
(2) _____ a group of people who have left a political party or other organization and formed a new separate organization
(3) _____ the state of being the most important thing
(4) _____ a situation in which there is no organization and control, especially in society because there is no effective government
(5) _____ to order someone to do something
(6) _____ to beat someone very hard with a whip or a stick, as a punishment
(7) _____ to end legally or officially by not being continued or made effective for a longer period

(8) _____ ending or stopping

B. Use the proper forms of the words to complete the sentences.
   (1) Since its _____ in 1968, the company has been at the forefront of computer development.
   (2) The Socialist Workers' Party seemed to split into several _____ groups.
   (3) The government insists on the _____ of citizens' rights.
   (4) If the pay deal isn't settled amicably there'll be _____ in the factories.
   (5) He _____ until he was on the verge of death.
   (6) The association needs to win back former members who have allowed their subscriptions to _____.
   (7) Our delegates _____ to vote against the proposal at the conference.
   (8) Religious leaders have called for a total _____ of the bombing campaign.

II. Fill in the blanks with the proper forms of the words.
   (1) Athletes must undergo a _____ (mandate) drugs test before competing in the championship.
   (2) A part of the year marked by a _____ (cease) or lessening of normal activity, as of a business.
   (3) He encouraged the use of finger-printing in _____ (identify).
   (4) The development of food and agriculture has been an important objective of the World Bank since its _____ (incept).
   (5) You will find religious groups ranging all the way from _____ (fundamental) Christianity to paganism to Buddhism.
   (6) _____ (Christian), Islam and Judaism are the names of religions or faiths followed by Christians, Muslims and Jews respectively.
   (7) The race of plants and the race of animals shrink under this great _____ (restrict) law.
   (8) It was essential that the Europeans break away from slavish _____ (adhere) to authority.

Comprehensive Work
I. Group Work
   1. Discuss the following question within a group of three or four members. Take down the answers of your group members and share them with other groups.
      How could *the Bible* and the Jewish Values have influenced the founding of America so deeply?
   2. Do you know Steven Spielberg, Ralph Lauren, Michael Eisner and Michael Dell? They are all successful, at the top of their fields. They're all fabulously wealthy. They're all Jewish. Those three characteristics, successful, wealthy and Jewish, are linked repeatedly in America today. And it is no accident. Jewish-Americans are, as a group, the wealthiest ethnic group in America. But what are the factors that work together to create Jewish wealth?

II. Pair Work
Discuss the following questions about the cartoon with you partner.
   (1) What is "Mayflower"?
   (2) What is the literal meaning of "power"?
   (3) What do they symbolize respectively in the cartoon?
   (4) What does the cartoon mean?

III. Essay Writing

This unseen power has indeed subjected America to its occult Jewish control. Perhaps the best proof of the constant expansion of Jewish financial power in America is furnished by the activities of the great Jewish banking houses and investment companies. Year by year, Goldman, Sachs and Co., Kuhn, Loeb and Co., Lazard Freres, Lehman Brothers and others, are pushing their financial control deeper and deeper into the American economy. It should be noted that though these banking houses have non-Jewish partners, they nonetheless remain firmly in Jewish hands. The Jews really have great influence on America and the world. Please write an essay entitled: *Is the New World Order "Jewish"?*

IV. Solo Work

1. Put in the missing words.

(1) Historically, when true Christianity came to any region, those who were practicing Christ's commands would begin to reach out to help the poor, the oppressed, the s_____, and needy. Most of our present day hospitals, charity centers, orphanages and rescue missions were all f_____ by Christians in keeping with the Biblical commands of Christ to demonstrate His love to a needy world. God has always been interested in helping the weak, the feeble and afflicted. Ungodly societies destroy their weak, helpless and burdensome members.

(2) *The Bible* gives us guidelines in the handling of the earth's resources and Christians are taught in the Word of God to manage them properly. The scriptures are not silent in regard to these things. Proverbs 12:10 says, "A righteous man regards the life of his beast; but the tender mercies of the wicked are cruel."

The Bible also teaches ecology by allowing the mother bird to go if you eat the e_____ she has lain.

Caring hearts will take care of the animals and the land. *The Bible* even instructed man to a_____ the land that crops were raised on to rest e_____ seventh year. Our crops are suffering from depleted vitality because we do not heed this admonition today. Farmers should rotate their crops so that every portion of their land could rest every seven years.

2. Proofreading and error correction.

    The Bible actually does not say anything specifically about the Stock Market. However, it is full of principles that directly affect any kind of investing.

    The basic principle of the stock market is not wrong if it is followed properly. What is that principle? When a man or a group of men have a good and righteous business or company that benefits humanity; yet they lack funding to make that business productive, it creates a need for another help. If another man or a group of men (investors) have surplus funds and could use the monies as additional or future support, it also creates a need for another's help. When the one group physically does the work and the other supports that work with his fund, it becomes mutually beneficial for both parties. However, today, many people invest without any research in the company they are investing in. They do not know if the company policies are based on good Biblical principles. They know nothing as to how their employees are treated. They know anything of the history of the company. They do not know the character of the one running the business; whether they are honest, reliable or trustworthy, etc. They know nothing of their alliances. Most of the stock market is run by lust and greed, instead of wise investment and help one another.

(1) _____
(2) _____
(3) _____
(4) _____
(5) _____

Read More

Text B The Jewish Influence on the Great Seal

    The Great Seal of the United States is used to **authenticate** certain documents issued by the United States federal government. The phrase is used both for the physical seal itself, and more generally for the design impressed upon it. The Great Seal was first used publicly in 1782.

    The design on the obverse of the Great Seal is the national coat of arms of the United States. It is

officially used on documents such as United States passports, military insignia, embassy **placards**, and various flags. As a coat of arms, the design has official colors; the physical Great Seal itself, as affixed to paper, is **monochrome**.

Since 1935, both sides of the Great Seal appear on the reverse of the one-dollar bill. The Seal of the President of the United States is directly based on the Great Seal, and its elements are used in numerous government agency and state seals.

Let's see what symbolic meanings can be reflected from the Great Seal.

The Eagle

Eagle is a famous Masonic symbol. In *the Bible* eagle is used as a metaphor for Israel's exodus from Egypt. This image also appears in the *New Testament Book of Revelation* where "two wings of a great eagle" portray God's intervention to deliver His people from persecution.

Thus, the eagle on the Great Seal could in fact echo the settlers' identification with the Israelites delivered from the Egyptian slavery, a theme that featured in the early designs of the *Dollar bill*.

Thirteen Stars

What symbolic meaning can we find in the image of the thirteen pentagrams forming a huge single hexagram?

Hexagram is also known as the "Seal of Solomon" and features prominently in the Masonic and Rosicrucian symbolism. Its place in the Western Mystery Tradition is firm, and as such it is originally a Jewish **Kabbalistic** sign.

In Hebrew the star is known as "The Shield of David". According to Jewish lore, the symbol was pictured on the famous, miraculous shield of King David, and the shield itself was believed to have followed the **Judahite** kings as an inheritance, all the way down to the hands of Judah the **Maccabean**, the legendary founder of the **Hasmonean** dynasty of the Hellenistic period. The association with King David, the progenitor of the future Messiah, made the star a powerful Messianic symbol.

During the Middle Ages the hexagram ultimately became the national emblem of the Jewish people itself, symbolizing the Divine providence that had accompanied the Israelites since time immemorial. If we assume that the hexagram of the Great Seal is a symbol of the Jewish people, then we can interpret the whole design in a new, meaningful way.

If we read *the Bible* carefully, it becomes evident that Jacob had actually not twelve but thirteen sons. Thus, Joseph became two, rising the total number of Jacob's offspring to thirteen, corresponding to the thirteen tribes of the nation that are here represented by the thirteen stars. These thirteen stars form the one big Star of David which represents the whole nation of Israel (Jacob), the reunion of which is one of the most important signs of the Messianic Age.

In Jewish **liturgical** use, Jacob and Israel are used not just as references to the famous patriarch but also as a title of the Jewish people in general. In this way the thirteen sons or tribes or stars are the extended body of their great forefather. Ultimately this symbol quite graphically echoes the Messianic prophecy of the Torah: *A star will emerge from Jacob.*

The Founding Fathers envisioned the Unites States in this very same way—a harmonious nation compound of diverse groups (or colonies). The words presented under the stars—E PLURIBUS UNUM—emphasize the idea of this union. United States as the New Zion, they no doubt claimed, was the fulfillment of the Judeo-Christian Messianic aspirations of freedom, peace and brotherly love.

We saw that the two psalms that functioned as the source of the arrow and olive branch symbols also mentioned the building of the Temple. We also noted that the word temple (bet) also means "nation" or "family". Here we have a connection between an architectural and a genealogical term.

The Founding Fathers' vision of them as the sons and builders of the New Israel is one of the reasons why the Exodus theme featured in the early designs of the Dollar bill.

Questions for discussion or reflection.
(1) How does *the Bible* influence the basic framework of America?
(2) Where are the opening sentences of the *Declaration of Independence* from?
(3) What is written on the inscription on the Liberty Bell at Independence Hall in Philadelphia?
(4) What is the symbolic meaning of the eagle?
(5) What is hexagram known as?

Text C Number Thirteen

Number thirteen is a **disturbing** number due to its famous association with bad luck. The origin of this belief is not easy to trace although it seems to have a Christian origin.

Some Christian traditions have it that at the Last Supper, Judas Iscariot, the disciple who betrayed Jesus, was the 13th to sit at the table. So, if the Founding Fathers were leaning solely on Christian thinking, it would be unlikely that this number would have found its way to the Great Seal, the symbol of America's divine success.

However, if there was a Jewish/*Old Testament* line of belief in their tradition, this number poses no problem.

Thirteen is actually a special number in Jewish tradition. First of all, thirteen signifies the age at which a boy matures and becomes a Bar Mitzvah, or "Son of the Commandment" which means that the responsibility of the religious duties are put on his shoulders.

Secondly, according to the Torah, God has thirteen attributes of mercy. There are also the famous thirteen principles of faith, compiled by medieval Jewish rabbi and philosopher Moshe benMaimon (Maimonides), outlining Judaism's tenets.

The foundation of the Oral Torah (basis of Talmud) is the thirteen **exegetical** principles which are enumerated in the introduction to ToratKohanim. Through these principles, the Oral Law is derived from the written text of the Torah. This is why the Midrash HaZohar on Bereshit teaches that the number thirteen serves as a metaphor for the Oral Torah.

The thirteen breaches made by the Greeks in the enclosing wall which surrounded the Temple Mount were repaired by the Hasmonean kings. These kings **decreed** that one must bow down when passing by each of these repaired breaches; a total of thirteen bowings.

The Elders made thirteen modifications in the text of the Torah when they translated it into Greek. This number represents the fact that inherent in the translation is the loss of the Oral Torah, which is derived through the thirteen exegetical principles. The thirteen breaches made by the Greeks and repaired by the Hasmoneans represent the entire focus of the Greek war against the Jews. The Greeks sought to eliminate the principles through their literal translation of the Torah into Greek, with the **resultant** loss of the Oral component of the Torah. The Hasmoneans succeeded in restoring these

indispensable tools of Torah interpretation. In order to commemorate and give thanks for this victory of authentic Torah ideology over the shallow, incomplete Sadducee misrepresentation of Torah, thirteen bowings were instituted at the sites of the repaired breaches. It may be further noted that according to Rashi, thirteen Hasmoneans commanded the Jewish army that overthrew the Greeks. These thirteen courageous men enabled the Jewish People to preserve the Oral Tradition and its thirteen principles.

In fact, the number thirteen holds great significance according to Kabbalah, the Jewish mystical tradition. The number indicates the ability to rise above the influence of the twelve signs of the Zodiac (12+1=13), not being bound by the influences of the cosmos.

Thus, the number thirteen can signify (a) reaching maturity and independence, (b) God's merciful blessings, (c) principles of true faith, (d) restoration of the Temple and the sovereignty and (e) rising above the clutches of dependence. All of these ideas were definitely significant to the Founding Fathers in their vision of the new, independent United States viewed in the *Old Testament/Jewish Messianic* light as "God's American Israel".

After-reading exercise:
Write down the 13's found in the Great Seal?
(1) _____
(2) _____
(3) _____
(4) _____
(5) _____
(6) _____
(7) _____
(8) _____
(9) _____

Notes

The Great Seal: On July 4, 1776, the same day that independence from Great Britain was declared by the thirteen states, the Continental Congress named the first committee to design a Great Seal, or national emblem, for the country. Similar to other nations, The United States of America needed an official symbol of sovereignty to formalize and seal (or sign) international treaties and transactions. It took six years, three committees, and the contributions of fourteen men before the Congress finally accepted a design (which included elements proposed by each of the three committees) in 1782.

Book to Read
In ***The Book of Jewish Values***, Rabbi Joseph Telushkin has combed *the Bible*, the Talmud, and

the whole spectrum of Judaism's sacred writings to give us a manual on how to lead a decent, kind, and honest life in a morally complicated world. Telushkin speaks to the major ethical issues of our time, issues that have, of course, been around since the beginning. He offers one or two pages a day of pithy, wise, and easily accessible teachings designed to be put into immediate practice.

In addition, Telushkin raises issues with ethical implications that may surprise you, such as the need to tip those whom you don't see, the right thing to do when you hear an ambulance siren, and why wasting time is a sin. Whether he is telling us what Jewish tradition has to say about insider trading or about the relationship between employers and employees, he provides fresh inspiration and clear guidance for every day of our lives.

Movie to See
Mayflower: The Pilgrims' Adventure (1979)

Originally titled *The Voyage of the Mayflower*, this made-for-TV historical drama was, not surprisingly, first telecast as a CBS Thanksgiving special. In the tradition of the 1952 theatrical feature Plymouth Adventure, the film meticulously recounted the journey in 1620 A.D. of 103 Pilgrim "separatists" from their religiously restrictive English homeland to the shores of the New World. The dramatic crux of the film was manifested in the conflict between mercenary, untrustworthy Mayflower captain Christopher Jones and idealistic but tough Pilgrim leader William Brewster. Also incorporated in the narrative are the intertwining relationships between Miles and Rose Standish, John Alden and Priscilla Mullens.

Song to Enjoy

Here is part of the lyrics of "Mayflower". Find the audio and enjoy the song. You can complete the lyrics while listening.

Mayflower
by Jon And Vangelis

The Sea like The Sea
The Wind like The Wind
The Stars in the Sky

The Sea like The Sea
The moon like The Moon
The Stars in The Sky

The Sea like The Sea
The Moon like The Moon
The Stars in the Sky

In the wind-on the ship-a lullaby
We sailing pass the moment of time
We sailing 'round the point
The kindly light
The kindly light
We go sailing thru' the waters of the summers end
Long ago, search for land

Looking to and fro,

We searching in the day
We searching in the night
We looking everywhere for land a helping hand

For there is hope if truth be there
How much more will we share
We pilgrims of the sea
Looking for a home-

In 1620, The Mayflower sailed from Plymouth westward,
Carrying the Pilgrims in search of a new land
In Star date 27X, year, minute 33, location earth, 16 degrees polar star west

The Mayflower was launched into space
In search of a new land.

....

Unit 15

Bible's Impact on English & American Culture

> I have always said, I always will say, that the studious perusal of the sacred volume will make better citizens, better fathers, and better husbands.
> —Thomas Jefferson (1743—1826)

Unit Goals

- To gain a general Bible impact on English and American culture
- To get acquainted with some words and expressions from *the Bible*
- To learn useful words and expressions about American culture
- To improve English language skills and western culture awareness

Before You Read

I. Please answer the following questions.

(1) How many people are there in the above picture?
(2) Can you guess who is the person standing in the middle?
(3) What story is the picture about?
(4) Who painted it?

II. Form groups of three or four students. Try to find, on the Internet or in the library, more information about literature works related to *the Bible*. Get ready for a 5-minute presentation in class.

《圣经》与文化
The Bible & Culture

Start to Read

Text A　English Culture and *the Bible*

A Unifying Factor

The Bible has been a significant component of English life for many centuries, particularly since the publication of the **Authorized** Version of *the Bible* in 1611, with which every citizen was expected to be familiar. Just as most people know television catch phrases today, so references to *the Bible* would be instantly recognized by almost everyone. It has contributed to developments in civil life, the arts and science.

Influence on the Law

The Bible features heavily in the architecture and decoration of the Houses of Parliament, paying silent tribute to its significance in English **jurisprudence**. Many old **parish** churches still have copies of the Ten Commandments on the walls, underlining the importance of *the Bible* for providing the moral cohesion of society. Most British law is ultimately derived from the codes of law within *the Bible*, of which the Ten Commandments is pre-eminent. The equality of all people before the law is another of its **legacies**.

Visual Arts

The Bible has for centuries fired and filled the imaginations of artists of all genres. The great masters—the painters of the European Renaissance and those who followed them frequently re-presented the great stories of *the Bible*, including the annunciation, birth, baptism and temptations of Jesus at the beginning of his ministry, the Last Supper and the crucifixion, followed by scenes of his resurrection. Sculptors have portrayed its characters such as Michael Angelo's *David* or Epstein's *Jacob*. Still today, *The Shawshank Redemption*, *The Messiah* and **Apocalypse** *Now*, with many more films, are echoing its main motifs.

Words and Music

The Bible is the main source of inspiration for some of Britain's greatest works of literature such as Milton's *Paradise Lost* or John Bunyan's *Pilgrim's Progress*. The foundations of English theatre were laid by medieval plays based on biblical events. Frequently biblical teachings are the subtext of Shakespeare's plays, which often refer to them. Even when authors may have been hardly conscious of the connections, *the Bible's* phrases have enriched their language and its themes provided them with avenues of exploration.

Many composers have produced major works exploring biblical accounts, such as Handel's *Elijah* and *The Messiah*, or more recently *Jesus Christ Superstar, GodSpell* and *Joseph and the Technicolour Dream Coat*.

The Bible and Science

Most people imagine that there is an inevitable conflict between *Genesis* and Darwin's theory of evolution, but right from the start there have been ministers and biblical scholars who have supported his essential insights, and scientists who have challenged them, as continues today.

More fundamentally, there is a strong case for claiming that it is the **consistency** and coherence of the biblical understanding of God, and the reliability of the universe which follows from this, which provided a substantial contribution to the development of the Enlightenment and the sciences which have flowed from it. From a philosophical standpoint these fundamental assumptions are a necessary foundation for science.

The Bible has also contributed to the wider cultural and social context in the United Kingdom:

- The debates about the **propriety** and nature of the monarchy have often been focused on biblical texts.
- The great social reforms of the eighteenth and nineteenth centuries were profoundly influenced by the biblical contribution to issues such as liberty, equality and fraternity, as the recent **commemoration** of The **Abolition** of the Transatlantic Slave Trade Act has reminded us.
- The debates concerning the limits of authority (whether of the monarchy or parliament) over individual conscience, were shaped by people like Milton and Thomas Helwys in the seventeenth century, who depended heavily on their biblical knowledge as a source of profound truth.
- Many of those involved in the Trades Union movement were also driven by the vision for fairness which they saw in *the Bible*.
- The celebrations of ordinary people through the year were shaped by the Christian festivals of Easter, Christmas, **Pentecost** and days set aside to commemorate saints—the word "holiday" originally meant "holy day".
- *The Bible* provided a common framework for social debate among the educated and from the eighteenth century onwards it was *the Bible* which lay at the heart of the developing **populist** education movements.

In short the social institutions and safeguards, as well as many of the benefits people take for granted, were supported by the understanding of human life which was found within *the Bible*. In this sense, the foundations of Britain's culture and society can truly be said to be biblical.

The Bible and the Environment

Today, as people are facing ever more clearly the perceived threats of global warming, *the Bible*, with its vision of man's position within creation and responsibility under God to care properly for it, still has a major contribution to make to the future of all humankind.

After You Read

Knowledge Focus

I. Pair Work: Work with your partner and consider the following questions.

(1) How does *the Bible* influence British law?

(2) How do visual arts echo Biblical themes according to Text A?

(3) Can you list some songs related to *the Bible*? (You may refer to the *Song to Enjoy* after each

《圣经》与文化
The Bible & Culture

unit.)

(4) Many pictures in this book are related to *the Bible*. Can you figure out some of the painters?

(5) How is *Paradise Lost* related to *the Bible*?

II. Solo Work: According to the knowledge mentioned above, write T if the statement is true and F if it is false.

(1) Bible's influence on English life began in 1611.   ( )
(2) Liberty, equality and fraternity were also influenced by *the Bible*.   ( )
(3) All British law derived from the Ten Commandments.   ( )
(4) *The Bible* played a key role in the developing populist education movements.   ( )
(5) Many British festivals originated from Christian festivals.   ( )

Language Focus
I. Build your vocabulary.

A. Use the proper forms of the words to complete the sentences.

propriety	populist	apocalypse	parish
renaissance	authorize	legacy	unify

(1) _____ to bring together; combine
(2) _____ to give official permission for something to happen,
(3) _____ something that is a part of your history or which stays from an earlier time
(4) _____ a new growth of activity or interest in something, especially art, literature or music
(5) _____ the last book of the *New Testament*; contains visionary descriptions of heaven and of conflicts between good and evil and of the end of the world
(6) _____ the rules of polite social behaviour
(7) _____ (in some Christian groups) an area cared for by one priest and which has its own church, or (in England) the smallest Unit of local government
(8) _____ representing or connected with the ideas and opinions of ordinary people

B. Use the proper forms of the words to complete the sentences.

(1) The _____ has welcomed the new vicar with open arms.
(2) The _____ Party is a political party that advocates individual liberty as the primary goal of government
(3) If the new leader does manage to _____ his warring party it will be quite an achievement.
(4) This is a restricted area, open to _____ personnel only.
(5) The Greeks have a rich _____ of literature.
(6) Opera in Britain is enjoying a long-awaited _____.
(7) The book offers a vision of the future in which there is a great nuclear _____.
(8) They'd invited us to dinner so we thought we'd better observe the _____ and invite them back.

II. Fill in the blanks with the proper forms of the words.

(1) The interest on this account will be paid at _____ (redeem).

(2) The plan has now been dropped, with little hope of _____ (resurrect).
(3) I have never felt more reverent at a _____ (baptize).
(4) Some people seemed to believe that with the _____ (abolish) of the emperor, China had become a democratic country and that hence forth everything would take its proper course.
(5) One of writer's favourite themes is the _____ (fraternal) of mankind.
(6) Doubts were expressed concerning the validity and _____ (rely) of the primary measuring instrument.
(7) Customer training and technical support costs are reduced because the _____ (consist) that standards bring improves ease of using and learning.
(8) The findings show a _____ (substance) difference between the opinions of men and women.

Comprehensive Work

I. Group Work

Work in groups and discuss the following questions.
(1) How were the social reforms of the eighteenth and nineteenth centuries influenced by *the Bible*? Give some examples.
(2) What was the Christian response to Darwin?

II. Pair Work: Work with your partner and discuss the influence of *The Ten Commandments* on modern society.

III. Essay Writing

Towards the end of his life Darwin wrote: "It seems to me absurd to doubt that a man may be an ardent Theist and an evolutionist. The science opens me not only to puzzles and to questions about the world I live in; it leads me to marvel at its complexity. Here, I find

science is a good friend to my faith. It also calls me to a journey of learning and understanding." One of the things that mars our culture is the fracture between faith and science. It impoverishes our inquiry into the realities that make up our life and world. This is a false opposition.

What's your understanding of the relationship between science and faith? Write an essay to illustrate your point of view.

IV. Solo Work

1. Put in the missing words.

Jewish Symbols in the American One Dollar Bill

A while ago, at the West Point Academy's Jewish Chapel, there was a display about Hyam Salomon and the Revolutionary War. He died penniless, having used all his resources to aid the newly formed and poorly supplied American Continental Army.

This is a wonderful story sent to me by a lawyer friend that shares my interest in history. I hope you will find it of interest to you:

《圣经》与文化
The Bible & Culture

General Washington's financial advisor and assistant was a Jewish man by the name of Hyam Salomon. During the cold w_____ months at Valley Forge when American soldiers were freezing and r_____ out of food, it was Hyam who marshaled all the J_____ in America and Europe to provide money in relief aid to these stranded American troops and turned the course of history. Without this help, Washington's Continental Army, and the f_____ of the American Colonies would have perished before they could have defeated the British.

If you take a one dollar bill out of your pocket and look at the back at the Eagle, the stars above the Eagle's head are in the six point Star of David to honor Jews. If you turn the Eagle upside d_____ you will see a configuration in the likeness of a Menorah....both at the insistence of George Washington who said we should never forget the Jewish people and what they have done in the interest of America.

2. Proofreading and error correction.

The names of Eastern children, after the familiar Bible custom, usually express the parents' gratitude to God, or something connected with the personal appearance of the child or the circumstances in which it was born. Very frequently the name is given in remembrance of some relative. These names are thus personal registers of the happiness and hope of their parents. Those of Jacob's family will be recalled as instances of this custom, and so do names as Isaac (Laughter), Ishmael (God is hearing), Moses (Drawn out), and Samuel (Heard of God).

(1) _____

(2) _____

It is not unusual to call a son after his own father. The father's name is added as a kind of surname, as David, son of Jesse, and Simon, son of Jonah. A child named after someone in a former generation is a memorial of that one who, though absent, is still living in the minds of the family members. Care is taken lest he or she is forgotten. Thus it is common to have family members' names reused every few generations. This also explains why the people were so amazing when Elizabeth declared that the name of her child would be "John," and said to her, "...There is none of thy kindred that is called by this name" (Luke 1:61). When a child was named after some honor relative, there was often the hope that the child would inherit the character of the departed.

(3) _____

(4) _____

(5) _____

A certain class of names is expressive of family anxiety and sorrow. Such are Dibb (bear), Nimr (leopard), and Saba (lion), given when one child after another has died in infancy, and it is hoped that the name of a common wild animal may take off the evil eye, and put a stop to such misfortune.

Text B American Literature and *the Bible*

Since *the Bible* has been kicked out of public education, students today have difficulty recognizing biblical expressions from great novels written before 1950. Students do not recognize literary references to "Jonah" or "the prodigal son." Professors are forced to decode these images so students **dumbed**-down in *the Bible* can understand the context of our masterpieces of literature.

Educator Allen Bloom suggests, "Imagine such a young person walking through the Louvre or the Uffizi, and you can immediately grasp the condition of his soul. In his innocence of the stories of Biblical and Greek or Roman antiquity, Raphael, Leonardo, Michelangelo, Rembrandt and all the others can say nothing to him. All he sees are colors and forms—modern art. In short, like almost everything else in his spiritual life, the paintings and statues are abstract."

You don't have to go to Paris or Venice to see the dazed looks on students' faces. Without a proper foundation in *the Bible*, American students betray those same faces in our own galleries and libraries.

American Literature

The world has been touched by *the Bible* in every discipline, and we in the United States have not escaped. Literature and art in this country are as much or more influenced by *the Bible* than in any other country.

Again, here are some of literary classics by American authors that use biblical themes, references or allusions, some even in their titles.

The Grapes of Wrath—John Steinbeck
The Song of Solomon—Toni Morrison
Moby Dick—Herman Melville
The Scarlet Letter—Nathaniel Hawthorne
Uncle Tom's Cabin—Harriet Beecher Stowe

In 38 of 45 chapters in the American classic *Uncle Tom's Cabin* there are references to *the Bible*. *Uncle Tom's Cabin* contains almost 100 quotations from or direct references to the King James version of *the Bible*. Most often it is the narrator who makes the connections between the story and *the Bible*, but among the characters, it is Tom himself who most frequently quotes *the Bible*. It is nearly impossible for American school children to understand this American novel without some knowledge of *the Bible*.

American Poetry

Poetry, by its very nature, is often brief. Even still, detecting the influence of *the Bible* on American poets is not impossible. Many American poets reference God or their longing for God in their poetry. As is the case in American film, American literature, and in other cultural genres, sometimes God doesn't fare well in American poetry; other times He does. Regardless, God and His Bible have left their imprint on the poetry of America.

Here are some representative titles:

"The Battle Hymn of the Republic" —Julia Ward Howe
"The Crowing of the Red Cock" —Emma Lazarus
"Snow-Bound: A Winter Idyl" —John Greenleaf Whittier
"Pilgrim at Tinker Creek" —Annie Dillard
"The Only News I Know" —Emily Dickinson
"The Living Temple" —Oliver Wendell Holmes
"Journey of the Magi" —T. S. Eliot

There is a growing band of Christians who are invading the once secular world of American poetry. *The Bible* has always had some influence on American poetry, but it is now coming front and center.

American Film

Believe it or not, even Hollywood has been impacted by *the Bible*. You only have to remember some Tinsel Town greats (and not-so-greats) to remember that *the Bible* or biblical themes were seminal to many of them. For example:

The Ten Commandments
The Passion of the Christ
King of Kings
Bruce Almighty
Pulp Fiction
The Lord of the Rings

Armageddon
The Chronicles of Narnia
The Prince of Egypt
The Matrix
Chariots of Fire
The Exorcist

Of course, *the Bible* is not always treated fairly by Hollywood, but in an essay in the *Journal of Religion and Film*, Adele Reinhartz discusses some of the movies popular with college students and concludes, "The many uses of *the Bible* in film are a powerful argument for biblical literacy. Should our students, university administrators or provincial ministers of education question the on-going relevance of biblical studies programs, let us simply point them to the nearest Cineplex and ask them, as Jules asks his **erstwhile** victims, 'Do you read *the Bible*?'"

The Bible's influence on our culture is everywhere. Old American society would not be the great society it is today without the impact of *the Bible*. Ironic, isn't it, that *the Bible* is everywhere in our culture but itself is neglected by our culture. It seems we'd rather see a bad movie based on biblical themes than read the Good Book. What will be the impact of that?

1. Please finish the following chart based on Text B.

Writer	Work
Nathaniel Hawthorne	
	Moby Dick
Harriet Beecher Stowe	
	The Grapes of Wrath
Toni Morrison	

Text C The Bible's Influence on American Culture

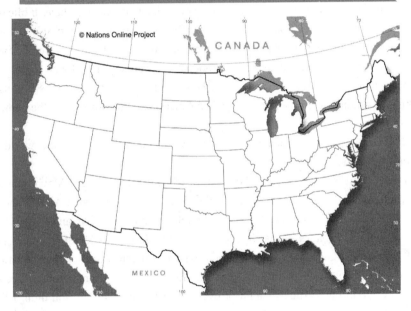

Naming Names

It is evident that *the Bible*'s influence on America's founding, American public education was both persuasive and pervasive. But what are its influences on our daily life? Did *the Bible* equally impact everyday life in "Old America", the America that reflected what our Founding Fathers desired? What can be said for its influence on our American culture? Often that influence flies just under our radar, but if you look carefully, it's clearly there.

When my wife, Linda, and I were naming our children, we stayed away from the typical names the flower children gave to their children—Cinnamon, Rainbow, Sunflower, Honeysuckle, etc.—and chose names we liked, not family names. *The Bible* has often significantly impacted the names Americans have given their children.

Naming Babies

John was the most popular boys' name from 1880 (the earliest year my research could trace) through 1924. Mary was the most popular girls' name from 1880 until 1947 (when it was knocked

out by Linda, only to return in 1953 to hold the top spot until Lisa knocked it out again in 1962). In 1972 it fell out of the top ten and has never returned.

In the early years of America, most children were named Jeremiah, Abigail, John, Josiah, Peter, Sarah, Paul, or Elizabeth. Today, many of these Bible names are making a comeback. In fact, of the top 50 names given to girls in America in 2005, 14 are Bible names. Of the top 50 names given to boys, 25 are Bible names.

Since historically Americans have been a Bible-reading people, that was bound to show up in naming our children.

Naming Places

Interesting, isn't it, that so many small towns and villages in America have biblical names. In eastern Pennsylvania you can begin at Philadelphia (a Bible name—Revelation 3:7) and in two hours you can visit both Bethlehem and Nazareth, as well as Emmaus, Bethesda, Shiloh, Bethel, Eden, Ephrata, Zionsville and New Jerusalem. If you choose, you can stop by Mount Nebo, Mount Zion, Mount Joy, Mount Lebanon, and Mount Carmel. Have you wondered why? It's because *the Bible* had a direct impact on the society and culture of Old America and it shows up in the names they gave their towns and villages.

America has more towns named after Bible towns than anywhere in the world, except, of course, *the Bible* lands themselves.

But you say, "That's Pennsylvania. Don't a lot of Amish live there?" Maybe you expect it in Pennsylvania, but take a drive through the Lone Star State and you can visit Athens and Corinth, as well as Karnack, Palestine, Hebron, Eden, Joshua, Temple, Bishop, Blessing, and Corpus Christi.

Again, you object. "That's Texas. It's part of *the Bible* belt. A lot of Southern Baptists live there." Okay, how about California? You wouldn't expect as much Amish or Baptist influence there. And yet in California you can visit Antioch, Carmel, Goshen, Bethel Island, Joshua Tree and Temple City. You could drive through Angels Camp or even go to Paradise, and if you didn't like that you could go to Diablo.

It doesn't matter where you go in the United States or whom you meet, when it comes to naming names, the influence of *the Bible* on America is undeniable.

Questions for discussion or reflection.
(1) Can you name all the U.S. States? You have 10 minutes to remember as many of the 50 United States. Are there any states' names related to *the Bible*?
(2) Do you agree naming places can reflect the influence of *the Bible* on America? Read Text C and you will find the answer.

For Fun

Book to Read

John F. A. Sawyer's ***The Blackwell Companion to the Bible and Culture*** provides readers with a concise, readable and scholarly introduction to twenty-first century approaches to *the Bible*. It consists of 30 articles written by distinguished specialists from around the world, draws on interdisciplinary and international examples to explore how *the Bible* has impacted on all the major social contexts where it has been influential and gives examples of how *the Bible* has influenced literature, art, music, history, religious studies, politics, ecology and sociology. Each article is accompanied by a comprehensive bibliography and offers guidance on how to read *the Bible* and its many interpretations.

Movie to See

Enjoy the film ***Shawshank Redemption***

In 1946, a banker named Andy Dufresne is convicted of a double murder, even though he stubbornly proclaims his innocence. He's sentenced to a life term at the Shawshank State Prison in Maine, where another lifer, Ellis "Red" Redding, picks him as the new recruit most likely to....

Song to Enjoy

Here is part of the lyrics of "When you believe". Find the audio and enjoy the song. You can complete the lyrics while listening.

When you believe
By Whitney Houston

Many nights we've prayed
With no proof anyone could hear
In our hearts a hopeful song
We barely understood

Now we are not afraid
Although we know there's much to fear
We were moving mountains long
Before we knew we could

There can be miracles, when you believe
Though hope is frail, it's hard to kill
Who knows what miracles you can achieve

When you believe, somehow you will
You will when you believe

In this time of fear
When prayers so often prove(s) in vain
Hope seems like the summer birds
Too swiftly flown away

Yet now I'm standing here
My heart's so full I can't explain
Seeking faith and speaking words
I never thought I'd say

There can be miracles, when you believe
Though hope is frail, it's hard to kill
Who knows what miracles you can achieve
When you believe, somehow you will
You will when you believe

They don't (always happen) when you ask
(Oh)
And it's easy to give in to your fears

(Oh...Ohhhh)
But when you're blinded by your pain
Can't see your way straight through the rain
(A small but) still resilient voice
Says (hope is very near)
(Ohhh)

There can be miracles
(Miracles)
When you believe
(Lord, when you believe)
Though hope is frail
(Though hope is frail)
It's hard to kill
(Hard to kill, Ohhh)
Who knows what miracles, you can achieve
When you believe, somehow you will(somehow, somehow, somehow)
somehow you will
You will when you believe

....

Appendix I
List of Biblical Names

1. 主要族长（出埃及前的）
   - Abraham 亚伯拉罕
   - Enoch 以诺
   - Issac 以撒
   - Jacob 雅各
   - Noah 挪亚

2. 希伯来历史中早期领袖
   - Aaron 亚伦
   - Joseph 约瑟
   - Joshua 约书亚
   - Moses 摩西

3. 主要的士师
   - Deborah 底波拉
   - Eli 以利
   - Gideon 基甸
   - Jephthah 耶弗他
   - Othniel 俄陀聂
   - Samson 参孙
   - Samuel 撒母耳

4. 国度未分裂之前的列王
   - David 大卫
   - Saul 扫罗
   - Solomon 所罗门

5. 以色列王
   - Ahab 亚哈
   - Baasha 巴沙
   - Jeroboam 耶罗波安
   - Nadab 拿答

6. 犹大王
   - Asaph 亚萨
   - Ethan 以探
   - Hezekiah 希西家
   - Job 约伯
   - Josiah 约西亚
   - Jotham 约坦

7. 主要的先知
   - Amos 阿摩司
   - Balaam 巴兰
   - Daniel 但以理
   - Elijah 以利亚
   - Elisha 利沙
   - Ezekiel 以西结
   - Haggai 哈该
   - Hosea 何西阿
   - Isaiah 以赛亚
   - Jeremiah 耶利米
   - Joel 约珥
   - Micaiah 米该雅
   - Nathanael 拿单

8. 勇敢的改革家
   - Daniel 但以理
   - Elisha 以利沙

9. 其他显要人物
   - Adam 亚当
   - Abel 亚伯
   - Absalom 押沙龙
   - Ahasuerus 亚哈随鲁
   - Bezal 比撒列
   - Cain 该隐
   - Caleb 迦勒
   - Dathan 大坍
   - Abiram 亚比兰
   - Eleazar 以利亚撒
   - Esau 以扫
   - Ezra 以斯拉
   - Goliah 歌利亚
   - Ishmael 以实玛利
   - Jesse 耶西
   - Joab 约押
   - Jonathan 约拿单
   - Judah 犹大
   - Levi 利未
   - Lot 罗得
   - Mordecai 末底改
   - Naboth 拿伯
   - Nadab 拿答
   - Nehemiah 尼希米
   - Uriah 乌利亚

10. 显要的妇女
    - Abigail 亚比该
    - Bathsheba 拔示巴
    - Deborah 底波拉
    - Esther 以斯帖
    - Eve 夏娃
    - Hannah 哈拿
    - Jael 雅亿
    - Jezebel 耶洗别
    - Leah 利亚
    - Michal 米甲
    - Miriam 米利暗
    - Naomi 拿俄米
    - Rachel 拉结
    - Rahab 喇合
    - Rebekah 利百加
    - Ruth 路得
    - Sarah 撒拉
    - Vashti 瓦实提

Appendix II

参考答案

Unit 1

Before You Read

I. Please match the words in the box with the pictures. And then figure out who wears them.

1. anklets   2. bracelets   3. sandals   4. loin cloth   5. ephod
6. headwear 7. circlet   8. veil   9. cloak

Knowledge Focus

II. Solo Work: Tell whether the following statements are true or false according to the knowledge you learned.

1. F   2. F   3. T   4. F   5. T

Language Focus

I. Build your vocabulary.

A. Write the correct word next to its definition.

1. penitence   2. embroidery   3. nomadic   4. festive
5. crucifixion   6. seam

B. Use the proper forms of the words to complete the sentences.

1. festivity   2. penitence   3. nomadic   4. embroidery
5. crucifixion   6. seam

II. Fill in the blanks with the proper forms of the words.

1. obtainable   2. royal   3. luxurious   4. penitent
5. cultivate   6. was crucified   7. inconsiderate   8. dissimilar

Comprehensive Work

IV. Solo Work

1. Put in the missing words.

   (1) message   (2) wealth   (3) to   (4) varies   (5) days

2. Proofreading and error correction.

   (1) woman's—women's   (2) so—but   (3) for∧a   (4) that—what
   (5) should—may

Unit 2

Knowledge Focus

II. Solo Work: According to the food knowledge mentioned above, write T if the statement is true and F if it is false.

1. F   2. T   3. F   4. F   5. T   6. F   7. F   8. T   9. T   10. F

Language Focus

I. Build your vocabulary.

A. Write the correct word next to its definition.
  1. cannibalism   2. gastronomic   3. cauldron   4. hierarchy
  5. culinary   6. culminate   7. grit   8. leaven

B. Use the proper forms of the words to complete the sentences.
  1. cauldron   2. hierarchy   3. Gastronomy   4. culinary
  5. cannibalistic   6. grits   7. culminate   8. unleavened

II. Fill in the blanks with the proper forms of the words.
  1. abundant   2. hospitality   3. depictions   4. revelation
  5. respectively   6. starvation   7. fundamentally   8. consumption
  9. Figuratively   10. indicative

Comprehensive Work

IV. Solo Work
  1. Put in the missing words.
    (1) saves   (2) point   (3) at   (4) until   (5) off
  2. Proofreading and error correction.
    (1) field—fields   (2) That—Such   (3) despite of—despite   (4) more—less
    (5) before—after

Unit 3

Before You Read

I. Are you familiar with the family problems in the Bible? Please try to identify the following pictures.
  1. C   2. D   3. B   4. A

Knowledge Focus

II. Solo Work: According to the knowledge mentioned above, write T if the statement is true and F if it is false.
  1. F   2. T   3. T   4. T   5. F

Language Focus

I. Build your vocabulary.

A. Write the correct word next to its definition.
  1. unrighteousness   2. brag   3. reverence   4. submissive
  5. adornment   6. subdue   7. eloquent

B. Use the proper forms of the words to complete the sentences.
  1. subdue   2. adorn   3. reverence   4. submissive
  5. eloquently   6. bragged   7. unrighteous

II. Fill in the blanks with the proper forms of the words.
  1. braided   2. embittered   3. disillusioned   4. unbecomingly
  5. abusiveness   6. unfading   7. considerately   8. indecently

Comprehensive Work
III. Solo Work
  1. Put in the missing words.
     (1) called   (2) positive   (3) key   (4) trained   (5) team
  2. Proofreading and error correction.
     (1) lies—lying   (2) visit∧a   (3) later—latter   (4) full—fully   (5) said—says

Unit 4

Before You Read
I. You can use the Internet and other resources to learn more about the wedding customs in America and China. Then finish the following exercises.
  1. Match the western wedding customs with their meanings
     (1) B   (2) A   (3) D   (4) C   (5) F   (6) E   (7) G
  2. Match Chinese wedding customs with their meanings
     (1) F   (2) D   (3) E   (4) B   (5) C   (6) A

Knowledge Focus
II. Solo Work: According to the marriage types mentioned above, write T if the statement is true and F if it is false.
  1. T   2. F   3. T   4. F   5. T

Language Focus
I. Build your vocabulary.
  A. Write the correct word next to its definition.
     1. perpetrator   2. dispose   3. transaction   4. consensual
     5. sire   6. pare   7. infertile   8. dismiss
  B. Use the proper forms of the words to complete the sentences.
     1. transaction   2. dispose   3. perpetrators   4. consensual
     5. sire   6. paring   7. infertile   8. be dismissed
II. Fill in the blanks with the proper forms of the words.
   1. disposal   2. perpetrated   3. theoretically   4. dismissal
   5. illegitimate   6. presumably   7. numerous   8. indications
   9. conceivable   10. captivity

Comprehensive Work
III. Solo Work
  1. Put in the missing words.
     (1) union   (2) permitted   (3) unmarried   (4) in   (5) spiritual
  2. Proofreading and error correction.
     (1) on—over   (2) requires∧a   (3) object—objective   (4) like—as
     (5) regular—regularized

Unit 5

Knowledge Focus

II. Solo Work: Write T in the blank if the statement is true and F if it is false according to Text A.
    1. F   2. T   3. F   4. F   5. T

Language Focus

Build your vocabulary.
    A. Write the correct word next to its definition.
        1. covet   2. candor   3. consecrate   4. gruesome
    B. Use the proper forms of the words to complete the sentences.
        1. coveted   2. candor   3. gruesome   4. consecrated

Comprehensive Work

IV. Solo Work
    1. Put in the missing words.
        (1) limited   (2) marriage   (3) allowed   (4) appear   (5) strangers
    2. Proofreading and error correction.
        (1) cheat—deceive   (2) number—amount   (3) question—questioning
        (4) act—acting   (5) weight—weigh

Unit 6

Knowledge Focus

I. Solo Work: According to the knowledge mentioned above, write T if the statement is true and F if it is false.
    1. F   2. F   3. T   4. F   5. T

Language Focus

II. Building your vocabulary
    A. Match the phrases in Column A with their meanings in Column B.
        1. C   2. F   3. D   4. A   5. B   6. H   7. E   8. G
    B. Use the proper forms of the phrases from the above box to complete the sentences.
        1. laid down their lives   2. get across   3. was likened to   4. stand up against
        5. sin against   6. pertaining to   7. rule over   8. feet of clay
II. Fill in the blanks with the proper forms of the words.
    1. sustainable   2. terrorizing   3. repentance   4. exemplify
    5. resignation   6. intermarrying   7. confronting   8. prompting

Comprehensive Work

III. Solo Work
    1. Put in the missing words.
        (1) watch   (2) apart   (3) member   (4) elder   (5) groups
    2. Proofreading and error correction.
        (1) country—nation   (2) talent—talented   (3) contact—contract
        (4) lonely—alone   (5) north—northern

Text C
After-reading exercise:
Biblical shepherds typically carry some implements with them. Please match the equipments with their functions.

a bag	carried food or other items
a sling	defending himself and the flock against wild animals
a flute	entertaining himself and the sheep
a cloak	used for night-time bedding
a stick (rod)	used for protection and a weapon against wild animals

Unit 7

Knowledge Focus

II. Solo Work: Test your knowledge about prophets in the Bible. Write T if the statement is true and F if it is false.
   1. F   2. T   3. F   4. F   5. F

Language Focus

I. Build your vocabulary
  A. Match the phrases in Column A with their meanings in Column B.
    1. F   2. D   3. H   4. E   5. B   6. G   7. A   8. C
  B. Use the proper forms of the phrases from the above box to complete the sentences.
    1. In light of   2. stray from   3. takes a dim view of   4. attest to
    5. alliances with   6. leading up to   7. hold out   8. access to

II. Fill in the blanks with the proper forms of the words.
    1. victimized   2. unwaveringly   3. assuredly   4. expansionism
    5. foredoomed   6. turbulent   7. exegetical   8. insufficient
    9. allegiance   10. uncompromising

Comprehensive Work

III. Solo Work
    1. Put in the missing words.
       (1) deaf   (2) of   (3) has   (4) rescue   (5) up
    2. Proofreading and error correction.
       (1) correspond—corresponding   (2) or—nor   (3) Either—Neither
       (4) droops—drops   (5) heaven—heavenly

Unit 8

Knowledge Focus

II. Solo Work: According to the food knowledge mentioned above, write T if the statement is true and F if it is false.
   1. T   2. T   3. F   4. T   5. F   6. F

Language Focus

Build your vocabulary.

A. Match the phrases in Column A with their meanings in Column B.
1. C   2. A   3. D   4. G   5. B   6. F   7. H   8. E

B. Use the proper forms of the phrases from the above box to complete the sentences.
1. on the basis of   2. paid off   3. draw a distinction   4. pull rank
5. first and foremost   6. getting involved in   7. make restitution   8. was charged with

Comprehensive Work

III. Solo Work
1. Put in the missing words.
   (1) character   (2) trade   (3) history   (4) force   (5) well
2. Proofreading and error correction.
   (1) somewhere—nowhere   (2) including—included   (3) hardship—hardships
   (4) historic—historical   (5) case—cases

Unit 9

Before You Read

1. Do you know the following weapons, which can be traced back to the Bible time? What are their English names? And where can you see them now?
   1. sword   2. dagger   3. spear   4. javelin   5. sling
2. The picture in the middle of the following is a military weapon used in the Bible time. What is its name? Which of the animals around could have been used to pull it in war?
   chariot   horse

Knowledge Focus

II. Solo Work: Fill in the blanks according to Text A.
1. combat   2. sword   3. dagger   4. spear   5. light
6. javelin   7. fired   8. sling   9. stones   10. arrows

Language Focus

I. Build your vocabulary.

A. Match the phrases in Column A with their meanings in Column B.
1. B   2. H   3. C   4. A   5. E   6. G   7. F   8. D

B. Use the proper forms of the phrases from the above box to complete the sentences.
1. in effect   2. dislodged the stone from   3. prevail against
4. stabbing (his wife) to death   5. is far superior to
6. be credited to   7. at the instance of   8. resulted in

II. Fill in the blanks with the proper forms of the words.
1. prevailing   2. monopolized   3. offensive   4. ineffective
5. strikingly   6. assassination   7. invaluable   8. implication
9. reinforcement   10. durability

Comprehensive Work

IV. Solo Work

    1. Put in the missing words.

        (1) beside   (2) pound   (3) fought   (4) Units   (5) develop

    2. Proofreading and error correction.

        (1) well—better   (2) everything—anything   (3) won—winning

        (4) stage—staged   (5) slowed∧down

Unit 10

Before You Read

    Cain   Eve   Cain   murder

Knowledge Focus

II. Solo Work: Fill in the blanks according to Text A.

    1.corrupt   2.sexual   3.absent   4.punishment   5.righteous

    6.metropolis   7.indifferent   8.destruction   9.repent   10.spiritual

Language Focus

I. Build your vocabulary.

    A. Match the phrases in Column A with their meanings in Column B.

       1. C   2. A   3. D   4. E   5. F   6. H   7. B   8. G

    B. Use the proper forms of the phrases from the above box to complete the sentences.

       1. prone to   2. lapse into   3. strive for

       4. was doomed to   5. as a consequence of   6. contrary to

       7. distinguish between   8. put an end to

II. Fill in the blanks with the proper forms of the words.

    1. undesirable   2. pluralistic   3.retributive   4. accordingly

    5. sinfulness   6. abolition   7. perverted   8. insignificantly

    9.heterogeneity   10. uncontrollable

Comprehensive Work

IV. Solo Work

    1. Put in the missing words.

       (1) languages   (2) wrong   (3) ancient   (4) heaven   (5) position

    2. Proofreading and error correction.

       (1) in—on   (2) Like—Unlike   (3) sent to—by   (4) ran∧away

       (5) harms—harm

Text B

Tell whether the following statements are True or false according to Text B.

    1. F   2. T   3. F   4. T

Text C

Please match the underlined words or phrases in the passage with their possible meaning.

    1. B   2. C   3. A   4. F   5. D   6. G   7. E

Unit 11

Before You Read

(1) What can you see in the following pictures? Actually they are about two Jewish holidays. Do you know what they are, how they are celebrated, and why?

    1. Trumpets 吹角节   2. Tabernacles 住棚节

(2) According to the following pictures, what are forbidden on Yom Kippur (Day of Atonement)?

    There are four things forbidden on Yom Kippur:

    1. wearing leather shoes and   2. eating and drinking

    3. washing oneself   4. anointing oneself with oil/ perfume/ makeup

Knowledge Focus

II. Solo Work: According to the food knowledge mentioned above, write T if the statement is true and F if it is false.

    1. F   2. T   3. T   4. F   5. T

Language Focus

I. Build your vocabulary.

  A. Write the correct word next to its definition.

    1. D   2. E   3. H   4. A   5. C   6. F   7. B   8. G

  B. Use the proper forms of the phrases from the above box to complete the sentences.

    1. justify myself   2. corresponds to   3. consisting (mainly) of   4. stands to reason

    5. fell short of   6. atone for   7. confessed to   8. in advance

II. Fill in the blanks with the proper forms of the words.

    1. expectation   2. redemptive   3. justification   4. correspondingly

    5. revelation   6. reminder   7. unrighteous   8. consistency

    9. approachable   10. prophesy

Comprehensive Work

IV. Solo Work

    1. Put in the missing words.

      (1) with   (2) slavery   (3) dinner   (4) chair   (5) served

    2. Proofreading and error correction.

      (1) light—lighting   (2) any—many   (3) turn—turns

      (4) gathers—collects   (5) adapted—adopted

Text C

    After-reading exercise.

    Tell whether the following statements are True or false based on Text C.

    1. T   2. F   3. F   4. F   5. T

Unit 12

Before You Read

(1) What colleges are the following seals about? Do you think they have something in common, especially at the top center?

    Columbia College, Dartmouth College; Both of them have Hebrew words at the top center. The Columbia seal has the Hebrew name for God; the Dartmouth seal has the Hebrew words meaning "God

Almighty".

(2) Do you know the following significant Founding Fathers of America? Can you match the pictures with their names and also the universities offering courses in Hebrew that they attended?

Thomas Jefferson (picture2) — William and Marry

James Madison (picture1) — Princeton

Alexander Hamilton (picture3) — King's College (i.e. Columbia)

Language Focus

I. Build your vocabulary.

Use the proper forms of the words to complete the sentences.

1. legalistic 2. ritualistic 3. justification 4. dissemination
5. commencemet 6. commissioner 7. auspicious 8. condemnation

II. Fill in the blanks with the proper forms of the words.

1. rebel against 2. in tune with 3. set aside 4. be acquainted with 5. submit to

Comprehensive Work

III. Solo Work

1. Put in the missing words.

   (1) work (2) founded (3) secondary (4) train (5) under

2. Proofreading and error correction.

   (1) by ∧ a (2) more—less (3) interesting—interested
   (4) alike—like (5) onto—into

Unit 13

Knowledge Focus

II. Solo Work: According to the knowledge mentioned above, write T if the statement is true and F if it is false.

1. F 2. F 3. T 4. T 5. T

Language Focus

I. Build your vocabulary.

A. Write the correct word next to its definition.

1. entail 2. assail 3. disrupt 4. fugitive
5. resultant 6. venue 7. unbidden 8. configure

B. Use the proper forms of the words to complete the sentences.

1. assailed 2. had disrupted 3. resultant 4. venue
5. be configured 6. fugitive 7. unbidden 8. entail

II. Fill in the blanks with the proper forms of the words.

1. disruption 2. Acquisitiveness 3. deprivation 4. perplexed
5. exploitative 6. destabilize 7. unreasonable 8. aggressively
9. vulnerability 10. intrusion

Comprehensive Work

III. Solo Work

1. Put in the missing words.
   (1) cultures   (2) worth   (3) falls   (4) play   (5) meaning
2. Proofreading and error correction.
   (1) about—with   (2) concern—concerning   (3) it's—its
   (4) knows—knew   (5) nearly—near

Unit 14

Knowledge Focus

II. Solo Work: According to the knowledge mentioned above, write T if the statement is true and F if it is false.
   1. F   2. T   3. T   4. F   5. T

Language Focus

I. Build your vocabulary.
   A. Write the correct word next to its definition.
      1. inception   2. splinter   3. primacy   4. anarchy
      5. mandate   6. flog   7. lapse   8. cessation
   B. Use the proper forms of the words to complete the sentences.
      1. inception   2. splinter   3. primacy   4. anarchy
      5. was flogged   6. lapse   7. have been mandated   8. cessation

II. Fill in the blanks with the proper forms of the words.
   1. mandatory   2. cessation   3. identification   4. inception
   5. fundamentalist 6. Christianity 7. restrictive   8. adherence

Comprehensive Work

IV. Solo Work

1. Put in the missing words.
   (1) sick   (2) founded   (3) eggs   (4) allow   (5) every
2. Proofreading and error correction.
   (1) another—another's   (2) fund—funds   (3) anything—nothing
   (4) one—ones   (5) help—helping

Text C
1. After-reading exercise:
   Write down the 13's found in the Great Seal?
   13 stars in the crest   13 stripes in the shield
   13 olive leaves   13 olives
   13 arrows (some like to include the 13 feathers of the arrows)
   13 letters in Annuit Coeptis   13 letters in E Pluribus Unum
   13 cources of stone in the Pyramid   13 X 9 dots in the divisions around the crest.

Unit 15

Knowledge Focus

II. Solo Work: According to the knowledge mentioned above, write T if the statement is true and F if it is false.

1. F   2. T   3. F   4. T   5. T

Language Focus

I. Build your vocabulary.

A. Use the proper forms of the words to complete the sentences.

1. unify   2. authorize   3. legacy   4. renaissance
5. apocalypse   6. propriety   7. parish   8. populist

B. Use the proper forms of the words to complete the sentences.

1. parish   2. populist   3. unify   4. authorize
5. legacy   6. renaissance   7. apocalypse   8. proprieties

II. Fill in the blanks with the proper forms of the words.

1. redemption   2. resurrection 3. baptism   4. abolition
5. fraternity   6. reliability   7. consistency   8. substantial

Comprehensive Work

IV. Solo Work

1. Put in the missing words.

   1. winter   2. running   3. Jews   4. fate   5. down

2. Proofreading and error correction.

   1. in which — under which   (2) hope—hopes   (3) unusual—usual
   (4) amazing—amazed   (5) honor—honored

Appendix III
Famous Bible Stories

Abraham

Abraham is an apparently wealthy and successful man who receives a mysterious call from God to leave the security of life in Haran (in the Middle East) and travel to a land which God will show him. In return, God promises he will bring blessing to the entire world through this act of obedience. Despite the great age of both Abraham and his wife Sarah, God also promises that they will have a son as proof of God's faithfulness to his promise. Abraham sets out in faith and Genesis records the many upsets and setbacks which he experiences. The most remarkable of these is God's command that he offer up his son Isaac "by now a youth" as a sacrifice, culminating in angelic intervention as Abraham is about to wield the knife. Abraham has met the supreme test of faith.

Bible Reference: Genesis 12:1-5 ¹The LORD had said to Abram, Go from your country, your people and your father's household to the land I will show you. ² "I will make you into a great nation, and I will bless you; I will make your name great, and you will be a blessing. ³I will bless those who bless you, and whoever curses you I will curse; and all peoples on earth will be blessed through you." ⁴So Abram went, as the LORD had told him; and Lot went with him. Abram was seventy-five years old when he set out from Harran. ⁵He took his wife Sarai, his nephew Lot, all the possessions they had accumulated and the people they had acquired in Harran, and they set out for the land of Canaan, and they arrived there.

Bible Reference: Genesis 17:1-16 ¹When Abram was ninety-nine years old, the LORD appeared to him and said, "I am God Almighty; walk before me faithfully and be blameless. ²Then I will make my covenant between me and you and will greatly increase your numbers." ³Abram fell face down, and God said to him, ⁴ "As for me, this is my covenant with you: you will be the father of many nations. ⁵No longer will you be called Abram; your name will be Abraham, for I have made you a father of many nations. ⁶I will make you very fruitful; I will make nations of you, and kings will come from you. ⁷I will establish my covenant as an everlasting covenant between me and you and your descendants after you for the generations to come, to be your God and the God of your descendants after you. ⁸The whole land of Canaan, where you now reside as a foreigner, I will give as an everlasting possession to you and your descendants after you; and I will be their God." ⁹Then God said to Abraham, "As for you, you must keep my covenant, you and your descendants after you for the generations to come. ¹⁰This is my covenant with you and your descendants after you, the covenant you are to keep: every male among you shall be circumcised. ¹¹You are to undergo circumcision, and it will be the sign of the covenant between me and you. ¹²For the generations to come every male among you who is eight days old must be circumcised, including those born in your household or bought with money from a foreigner—those who are not your offspring. ¹³Whether born in your household or bought with your money, they must be circumcised. My covenant in your flesh is to be an everlasting covenant. ¹⁴Any uncircumcised male, who has not been circumcised in the flesh, will be cut off from his people; he has broken my covenant." ¹⁵God also said to Abraham, "As for Sarai your wife, you are no longer to call her Sarai; her name will be Sarah. ¹⁶I will bless her and will surely give you a son by her. I will bless her so that she will be the mother of nations; kings of peoples will come from her."

Bible Reference: Genesis 22:1-18 ¹Some time later God tested Abraham. He said to him, "Abraham!" "Here I am," he replied. ²Then God said, "Take your son, your only son, whom you love—Isaac—and go to the region of Moriah. Sacrifice him there as a burnt offering on a mountain that I will show you." ³Early the next morning Abraham got up and loaded his donkey. He took with him two of his servants and his son Isaac. When he had cut enough wood for the burnt offering, he set out for the place God had told him about. ⁴On the third day Abraham looked up and saw the place in the distance. ⁵He said to his servants, "Stay here with the donkey while I and the boy go over there. We will worship and then we will come back to you." ⁶Abraham took the wood for the burnt offering and placed it on his son Isaac, and he himself carried the fire and the knife. As the two of them went on together, ⁷Isaac spoke up and said to his father Abraham, "Father?" "Yes, my son?" Abraham replied. "The fire and wood are here," Isaac said, "but where is the lamb for the burnt offering?" ⁸Abraham answered, "God himself will provide the lamb for the burnt offering, my son." And the two of them went on together. ⁹When they reached the place God had told him about, Abraham built an altar there and arranged the wood on it. He bound his son Isaac and laid him on the altar, on top of the wood. ¹⁰Then he reached out his hand and took the knife to slay his son. ¹¹But the angel of the LORD called out to him from heaven, "Abraham! Abraham!" "Here I am," he replied. ¹² "Do not lay a hand on the boy," he said. "Do not do anything to him. Now I know that you fear God, because you have not withheld from me your son, your only son." ¹³Abraham looked up and there in a thicket he saw a ram caught by its horns. He went over and took the ram and sacrificed it as a burnt offering instead of his son. ¹⁴So Abraham called that place The LORD Will Provide. And to this day it is said, "On the mountain of the LORD it will be provided." ¹⁵The angel of the LORD called to Abraham from heaven a second time ¹⁶and said, "I swear by myself, declares the LORD, that because you have done this and have not withheld your son, your only son, ¹⁷I will surely bless you and make your descendants as numerous as the stars in the sky and as the sand on the seashore. Your descendants will take possession of the cities of their enemies, ¹⁸and through your offspring all nations on earth will be blessed, because you have obeyed me."

Adam and Eve

The story of Adam and Eve happens in Genesis chapter two and three. Their creation is the focus of chapter two with their fall and punishment in chapter three. God fashions Adam from dust and plants a garden (the Garden of Eden) and causes to grow in the middle of the garden the Tree of the knowledge of good and evil and the Tree of life. God sets the man in the garden where he is to have dominion over the plants and animals. Eve is later created to be his companion from a part of his body. God prohibits Adam and Eve from eating the fruit from the forbidden tree. However, a serpent tricks Eve into eating from it. Adam also eats from it. They are subsequently expelled from the garden for disobeying God who visits upon them and their progeny numerous hardships as punishment. Adam and Eve are the first humans, the first gardeners, the first parents and the first people to do wrong thing. They begin to experience spiritual death, and soon physical death. Adam and Eve sin by placing their desires above what God had told them and through this act sin entered the world.

Bible Reference: Genesis 2:7-25 ⁷ Then the LORD God formed a man from the dust of the ground and breathed into his nostrils the breath of life, and the man became a living being.⁸ Now the LORD God had planted a garden in the east, in Eden; and there he put the man he had formed.⁹ The LORD God made all kinds of trees grow out of the ground—trees that were pleasing to the eye and good for food. In the middle of the garden were the tree of life and the tree of the knowledge of good and evil. ¹⁰ A river watering the garden flowed from Eden; from there it was separated into four headwaters.¹¹ The name of the first is the Pishon; it winds through the entire land of Havilah, where there is gold.¹² (The gold of that land is good; aromatic resin and onyx are also there.)¹³ The name of the second river is the Gihon; it winds through the entire land of Cush.¹⁴ The name of the third river is the Tigris; it runs along the east side of Ashur. And the fourth river is the Euphrates.¹⁵ The LORD God took the man and put him in the Garden of Eden to work it and take care of it.¹⁶ And the LORD God commanded the man, "You are free to eat from any tree in the garden;¹⁷ but you must not eat from the tree of the knowledge of good and evil, for when you eat from it you will certainly die."¹⁸ The LORD God said, "It is not good for the man to be alone. I will make a helper suitable for him."¹⁹ Now the LORD God had formed out of the ground all the wild animals and all the birds in the sky. He brought them to the man to see what he would name them; and whatever the man called each living creature, that was its name.[20] So the man gave names to all the livestock, the birds in the sky and all the wild animals. But for Adam no suitable helper was found.[21] So the LORD God caused the man to fall into a deep sleep; and while he was sleeping, he took one of the man's ribs and then closed up the place with flesh.[22] Then the LORD God made a woman from the rib he had taken out of the man, and he brought her to the man.[23] The man said, "This is now bone of my bones and flesh of my flesh; she shall be called 'woman,' for she was taken out of man."[24] That is why a man leaves his father and mother and is united to his wife, and they become one flesh.[25] The man and his wife were both naked and they felt no shame.

Bible Reference: Genesis 3:1-24 [1] Now the serpent was more crafty than any of the wild animals the LORD God had made. He said to the woman, "Did God really say, 'You must not eat from any tree in the garden'?"[2] The woman said to the serpent, "We may eat fruit from the trees in the garden,[3] but God did say, 'You must not eat fruit from the tree that is in the middle of the garden, and you must not touch it, or you will die.'"[4] "You will not certainly die," the serpent said to the woman.[5] "For God knows that when you eat of it your eyes will be opened, and you will be like God, knowing good and evil."[6] When the woman saw that the fruit of the tree was good for food and pleasing to the eye, and also desirable for gaining wisdom, she took some and ate it. She also gave some to her husband, who was with her, and he ate it.[7] Then the eyes of both of them were opened, and they realized they were naked; so they sewed fig leaves together and made coverings for themselves.[8] Then the man and his wife heard the sound of the LORD God as he was walking in the garden in the cool of the day, and they hid from the LORD God among the trees of the garden.[9] But the LORD God called to the man, "Where are you?"[10] He answered, "I heard you in the garden, and I was afraid because I was naked; so I hid."[11] And he said, "Who told you that you were naked? Have you eaten from the tree that I commanded you not to eat from?"[12] The man said, "The woman you put here with me—she gave me some fruit from the tree, and I ate it."[13] Then the LORD God said to the woman, "What is this you have done?" The woman said, "The serpent deceived me, and I ate."[14] So the LORD God said to the serpent, "Because you have done this, "Cursed are you above all livestock and all wild animals! You will crawl on your belly and you will eat dust all the days of your life.[15] And I will put enmity between you and the woman, and between your offspring and hers; he will crush your head, and you will strike his heel."[16] To the woman he said, "I will make your pains in childbearing very severe; with painful labor you will give birth to children. Your desire will be for your husband, and he will rule over you."[17] To Adam he said, "Because you listened to your wife and ate fruit from the tree about which I commanded you, 'You must not eat from it,' "Cursed is the ground because of you; through painful toil you will eat food from it all the days of your life.[18] It will produce thorns and thistles for you, and you will eat the plants of the field.[19] By the sweat of your brow you will eat your food until you return to the ground, since from it you were taken; for dust you are and to dust you will return."[20] Adam named his wife Eve, because she would become the mother of all the living.[21] The LORD God made garments of skin for Adam and his wife and clothed them.[22] And the LORD God said, "The man has now become like one of us, knowing good and evil. He must not be allowed to reach out his hand and take also from the tree of life and eat, and live forever."[23] So the LORD God banished him from the Garden of Eden to work the ground from which he had been taken.[24] After he drove the man out, he placed on the east side of the Garden of Eden cherubim and a flaming sword flashing back and forth to guard the way to the tree of life.

Bartimaeus

Bible Reference: Mark 10:46-52 [46]Then they came to Jericho. As Jesus and his disciples, together with a large crowd, were leaving the city, a blind man, Bartimaeus (which means "son of Timaeus"), was sitting by the roadside begging. [47]When he heard that it was Jesus of Nazareth, he began to shout, "Jesus, Son of David, have mercy on me!" [48]Many rebuked him and told him to be quiet, but he shouted all the more, "Son of David, have mercy on me!" [49]Jesus stopped and said, "Call him." So they called to the blind man, "Cheer up! On your feet!

He's calling you." ⁵⁰Throwing his cloak aside, he jumped to his feet and came to Jesus. ⁵¹ "What do you want me to do for you?" Jesus asked him. The blind man said, "Rabbi, I want to see." ⁵² "Go," said Jesus, "your faith has healed you." Immediately he received his sight and followed Jesus along the road.

Crossing the Red Sea

The Israelites, escaping from slavery in Egypt under the leadership of Moses, camped near the Red Sea. Suddenly, they saw that the Egyptians were marching towards them. Pharaoh had realised that he had lost his slaves. He was at the head of his army and determined to recapture them. The Israelites panicked. They knew they did not stand a chance against the well equipped army. They blamed Moses for bringing them out of Egypt.

"Now we shall all die," they said. "At least in Egypt we were alive, even if we were slaves."

Moses asked God what he was to do. God said,

"I will fight for you: all you have to do is to be still."

The pillar of cloud, which had been guiding them, left the front of the Israelite column and moved to the rear. There, it cast darkness over the Egyptians.

When Moses reached the Red Sea, he stretched out his hand over the Sea, as God had told him to. All night, the wind blew, dividing the water so that the Israelites were then able to cross over the area on dry land. Then God told Moses to stretch out his hand again—and this time the waters flowed back and engulfed the Egyptians who were pursuing the Israelites. Then the Israelites realized how powerful God was.

Bible Reference: Exodus 14:1-31 ¹Then the LORD said to Moses, ² "Tell the Israelites to turn back and camp near Pi Hahiroth, between Migdol and the sea. They are to camp by the sea, directly opposite Baal Zephon. ³Pharaoh will think, 'The Israelites are wandering around the land in confusion, hemmed in by the desert.' ⁴And I will harden Pharaoh's heart, and he will pursue them. But I will gain glory for myself through Pharaoh and all his army, and the Egyptians will know that I am the LORD." So the Israelites did this. ⁵When the king of Egypt was told that the people had fled, Pharaoh and his officials changed their minds about them and said, "What have we done? We have let the Israelites go and have lost their services!" ⁶So he had his chariot made ready and took his army with him. ⁷He took six hundred of the best chariots, along with all the other chariots of Egypt, with officers over all of them. ⁸The LORD hardened the heart of Pharaoh king of Egypt, so that he pursued the Israelites, who were marching out boldly. ⁹The Egyptians—all Pharaoh's horses and chariots, horsemen and troops—pursued the Israelites and overtook them as they camped by the sea near Pi Hahiroth, opposite Baal Zephon. ¹⁰As Pharaoh approached, the Israelites looked up, and there were the Egyptians, marching after them. They were terrified and cried out to the LORD. ¹¹They said to Moses, "Was it because there were no graves in Egypt that you brought us to the desert to die? What have you done to us by bringing us out of Egypt? ¹²Didn't we say to you in Egypt, 'Leave us alone; let us serve the Egyptians'? It would have been better for us to serve the Egyptians than to die in the desert!" ¹³Moses answered the people, "Do not be afraid. Stand firm and you will see the deliverance the LORD will bring you today. The Egyptians you see today you will never see again. ¹⁴The LORD will fight for you; you need only to be still." ¹⁵Then the LORD said to Moses, "Why are you crying out to me? Tell the Israelites to move on. ¹⁶Raise your staff and stretch out your hand over the sea to divide the water so that the Israelites can go through the sea on dry ground. ¹⁷I will harden the hearts of the Egyptians so that they will go in after them. And I will gain glory through Pharaoh and all his army, through his chariots and his horsemen. ¹⁸The Egyptians will know that I am the LORD when I gain glory through Pharaoh, his chariots and his horsemen." ¹⁹Then the angel of God, who had been travelling in front of Israel's army, withdrew and went behind them. The pillar of cloud also moved from in front and stood behind them, ²⁰coming between the armies of Egypt and Israel. Throughout the night the cloud brought darkness to the one side and light to the other; so neither went near the other all night long. ²¹Then Moses stretched out his hand over the sea, and all that night the LORD drove the sea back with a strong east wind and turned it into dry land. The waters were divided, ²²and the Israelites went through the sea on dry ground, with a wall of water on their right and on their left. ²³The

Egyptians pursued them, and all Pharaoh's horses and chariots and horsemen followed them into the sea. ²⁴During the last watch of the night the LORD looked down from the pillar of fire and cloud at the Egyptian army and threw it into confusion. ²⁵He jammed the wheels of their chariots so that they had difficulty driving. And the Egyptians said, "Let's get away from the Israelites! The LORD is fighting for them against Egypt." ²⁶Then the LORD said to Moses, "Stretch out your hand over the sea so that the waters may flow back over the Egyptians and their chariots and horsemen." ²⁷Moses stretched out his hand over the sea, and at daybreak the sea went back to its place. The Egyptians were fleeing towards it, and the LORD swept them into the sea. ²⁸The water flowed back and covered the chariots and horsemen—the entire army of Pharaoh that had followed the Israelites into the sea. Not one of them survived. ²⁹But the Israelites went through the sea on dry ground, with a wall of water on their right and on their left. ³⁰That day the LORD saved Israel from the hands of the Egyptians, and Israel saw the Egyptians lying dead on the shore. ³¹And when the Israelites saw the great power the LORD displayed against the Egyptians, the people feared the LORD and put their trust in him and in Moses his servant.

Daniel and the Lions

Daniel is an Israelite exiled in Persia, the successor empire to the Babylonians. He has risen to prominence at the royal court, but, in doing so he has made enemies who are determined to bring him down. They persuade King Darius to issue a decree that for a period of thirty days nobody may pray to anyone other than the king, on pain of being thrown into a lions' den. Faithful Daniel refuses to comply and continues to pray to God three times daily. This is reported to the king who has no option but to do as he had decreed. Next morning, Darius rushes down to the den after a sleepless night and is overjoyed to find Daniel—a favourite courtier—unharmed. He is immediately released and his accusers and their families take his place in the den with predictable results! The purpose of the story is to: "encourage faithfulness under persecution" show that Israel's God can and will rescue his people even from certain death, sometimes by the most unlikely means.

Bible Reference: Daniel 6:1-28 ¹It pleased Darius to appoint 120 satraps to rule throughout the kingdom, ²with three chief ministers over them, one of whom was Daniel. The satraps were made accountable to them so that the king might not suffer loss. ³Now Daniel so distinguished himself among the chief ministers and the satraps by his exceptional qualities that the king planned to set him over the whole kingdom. ⁴At this, the chief ministers and the satraps tried to find grounds for charges against Daniel in his conduct of government affairs, but they were unable to do so. They could find no corruption in him, because he was trustworthy and neither corrupt nor negligent. ⁵Finally these men said, "We will never find any basis for charges against this man Daniel unless it has something to do with the law of his God." ⁶So these chief ministers and satraps went as a group to the king and said: "May King Darius live for ever! ⁷The royal ministers, prefects, satraps, advisors and governors have all agreed that the king should issue an edict and enforce the decree that anyone who prays to any god or human being during the next thirty days, except to you, Your Majesty, shall be thrown into the lions' den. ⁸Now, Your Majesty, issue the decree and put it in writing so that it cannot be altered—in accordance with the law of the Medes and Persians, which cannot be repealed." ⁹So King Darius put the decree in writing. ¹⁰Now when Daniel learned that the decree had been published, he went home to his upstairs room where the windows opened towards Jerusalem. Three times a day he got down on his knees and prayed, giving thanks to his God, just as he had done before. ¹¹Then these men went as a group and found Daniel praying and asking God for help. ¹²So they went to the king and spoke to him about his royal decree: "Did you not publish a decree that during the next thirty days anyone who prays to any god or human being except to you, Your Majesty, would be thrown into the lions' den?" The king answered, "The decree stands—in accordance with the law of the Medes and Persians, which cannot be repealed." ¹³Then they said to the king, "Daniel, who is one of the exiles from Judah, pays no attention to you, Your Majesty, or to the decree you put in writing. He still prays three times a day." ¹⁴When the king heard this, he was greatly distressed; he was determined to rescue Daniel and made every effort until sunset to save him. ¹⁵Then the men went as a group to King Darius and said to him, "Remember, Your Majesty, that according to the law of the Medes and Persians no decree or edict that the king issues can be changed." ¹⁶So the king gave the order, and they brought Daniel and threw him into the lions' den. The king said to Daniel, "May your God, whom you serve continually, rescue you!" ¹⁷A stone was brought and placed over the mouth of the den, and the king sealed it with his own signet ring and with the rings of his nobles, so that Daniel's situation might not be changed. ¹⁸Then the king returned to his palace and spent the night without eating and without any entertainment being brought to him. And he could not sleep. ¹⁹At the first light of dawn, the king got up and hurried to the lions' den. ²⁰When he came near the den, he called to Daniel in an anguished voice, "Daniel, servant of the living God, has your God, whom you serve continually, been able to rescue you from the lions?" ²¹Daniel answered, "May the king live for ever! ²²My God sent his angel, and he shut the mouths of the lions. They have not hurt me, because I was found innocent in his sight. Nor have I ever done any wrong before you, Your Majesty." ²³The king was overjoyed and gave orders to lift Daniel out of the den. And when Daniel was lifted from the den, no wound was found on him, because he had trusted in his God. ²⁴At the king's command, the men who had falsely accused Daniel were brought in and thrown into the lions' den, along with their wives and children. And before they reached the floor of the den, the lions overpowered them and crushed all their bones. ²⁵Then King Darius wrote to all the nations and peoples of every language in all the earth: "May you prosper greatly!" ²⁶I issue a decree that in every part of my kingdom people must fear and reverence the God of Daniel. "For he is the living God and he endures for ever; his kingdom will not be destroyed, his dominion will never end. ²⁷He rescues and he saves; he performs signs and wonders in the heavens and on the earth. He has rescued Daniel from the power of the lions." ²⁸So Daniel prospered during the reign of Darius and the reign of Cyrus the Persian.

David and Goliath

    This is one of the most famous stories from the Old Testament. Set in the time of Saul, Israel's first king, it tells of a time when Israel was oppressed by the Philistines, a neighbouring war-like tribe who had already several times defeated the Israelites in battle. On this occasion, the Philistines parade their champion, Goliath, a giant of a man, in font of the terrified Israelites. He issues a challenge to them, to send one of their number to engage him in single-handed combat. Up steps a young shepherd boy, David (destined to be Israel's king), enraged by Goliath's taunts and insults and convinced that God will help him overcome the enemy. He confronts Goliath armed only with a sling and a stone, but hits him on the forehead and kills him instantly, leading to a Philistine retreat. The story illustrates: "that Israel's God cannot be defied without consequences" the need to trust that God can bring victory without military paraphernalia.

    Bible Reference: 1 Samuel 17:1-58 ¹Now the Philistines gathered their forces for war and assembled at Sokoh in Judah. They pitched camp at Ephes Dammim, between Sokoh and Azekah. ²Saul and the Israelites assembled and camped in the Valley of Elah and drew up their battle line to meet the Philistines. ³The Philistines occupied one hill and the Israelites another, with the valley between them. ⁴A champion named Goliath, who was from Gath, came out of the Philistine camp. His height was six cubits and a span. ⁵He had a bronze helmet on his head and wore a coat of scale armour of bronze weighing five thousand shekels; ⁶on his legs he wore bronze greaves, and a bronze javelin was slung on his back. ⁷His spear shaft was like a weaver's rod, and its iron point weighed six hundred shekels. His shield-bearer went ahead of him. ⁸Goliath stood and shouted to the ranks of Israel, "Why do you come out and line up for battle? AmI not a Philistine, and are you not the servants of Saul? Choose a man and let him come down to me. ⁹If he is able to fight and kill me, we will become your subjects; but if I overcome him and kill him, you will become our subjects and serve us." ¹⁰Then the Philistine said, "This day I defy the armies of Israel! Give me a man and let us fight each other." ¹¹On hearing the Philistine's words, Saul and all the Israelites were dismayed and terrified. ¹²Now David was the son of an Ephrathite named Jesse, who was from Bethlehem in Judah. Jesse had eight sons, and in Saul's time he was very old. ¹³Jesse's three eldest sons had followed Saul to the war: the firstborn was Eliab; the second, Abinadab; and the third, Shammah. ¹⁴David was the youngest. The three eldest followed Saul, ¹⁵but David went back and forth from Saul to tend his father's sheep at Bethlehem. ¹⁶For forty days the Philistine came forward every morning and evening and took his stand. ¹⁷Now Jesse said to his son David, "Take this ephah of roasted grain and these ten loaves of bread for your brothers and hurry to their camp. ¹⁸Take along these ten cheeses to the commander of their Unit. See how your brothers are and bring back some assurance from them. ¹⁹They are with Saul and all the men of Israel in the Valley of Elah, fighting against the Philistines." ²⁰Early in the morning David left the flock in the care of a shepherd, loaded up and set out, as Jesse had directed. He reached the camp as the army was going out to its battle positions, shouting the war cry. ²¹Israel and the Philistines were drawing up their lines facing each other. ²²David left his things with the keeper of supplies, ran to the battle lines and asked his brothers how they were. ²³As he was talking with them, Goliath, the Philistine champion from Gath, stepped out from his lines and shouted his usual defiance, and David heard it. ²⁴Whenever the Israelites saw the man, they all fled from him in great fear. ²⁵Now the Israelites had been saying, "Do you see how this man keeps coming out? He comes out to defy Israel. The king will give great wealth to the man who kills him. He will also give him his daughter in marriage and will exempt his family line from taxes in Israel." ²⁶David asked those standing near him, "What will be done for the man who kills this Philistine and removes this disgrace from Israel? Who is this uncircumcised Philistine that he should defy the armies of the living God?" ²⁷They repeated to him what they had been saying and told him, "This is what will be done for the man who kills him." ²⁸When Eliab, David's eldest brother, heard him speaking with the men, he burned with anger at him and asked, "Why have you come down here? And with whom did you leave those few sheep in the wilderness? I know how conceited you are and how wicked your heart is; you came down only to watch the battle." ²⁹ "Now what have I done?" said David. "Can't I even speak?" ³⁰He then turned away to someone else and brought up the same matter, and the men answered him as before. ³¹What David said was overheard and reported to Saul, and Saul sent for him. ³²David said to Saul, "Let no-one lose heart on account of this Philistine; your servant will go and fight him." ³³Saul replied, "You are not able to go out against this Philistine and fight him; you are little more than a boy, and he has been a warrior from his youth." ³⁴But David said to Saul, "Your servant has been keeping his father's sheep. When a lion or a bear came and carried off a sheep from the flock, ³⁵I went after it, struck it and rescued the sheep from its mouth. When it turned on me, I seized it by its hair, struck it and killed it. ³⁶Your servant has killed both the lion and the bear; this uncircumcised Philistine will be like one of them, because he has defied the armies of the living God. ³⁷The LORD who rescued me from the paw of the lion and the paw of the bear will rescue me from the hand of this Philistine." Saul said to David, "Go, and the LORD be with you." ³⁸Then Saul dressed David in his own tunic. He put a coat of armour on him and a bronze helmet on his head. ³⁹David fastened on his sword over the tunic and tried walking around, because he was not used to them. "I cannot go in these," he said to Saul, "because I am not used to them." So he took them off. ⁴⁰Then he took his staff in his hand, chose five smooth stones from the stream, put them in the pouch of his shepherd's bag and, with his sling in his hand, approached the Philistine. ⁴¹Meanwhile, the Philistine, with his shield-bearer in front of him, kept coming closer to David. ⁴²He looked David over and saw that he was little more than a boy, glowing with health and handsome, and he despised him. ⁴³He said to David, "Am I a dog, that you come at me with sticks?" And the Philistine cursed David by his gods. ⁴⁴ "Come here," he said, "and I'll give your flesh to the birds and the wild animals!" ⁴⁵David said to the Philistine, "You come against me with sword and spear and javelin, but I come against you in the name of the LORD Almighty, the God of the armies of Israel, whom you have defied. ⁴⁶This day the LORD will deliver you into my hands, and I'll strike you down and cut off your head. This very day I will give the carcasses of the Philistine army to the birds and the wild animals, and the whole world will know that there is a God in Israel. ⁴⁷All those gathered here will know that it is not by sword or spear that the LORD saves; for the battle is the LORD's, and he will give all of you into our hands." ⁴⁸As the Philistine moved closer to attack him, David ran quickly towards the battle line to meet him. ⁴⁹Reaching into his bag and taking out a stone, he slung it and struck the Philistine on the forehead. The stone sank into his forehead, and he fell face down on the ground. ⁵⁰So David triumphed over the Philistine with a sling and a stone; without a sword in his hand he struck down the Philistine and killed him. ⁵¹David ran and stood over him. He took hold of the Philistine's sword and drew it from the sheath. After he killed him, he cut off his head with the sword. When the Philistines saw that their hero was dead, they turned and ran. ⁵²Then the men of Israel and Judah surged forward with a shout and pursued the Philistines to the entrance of Gath and to the gates of Ekron. Their dead were strewn along the Shaaraim road to Gath and Ekron. ⁵³When the Israelites returned from chasing the Philistines, they plundered their camp. ⁵⁴David took the Philistine's head and brought it to Jerusalem; he put the Philistine's weapons in his own tent. ⁵⁵As Saul

watched David going out to meet the Philistine, he said to Abner, commander of the army, "Abner, whose son is that young man?" Abner replied, "As surely as you live, Your Majesty, I don't know." ⁵⁶The king said, "Find out whose son this young man is." ⁵⁷As soon as David returned from killing the Philistine, Abner took him and brought him before Saul, with David still holding the Philistine's head. ⁵⁸ "Whose son are you, young man?" Saul asked him. David said, "I am the son of your servant Jesse of Bethlehem."

Feeding of the 5000

This is the account of a <u>miraculous</u> feeding of a large crowd in the desert. It recalls <u>God</u>'s provision for his people of <u>manna</u> during their forty years wandering in the <u>wilderness</u> during the <u>Exodus</u> which is described in the <u>Old Testament</u>. At the end of a long day, the <u>disciples</u> of <u>Jesus</u> are unprepared when he challenges them to feed the large crowd who have been listening to Jesus. They wrongly assume that they have to buy bread, but Jesus takes charge and miraculously enables the crowd to be fed using only the five loaves and two fish which a young boy makes available. The story has two clear points "Jesus is shown as being like a new <u>Moses</u>, supplying the needs of his people in the desert" in <u>John</u>'s <u>gospel</u>, Jesus portrays himself as "the living bread from heaven", which reminds <u>Christian</u>s of their celebration of <u>holy communion</u> / the <u>eucharist</u> / the <u>Last Supper</u>, and its reference to the bread of life.

Bible Reference: <u>John 6:3-13</u> ³Then Jesus went up on a mountainside and sat down with his disciples. ⁴The Jewish Passover Feast was near. ⁵When Jesus looked up and saw a great crowd coming towards him, he said to Philip, "Where shall we buy bread for these people to eat?" ⁶He asked this only to test him, for he already had in mind what he was going to do. ⁷Philip answered him, "It would take almost a year's wages to buy enough bread for each one to have a bite!" ⁸Another of his disciples, Andrew, Simon Peter's brother, spoke up, ⁹ "Here is a boy with five small barley loaves and two small fish, but how far will they go among so many?" ¹⁰Jesus said, "Make the people sit down." There was plenty of grass in that place, and they sat down (about five thousand men were there). ¹¹Jesus then took the loaves, gave thanks, and distributed to those who were seated as much as they wanted. He did the same with the fish. ¹²When they had all had enough to eat, he said to his disciples, "Gather the pieces that are left over. Let nothing be wasted." ¹³So they gathered them and filled twelve baskets with the pieces of the five barley loaves left over by those who had eaten.

Food and Water in the Desert and the First Covenant

As the Israelites escaped from slavery in Egypt, travelling into the desert, they soon started to complain again. First, they ran out of food.

"At least in Egypt we had enough to eat," they said.

So God sent quail around their camp each evening and each morning the ground was covered in manna. Next, they could find no water. So God told Moses to strike a great rock with his staff, and fresh water flowed out for the Israelites to drink.

Three months after they left Egypt, the Israelites came to the Desert of Sinai. There, God made a covenant, a solemn agreement, with them:

"You have seen how I brought you out of Egypt. Now, if you keep all my commandments, I will make you my treasured possession. The whole earth is mine, but you will be my own nation."

The leaders of the people agreed that they would do everything that God required of them. So Moses went up Mount Sinai to meet with God and he gave Moses the Ten Commandments.

Bible Reference: <u>Exodus 16:1-36</u> ¹The whole Israelite community set out from Elim and came to the Desert of Sin, which is between Elim and Sinai, on the fifteenth day of the second month after they had come out of Egypt. ²In the desert the whole community grumbled against Moses and Aaron. ³The Israelites said to them, "If only we had died by the LORD's hand in Egypt! There we sat round pots of meat and ate all the food we wanted, but you have brought us out into this desert to starve this entire assembly to death." ⁴Then the LORD said to Moses, "I will rain down bread from heaven for you. The people are to go out each day and gather enough for that day. In this way I will test them and see whether they will follow my instructions. ⁵On the sixth day they are to prepare what they bring in, and that is to be twice as much as they gather on the other days." ⁶So Moses and Aaron said to all the Israelites, "In the evening you will know that it was the LORD who brought you out of Egypt, ⁷and in the morning you will see the glory of the LORD, because he has heard your grumbling against him. Who are we, that you should grumble against us?" ⁸Moses also said, "You will know that it was the LORD when he gives you meat to eat in the evening and all the bread you want in the morning, because he has heard your grumbling against him. Who are we? You are not grumbling against us, but against the LORD." ⁹Then Moses told Aaron, "Say to the entire Israelite community, 'Come before the LORD, for he has heard your grumbling.'" ¹⁰While Aaron was speaking to the whole Israelite commUnity, they looked towards the desert, and there was the glory of the LORD appearing in the cloud. ¹¹The LORD said to Moses, ¹² "I have heard the grumbling of the Israelites. Tell them, 'At twilight you will eat meat, and in the morning you will be filled with bread. Then you will know that I am the LORD your God.'" ¹³That evening quail came and covered the camp, and in the morning there was a layer of dew around the camp. ¹⁴When the dew was gone, thin flakes like frost on the ground appeared on the desert floor. ¹⁵When the Israelites saw it, they said to each other, "What is it?" For they did not know what it was. Moses said to them, "It is the bread the LORD has given you to eat. ¹⁶This is what the LORD has commanded: 'Each one is to gather as much as they need. Take an omer for each person you have in your tent.'" ¹⁷The Israelites did as they were told; some gathered much, some little. ¹⁸And when they measured it by the omer, the one who gathered much did not have too much, and the one who gathered little did not have too little. Each one had gathered just as much as they needed. ¹⁹Then Moses said to them, "No-one is to keep any of it until morning." ²⁰However, some of them paid no attention to Moses; they kept part of it until morning, but it was full of maggots and began to smell. So Moses was angry with them. ²¹Each morning everyone gathered as much as they needed, and when the sun grew hot, it melted away. ²²On the sixth day, they gathered twice as much—two omers for each person —and the leaders of the commUnity came and reported this to Moses. ²³He said to them, "This is what the LORD commanded: 'Tomorrow is to be a day of sabbath rest, a holy sabbath to the LORD. So bake what you want to bake and boil what you want to boil. Save whatever is left and keep it until morning." ²⁴So they saved it until morning, as Moses commanded, and it did not stink or get maggots in it. ²⁵ "Eat it today," Moses said, "because today is a sabbath to the LORD. You will not find any of it on the ground today. ²⁶Six days you are to gather it, but on the seventh day, the Sabbath, there will not be any." ²⁷Nevertheless, some of the people went out on the seventh day to gather it, but they found none. ²⁸Then the LORD said to Moses, "How long will you refuse to keep my commands and my instructions? ²⁹Bear in mind that the LORD has given you the Sabbath; that is why on the sixth day he gives you bread for two days. Everyone is to stay where they are on the seventh day; no-one is to go out." ³⁰So the people rested on the seventh day. ³¹The people of Israel called the bread manna. It was white like coriander seed and tasted like wafers made with honey. ³²Moses said, "This is what the LORD has commanded: 'Take an omer of manna and keep it for the generations to come, so they can see the bread I gave you to eat in the wilderness when I brought you out of Egypt.'" ³³So Moses said to Aaron, "Take a jar and put an omer of manna in it. Then place it before the LORD to be kept for the generations to come." ³⁴As the LORD commanded Moses, Aaron put the manna with the tablets of the covenant law, that it might be preserved. ³⁵The Israelites ate manna for forty years, until they came to a land that was settled; they ate manna until they reached the border of Canaan. ³⁶(An omer is one tenth of an ephah.)

Bible Reference: Exodus 17:1-6 ¹The whole Israelite commUnity set out from the Desert of Sin, travelling from place to place as the LORD commanded. They camped at Rephidim, but there was no water for the people to drink. ²So they quarrelled with Moses and said, "Give us water to drink." Moses replied, "Why do you quarrel with me? Why do you put the LORD to the test?" ³But the people were thirsty for water there, and they grumbled against Moses. They said, "Why did you bring us up out of Egypt to make us and our children and livestock die of thirst?" ⁴Then Moses cried out to the LORD, "What am I to do with these people? They are almost ready to stone me." ⁵The LORD answered Moses, "Go out in front of the people. Take with you some of the elders of Israel and take in your hand the staff with which you struck the Nile, and go. ⁶I will stand there before you by the rock at Horeb. Strike the rock, and water will come out of it for the people to drink." So Moses did this in the

sight of the elders of Israel.

Bible Reference: Exodus 19:1-8 ¹On [the first day of] the third month after the Israelites left Egypt—on that very day—they came to the Desert of Sinai. ²After they set out from Rephidim, they entered the Desert of Sinai, and Israel camped there in the desert in front of the mountain. ³Then Moses went up to God, and the LORD called to him from the mountain and said, "This is what you are to say to the house of Jacob and what you are to tell the people of Israel: ⁴ 'You yourselves have seen what I did to Egypt, and how I carried you on eagles' wings and brought you to myself. ⁵Now if you obey me fully and keep my covenant, then out of all nations you will be my treasured possession. Although the whole earth is mine, ⁶you will be for me a kingdom of priests and a holy nation.' These are the words you are to speak to the Israelites." ⁷So Moses went back and summoned the elders of the people and set before them all the words the LORD had commanded him to speak. ⁸The people all responded together, "We will do everything the LORD has said." So Moses brought their answer back to the LORD.

Gabriel Visits Mary

Mary lived in Nazareth. She was engaged to be married to a man called Joseph, a descendant of King David. One day, an angel called Gabriel, one of God's messengers, came to her, greeting her as someone greatly favoured by God.

"The Lord is with you," he said.

Then Mary was worried, unsure of what he meant. Gabriel saw how she felt and said,

"Don't be frightened. God is very pleased with you. Soon, you will become pregnant with a son. When he is born, you are to call him 'Jesus'. He will be a special person and will be called the Son of God. God himself will make him ruler for ever of David's kingdom."

This confused Mary even more.

"How can all this happen," she asked, "when I am still a virgin?"

So the angel explained to her that the Holy Spirit would come to her and the baby would be conceived by the power of God.

"Nothing is impossible for God to do," he said. "Your relative Elizabeth is pregnant now, even though she has been barren for many years."

(Elizabeth's baby was to be John the Baptist.)

Mary said,

"I am God's follower. Let everything happen to me, just as you have said."

Then Gabriel left her.

Bible Reference: Luke 1:26-38 ²⁶In the sixth month of Elizabeth's pregnancy, God sent the angel Gabriel to Nazareth, a town in Galilee, ²⁷to a virgin pledged to be married to a man named Joseph, a descendant of David. The virgin's name was Mary. ²⁸The angel went to her and said, "Greetings, you who are highly favoured! The Lord is with you." ²⁹Mary was greatly troubled at his words and wondered what kind of greeting this might be. ³⁰But the angel said to her, "Do not be afraid, Mary, you have found favour with God. ³¹You will conceive and give birth to a son, and you are to call him Jesus. ³²He will be great and will be called the Son of the Most High. The Lord God will give him the throne of his father David, ³³and he will reign over the house of Jacob for ever; his kingdom will never end." ³⁴ "How will this be," Mary asked the angel, "since I am a virgin?" ³⁵The angel answered, "The Holy Spirit will come on you, and the power of the Most High will overshadow you. So the holy one to be born will be called the Son of God. ³⁶Even Elizabeth your relative is going to have a child in her old age, and she who was said to be unable to conceive is in her sixth month. ³⁷For no word from God will ever fail."
³⁸ "I am the Lord's servant," Mary answered. "May it be to me according to your word." Then the angel left her.

Jesus and Nicodemus

Nicodemus was a leading Jewish rabbi who comes to ask questions of Jesus "by night". Jesus informs Nicodemus that he needs to be born again. This account contains: "The central teaching that people seeking God have to start seeing things in an entirely new light. Jesus is the one charged by God to reveal spiritual truths in a way that Nicodemus has no inkling of, and above all, to save the world. " One of the most quoted verses of the Bible: For God so loved the world that he gave his one and only Son, that whoever believes in him shall not perish but have eternal life (John 3:16 TNIV) In a telling detail later in his gospel, John tells us that it was Nicodemus who helped Joseph of Arimathaea to bury the body of Jesus with a mixture of myrrh and aloes.

Bible Reference: John 3: 1-21 [16] ¹Now there was a Pharisee, a man named Nicodemus who was a member of the Jewish ruling council. ²He came to Jesus at night and said, "Rabbi, we know that you are a teacher who has come from God. For no-one could perform the signs you are doing if God were not with him." ³Jesus replied, "Very truly I tell you, no-one can see the kingdom of God without being born again." ⁴ "How can anyone be born when they are old?" Nicodemus asked. "Surely they cannot enter a second time into their mother's womb to be born!" ⁵Jesus answered, "Very truly I tell you, no-one can enter the kingdom of God without being born of water and the Spirit. ⁶Flesh gives birth to flesh, but the Spirit gives birth to spirit. ⁷You should not be surprised at my saying, 'You must be born again.' ⁸The wind blows wherever it pleases. You hear its sound, but you cannot tell where it comes from or where it is going. So it is with everyone born of the Spirit." ⁹"How can this be?" Nicodemus asked. ¹⁰"You are Israel's teacher," said Jesus, "and do you not understand these things? ¹¹Very truly I tell you, we speak of what we know, and we testify to what we have seen, but still you people do not accept our testimony. ¹²I have spoken to you of earthly things and you do not believe; how then will you believe if I speak of heavenly things? ¹³No-one has ever gone into heaven except the one who came from heaven—the Son of Man. ¹⁴Just as Moses lifted up the snake in the wilderness, so the Son of Man must be lifted up, ¹⁵that everyone who believes may have eternal life in him." ¹⁶For God so loved the world that he gave his one and only Son, that whoever believes in him shall not perish but have eternal life. ¹⁷For God did not send his Son into the world to condemn the world, but to save the world through him. ¹⁸Whoever believes in him is not condemned, but whoever does not believe stands condemned already because they have not believed in the name of God's one and only Son. ¹⁹This is the verdict: light has come into the world, but people loved darkness instead of light because their deeds were evil. ²⁰All those who do evil hate the light, and will not come into the light for fear that their deeds will be exposed. ²¹But those who live by the truth come into the light, so that it may be seen plainly that what they have done has been done in the sight of God.

Jesus and Peter

On the night Jesus had been arrested, Peter had panicked and denied knowing him. The next day Jesus had been put to death by the authorities. Some time later, confused and needing some normality in his life, Peter decided to go fishing. Some of the other disciples went with him. But all night they caught no fish. As dawn broke, they saw a man standing on the shore. He shouted,

"Have you caught anything? Then throw your net out on the right side of the boat!"

As soon as they did this, so many fish swam into the net that they could not lift it. Then one of them said, "It's Jesus!"

As soon as he heard this, Peter leapt out of the boat and waded ashore to get to him quickly. Jesus had already cooked some fish for them. They all ate on the quiet shore. Then Jesus said,

"Peter, do you love me most of all?"

Peter said that Jesus knew he did.

"Feed my lambs," Jesus replied.

But then Jesus asked him,

"Do you really love me?"

Again, Peter said,

"Lord, you know that I do."

Jesus told him to look after his sheep for him.

Then he asked Peter the question a third time. Peter was hurt that Jesus did not seem to believe him, so he said,

"Lord, you know everything. You know that I do love you."

Jesus said,

"Feed my sheep."

In this way, Jesus showed Peter that the three times he had denied knowing Jesus after Jesus had been arrested were cancelled out and forgiven by the three questions and answers. Now Peter had once again been given the task of caring for Jesus' followers.

Bible Reference: John 21:1-19 [1]Afterwards Jesus appeared again to his disciples, by the Sea of Gallilee. It happened this way: [2]Simon Peter, Thomas (also known as Didymus), Nathanael from Cana in Galilee, the sons of Zebedee, and two other disciples were together. [3] "I'm going out to fish," Simon Peter told them, and they said, "We'll go with you." So they went out and got into the boat, but that night they caught nothing. [4]Early in the morning, Jesus stood on the shore, but the disciples did not realize that it was Jesus. [5]He called out to them, "Friends, haven't you any fish?" "No," they answered. [6]He said, "Throw your net on the right side of the boat and you will find some." When they did, they were unable to haul the net in because of the large number of fish. [7]Then the disciple whom Jesus loved said to Peter, "It is the Lord!" As soon as Simon Peter heard him say, "It is the Lord," he wrapped his outer garment round him (for he had taken it off) and jumped into the water. [8]The other disciples followed in the boat, towing the net full of fish, for they were not far from shore, about a hundred metres. [9]When they landed, they saw a fire of burning coals there with fish on it, and some bread. [10]Jesus said to them, "Bring some of the fish you have just caught." [11]Simon Peter climbed aboard and dragged the net ashore. It was full of large fish, 153, but even with so many the net was not torn. [12]Jesus said to them, "Come and have breakfast." None of the disciples dared ask him, "Who are you?" They knew it was the Lord. [13]Jesus came, took the bread and gave it to them, and did the same with the fish. [14]This was now the third time Jesus appeared to his disciples after he was raised from the dead. [15]When they had finished eating, Jesus said to Simon Peter, "Simon son of John, do you love me more than these?" "Yes, Lord," he said, "you know that I love you." Jesus said, "Feed my lambs." [16]Again Jesus said, "Simon son of John, do you love me?" He answered, "Yes, Lord, you know that I love you." Jesus said, "Take care of my sheep." [17]The third time he said to him, "Simon son of John, do you love me?" Peter was hurt because Jesus asked him the third time, "Do you love me?" He said, "Lord, you know all things; you know that I love you." Jesus said, "Feed my sheep. [18]Very truly I tell you, when you were younger you dressed yourself and went where you wanted; but when you are old you will stretch out your hands, and someone else will dress you and lead you where you do not want to go." [19]Jesus said this to indicate the kind of death by which Peter would glorify God. Then he said to him, "Follow me!"

Jesus and the Children

Jesus had spent a long time teaching the crowds. Some women, believing him to be special and sent from God, brought their children to him. They hoped that he would place his hands on them and pray for them. But the disciples tried to send the women away, telling them that Jesus could not be bothered with their children, as he was too busy.

Jesus, however, insisted that the children should not be prevented from coming to him and declared that they represented those to whom a place in God's kingdom is given. Then he placed his hands on them in blessing.

Bible Reference: Matthew19:13-15 [13]Then people brought little children to Jesus for him to place his hands on them and pray for them. But the disciples rebuked them. [14]Jesus said, "Let the little children come to me, and do not hinder them, for the kingdom of heaven belongs to such as these." [15]When he had placed his hands on them, he went on from there.

Jesus Calms a Storm

All day, Jesus had been teaching the crowds by the side of the lake known as the Sea of Galilee. Now, it was late and he was tired. He asked the disciples to take him over to the other side of the lake. They climbed into a boat, and the disciples began to row across. Soon, Jesus was asleep in the stern of the boat.

Suddenly, one of the lake's unpredictable storms blew up. The small boat was tossed violently about. Even the fishermen among the disciples panicked. They shook Jesus awake, crying,

"Teacher! Don't you even care that we might drown?"

Jesus stood up immediately and said to the rough water,

"Quiet! Be calm!"

At once the wind died down and the water was calm and flat.

Jesus asked the disciples,

"Why were you so frightened? Do you have no trust in me?"

The disciples were troubled. They asked each other just who this man was who could command even the wind and the water.

Bible Reference: Mark 4:35-41 [35]That day when evening came, he said to his disciples, "Let us go over to the other side." [36]Leaving the crowd behind, they took him along, just as he was, in the boat. There were also other boats with him. [37]A furious squall came up, and the waves broke over the boat, so that it was nearly swamped. [38]Jesus was in the stern, sleeping on a cushion. The disciples woke him and said to him, "Teacher, don't you care if we drown?" [39]He got up, rebuked the wind and said to the waves, "Quiet! Be still!" Then the wind died down and it was completely calm. [40]He said to his disciples, "Why are you so afraid? Do you still have no faith?" [41]They were terrified and asked each other, "Who is this? Even the wind and the waves obey him!"

Joseph and His Brothers—Part I

Jacob had twelve sons, but he made it clear to all of them that Joseph was his favourite, buying him a special robe. Joseph told his brothers about some dreams he had experienced, which, he believed, proved that he would rule over all of them one day. Angry and jealous, they saw an opportUnity to kill Joseph when he was sent by his father to take supplies to them as they looked after the family's herds. Reuben, the eldest, persuaded them to throw Joseph down a well: he hoped to save his younger brother later. However, before he could do this, the other brothers sold Joseph to some Midianite traders who were on their way to Egypt. When the traders arrived there, they sold Joseph to Potiphar, Pharaoh's captain of the guard.

Meanwhile, the brothers told Jacob that Joseph had been killed by a wild animal. He was heart-broken.

Bible Reference: Genesis 37:1-11 [1]Jacob lived in the land where his father had stayed, the land of Canaan. [2]This is the account of Jacob's family line. Joseph, a young man of seventeen, was tending the flocks with his brothers, the sons of Bilhah and the sons of Zilpah, his father's wives, and he brought their father a bad report about them. [3]Now Israel loved Joseph more than any of his other sons, because he had been born to him in his old age; and he made a richly ornamented robe for him. [4]When his brothers saw that their father loved him more than any of them, they hated him and could not speak a kind word to him. [5]Joseph had a dream, and when he told it to his brothers, they hated him all the more. [6]He said to them, "Listen to this dream I had: [7]we were binding sheaves of corn out in the field when suddenly my sheaf rose and stood upright, while your sheaves gathered round mine and bowed down to it." [8]His brothers said to him, "Do you intend to reign over us? Will you actually rule us?" And they hated him all the more because of his dream and what he had said. [9]Then he had another dream, and he told it to his brothers. "Listen," he said, "I had another dream, and this time the sun and moon and eleven stars were bowing down to me." [10]When he told his father as well as his brothers, his father rebuked him and said, "What is this dream you had? Will your mother and I and your brothers actually come and bow down to the ground before you?" [11]His brothers were jealous of him, but his father kept the matter in mind.

Bible Reference: Genesis 37:17-28 [17] "They have moved on from here," the man answered. "I heard them say, 'Let's go to Dothan.'" So Joseph went after his brothers and found them near Dothan. [18]But they saw him in the distance, and before he reached them, they plotted to kill him. [19] "Here comes that dreamer!" they said to each other. [20] "Come now, let's kill him and throw him into one of these cisterns and say that a ferocious animal devoured him. Then we'll see what comes of his dreams." [21]When Reuben heard this, he tried to rescue him from their hands. "Let's not take his life," he said. [22] "Don't shed any blood. Throw him into this cistern here in the

wilderness, but don't lay a hand on him." Reuben said this to rescue him from them and take him back to his father. ²³So when Joseph came to his brothers, they stripped him of his robe—the richly ornamented robe he was wearing—²⁴and they took him and threw him into the cistern. The cistern was empty; there was no water in it. ²⁵As they sat down to eat their meal, they looked up and saw a caravan of Ishmaelites coming from Gilead. Their camels were loaded with spices, balm and myrrh, and they were on their way to take them down to Egypt. ²⁶Judah said to his brothers, "What will we gain if we kill our brother and cover up his blood? ²⁷Come, let's sell him to the Ishmaelites and not lay our hands on him; after all, he is our brother, our own flesh and blood." His brothers agreed. ²⁸So when the Midianite merchants came by, his brothers pulled Joseph up out of the cistern and sold him for twenty shekels of silver to the Ishmaelites, who took him to Egypt.

Bible Reference: Genesis 37:36 ³⁶Meanwhile, the Midianites sold Joseph in Egypt to Potiphar, one of Pharaoh's officials, the captain of the guard.

Joseph and His Brothers—Part II

As the famine in Egypt worsened, the people survived, but other countries suffered. Joseph's older brothers came from their homeland to buy food. They did not recognise Joseph now he was a high ranking Egyptian official, but he knew them immediately. He ordered them to leave Simeon in prison while they returned home to their father Jacob with the food they had purchased. When they needed more, they were to return with Benjamin, the youngest brother.

On the journey they discovered that the silver with which they had paid for the food had been replaced in their grain sacks. Terrified to return but desperately needing more food, they brought Benjamin back to Egypt with them. This time, Joseph had his own silver cup hidden in Benjamin's sack, and sent his steward after them. Joseph told them that Benjamin must stay as his slave. Judah begged him to spare their youngest brother, saying that this loss, on top of the loss of Joseph in the past, would kill their father. He offered to stay in Benjamin's place.

Then Joseph knew that the brothers realised what they had done in the past (harming Joseph and lying about his death) was wrong and were sorry for the grief they had brought to their father Jacob. He told them who he was. The brothers were terrified: the helpless young brother they had once sold into slavery was now very powerful.

Joseph said,

"God sent me to Egypt, not you. He sent me ahead of you so that I could save many lives, including your own."

On Joseph's orders, the brothers brought Jacob to Egypt. For the rest of the famine, the family lived there safely and with honour.

Bible Reference: Genesis 42:1-38 ¹When Jacob learned that there was grain in Egypt, he said to his sons, "Why do you just keep looking at each other?" ²He continued, "I have heard that there is grain in Egypt. Go down there and buy some for us, so that we may live and not die." ³Then ten of Joseph's brothers went down to buy grain from Egypt. ⁴But Jacob did not send Benjamin, Joseph's brother, with the others, because he was afraid that harm might come to him. ⁵So Israel's sons were among those who went to buy grain, for the famine was in the land of Canaan also. ⁶Now Joseph was the governor of the land, the person who sold grain to all its people. So when Joseph's brothers arrived, they bowed down to him with their faces to the ground. ⁷As soon as Joseph saw his brothers, he recognized them, but he pretended to be a stranger and spoke harshly to them. "Where do you come from?" he asked. "From the land of Canaan," they replied, "to buy food." ⁸Although Joseph recognized his brothers, they did not recognize him. ⁹Then he remembered his dreams about them and said to them, "You are spies! You have come to see where our land is unprotected." ¹⁰ "No, my lord," they answered. "Your servants have come to buy food. ¹¹We are all the sons of one man. Your servants are honest men, not spies." ¹² "No!" he said to them. "You have come to see where our land is unprotected." ¹³But they replied, "Your servants were twelve brothers, the sons of one man, who lives in the land of Canaan. The youngest is now with our father, and one is no more." ¹⁴Joseph said to them, "It is just as I told you: you are spies! ¹⁵And this is how you will be tested: as surely as Pharaoh lives, you will not leave this place unless your youngest brother comes here. ¹⁶Send one of your number to get your brother; the rest of you will be kept in prison, so that your words may be tested to see if you are telling the truth. If you are not, then as surely as Pharaoh lives, you are spies!" ¹⁷And he put them all in custody for three days. ¹⁸On the third day, Joseph said to them, "Do this and you will live, for I fear God: ¹⁹if you are honest men, let one of your brothers stay here in prison, while the rest of you go and take grain back for your starving households. ²⁰But you must bring your youngest brother to me, so that your words may be verified and that you may not die." This they proceeded to do. ²¹They said to one another, "Surely we are being punished because of our brother. We saw how distressed he was when he pleaded with us for his life, but we would not listen; that's why this distress has come on us." ²²Reuben replied, "Didn't I tell you not to sin against the boy? But you wouldn't listen! Now we must give an accounting for his blood." ²³They did not realize that Joseph could understand them, since he was using an interpreter. ²⁴He turned away from them and began to weep, but then came back and spoke to them again. He had Simeon taken from them and bound before their eyes. ²⁵Joseph gave orders to fill their bags with grain, to put each man's silver back in his sack, and to give them provisions for their journey. After this was done for them, ²⁶they loaded their grain on their donkeys and left. ²⁷At the place where they stopped for the night one of them opened his sack to get feed for his donkey, and he saw his silver in the mouth of his sack. ²⁸ "My silver has been returned," he said to his brothers. "Here it is in my sack." Their hearts sank and they turned to each other trembling and said, "What is this that God has done to us?" ²⁹When they came to their father Jacob in the land of Canaan, they told him all that had happened to them. They said, ³⁰ "The man who is lord over the land spoke harshly to us and treated us as though we were spying on the land. ³¹But we said to him, 'We are honest men; we are not spies. ³²We were twelve brothers, sons of one father. One is no more, and the youngest is now with our father in Canaan.' " ³³ "Then the man who is lord over the land said to us, 'This is how I will know whether you are honest men: leave one of your brothers here with me, and take food for your starving households and go. ³⁴But bring your youngest brother to me so I will know that you are not spies but honest men. Then I will give your brother back to you, and you can trade in the land.' " ³⁵As they were emptying their sacks, there in each man's sack was his pouch of silver! When they and their father saw the money pouches, they were frightened. ³⁶Their father Jacob said to them, "You have deprived me of my children. Joseph is no more and Simeon is no more, and now you want to take Benjamin. Everything is against me!" ³⁷Then Reuben said to his father, "You may put both of my sons to death if I do not bring him back to you. Entrust him to my care, and I will bring him back." ³⁸But Jacob said, "My son will not go down there with you; his brother is dead and he is the only one left. If harm comes to him on the journey you are taking, you will bring my grey head down to the grave in sorrow."

Bible Reference: Genesis 43:1-34 ¹Now the famine was still severe in the land. ²So when they had eaten all the grain they had brought from Egypt, their father said to them, "Go back and buy us a little more food." ³But Judah said to him, "The man warned us solemnly, 'You will not see my face again unless your brother is with you.' " ⁴If you will send our brother along with us, we will go down and buy food for you. ⁵But if you will not send him, we will not go down, because the man said to us, "You will not see my face again unless your brother is with you." ⁶Israel asked, "Why did you bring this trouble on me by telling the man you had another brother?" ⁷They replied, "The man questioned us closely about ourselves and our family. 'Is your father still living?' " he asked us. "Do you have another brother?" We simply answered his questions. How were we to know he would say, "Bring your brother down here?" ⁸Then Judah said to Israel his father, "Send the boy along with me and we will go at once, so that we and you and our children may live and not die. ⁹I myself will guarantee his safety; you can hold me personally responsible for him. If I do not bring him back to you and set him here before you, I will bear the blame before you all my life. ¹⁰As it is, if we had not delayed, we could have gone and returned twice." ¹¹Then their father Israel said to them, "If it must be, then do this: put some of the best products of the land in your bags and take them down to the man as a gift—a little balm and a little honey, some spices and myrrh, some pistachio nuts and almonds. ¹²Take double the amount of silver with you, for you must return the silver that was put back into the mouths of your sacks. Perhaps it was a mistake. ¹³Take your brother also and go back to the man at once. ¹⁴And may God Almighty grant you mercy before the man so that he will let your other brother and Benjamin come back with you. As for me, if I am bereaved, I am bereaved." ¹⁵So the men took the gifts and double the amount of silver, and Benjamin also. They hurried down to Egypt and presented themselves to Joseph. ⁱ⁶When Joseph saw Benjamin with them, he said to the steward of his house, "Take these men to my house, slaughter an animal and prepare a meal; they are to eat with me at noon." ¹⁷The man did as Joseph told him and took the men to Joseph's house. ¹⁸Now the men were frightened when they were taken to his house. They thought, "We were brought here because of the silver that was put back into our sacks the first time. He wants to attack us and overpower us and seize us as slaves and take our donkeys." ¹⁹So they went up to Joseph's steward and spoke to him at the entrance to the house. ²⁰ "We beg your pardon, our lord," they said, "we came down here the first time to buy food. ²¹But at the place where we stopped for the night we opened our sacks and each of us found his silver—the exact weight—in the mouth of his sack. So we have brought it back with us. ²²We have also brought additional silver with us to buy food. We don't know who put our silver in our sacks." ²³ "It's all right," he said. "Don't be afraid. Your God, the God of your father, has given you treasure in your sacks; I received your silver." Then he brought Simeon out to them. ²⁴The steward took the men into Joseph's house, gave them water to wash their feet and provided fodder for their donkeys. ²⁵They prepared their gifts for Joseph's arrival at noon, because they had heard that they were to eat there. ²⁶When Joseph came home, they presented to him the gifts they had brought into the house, and they bowed down before him to the ground. ²⁷He asked them how they were, and then he said, "How is your aged father you told me about? Is he still living?" ²⁸They replied, "Your servant our father is still alive and well." And they bowed down, prostrating themselves before him. ²⁹As he looked about and saw his brother Benjamin, his own mother's son, he asked, "Is this your youngest brother, the one you told me about?" And he said, "God be gracious to you, my son." ³⁰Deeply moved at the sight of his brother, Joseph hurried out and looked for a place to weep. He went into his private room and wept there. ³¹After he had washed his face, he came out and, controlling himself, said, "Serve the food." ³²They served him by himself, the brothers by themselves, and the Egyptians who ate with him by themselves, because Egyptians could not eat with Hebrews, for that is detestable to Egyptians. ³³The men had been seated before him in the order of their ages, from the firstborn to the youngest; and they looked at each other in astonishment. ³⁴When portions were served to them from Joseph's table, Benjamin's portion was five times as much as anyone else's. So they feasted and drank freely with him.

Bible Reference: Genesis 44:1-34 ¹Now Joseph gave these instructions to the steward of his house: "Fill the men's sacks with as much food as they can carry, and put each man's silver in the mouth of his sack. ²Then put my cup, the silver one, in the mouth of the youngest one's sack, along with the silver for his grain." And he did as Joseph said. ³As morning dawned, the men were sent on their way with their donkeys. ⁴They had not gone far from the city when Joseph said to his steward, "Go after those men at once, and when you catch up with them, say to them, 'Why have you repaid good with evil? ⁵Isn't this the cup my master drinks from and also uses for divination? This is a wicked thing you have done.'" ⁶When he caught up with them, he repeated these words to them. ⁷But they said to him, "Why does my lord say such things? Far be it from your servants to do anything like that! ⁸We even brought back to you from the land of Canaan the silver we found inside the mouths of our sacks. So why would we steal silver or gold from your master's house? ⁹If any of your servants is found to have it, he will die; and the rest of us will become my lord's slaves." ¹⁰ "Very well, then," he said, "let it be as you say. Whoever is found to have it will become my slave; the rest of you will be free from blame." ¹¹Each of them quickly lowered his sack to the ground and opened it. ¹²Then the steward proceeded to search, beginning with the eldest and ending with the youngest. And the cup was found in Benjamin's sack. ¹³At this, they tore their clothes. Then they all loaded their donkeys and returned to the city. ¹⁴Joseph was still in the house when Judah and his brothers came in, and they threw themselves to the ground before him. ¹⁵Joseph said to them, "What is this you have done? Don't you know that a man like me can find things out by divination?" ¹⁶ "What can we say to my lord?" Judah replied. "What can we say? How can we prove our innocence? God has uncovered your servants' guilt. We are now my lord's slaves - we ourselves and the one who was found to have the cup." ¹⁷But Joseph said, "Far be it from me to do such a thing! Only the man who was found to have the cup will become my slave. The rest of you, go back to your father in peace." ¹⁸Then Judah went up to him and said: "Pardon your servant, my lord, let me speak a word to my lord. Do not be angry with your servant, though you are equal to Pharaoh himself. ¹⁹My lord asked his servants, 'Do you have a father or a brother?'" ²⁰And we answered, 'We have an aged father, and there is a young son born to him in his old age. His brother is dead, and he is the only one of his mother's sons left, and his father loves him.'" ²¹Then you said to your servants, "Bring him down to me so I can see him for myself." ²²And we said to my lord, "The boy cannot leave his father; if he leaves him, his father will die." ²³But you told your servants, "Unless your youngest brother comes down with you, you will not see my face again." ²⁴When we went back to your servant my father, we told him what my lord had said. ²⁵Then our father said, "Go back and buy a little more food." ²⁶But we said, "We cannot go down. Only if our youngest brother is with us will we go. We cannot see the man's face unless our youngest brother is with us." ²⁷Your servant my father said to us, "You know that my wife bore me two sons. ²⁸One of them went away from me, and I said, 'He has surely been torn to pieces.' And I have not seen him since. ²⁹If you take this one from me too and harm comes to him, you will bring my grey head down to the grave in misery." ³⁰ "So now, if the boy is not with us when I go back to your servant my father, and if my father, whose life is closely bound up with the boy's life, ³¹sees that the boy isn't there, he will die. Your servants will bring the grey head of our father down to the grave in sorrow. ³²Your servant guaranteed the boy's safety to my father. I said, "If I do not bring him back to you, I will bear the blame before you, my father, all my life!" ³³ "Now then, please let your servant remain here as my lord's slave in place of the boy, and let the boy return with his brothers. ³⁴How can I go back to my father if the boy is not with me? No! Do not let me see the misery that would come on my father."

Bible Reference: Genesis 45:1-28 ¹Then Joseph could no longer control himself before all his attendants, and he cried out, "Make everyone leave my presence!" So there was no-one with Joseph when he made himself known to his brothers. ²And he wept so loudly that the Egyptians heard him, and Pharaoh's household heard about it. ³Joseph said to his brothers, "I am Joseph! Is my father still living?" But his brothers were not able to answer him, because they were terrified at his presence. ⁴Then Joseph said to his brothers, "Come close to me." When they had done so, he said, "I am your brother Joseph, the one you sold into Egypt! ⁵And now, do not be distressed and do not be angry with yourselves for selling me here, because it was to save lives that God sent me ahead of you. ⁶For two years now there has been famine in the land, and for the next five years there will be no ploughing and reaping. ⁷But God sent me ahead of you to preserve for you a remnant on earth and to save your lives by a great deliverance." ⁸So then, it was not you who sent me here, but God. He made me father to Pharaoh, lord of his entire household and ruler of all Egypt. ⁹Now hurry back to my father and say to him, "This is what your son Joseph says: God has made me lord of all Egypt. Come down to me; don't delay. ¹⁰You shall live in the region of Goshen and be near me—you, your children and grandchildren, your flocks and herds, and all you have. ¹¹I will provide for you there, because five years of famine are still to come. Otherwise you and your household and all who belong to you will become destitute." ¹² "You can see for yourselves, and so can my brother Benjamin, that it is really I who am speaking to you. ¹³Tell my father about all the honour accorded me in Egypt and about everything you have seen. And bring my father down here quickly." ¹⁴Then he threw his arms around his brother Benjamin and wept, and Benjamin embraced him, weeping. ¹⁵And he kissed all his brothers and wept over them. Afterwards his brothers talked with him. ¹⁶When the news reached Pharaoh's palace that Joseph's brothers had come, Pharaoh and all his officials were pleased. ¹⁷Pharaoh said to Joseph, "Tell your brothers, "Do this: load your animals and return to the land of Canaan, ¹⁸and bring your father and your families back to me. I will give you the best of the land of Egypt and you can enjoy the fat of the land." ¹⁹You are also instructed to tell them, "Do this: take some carts from Egypt for your children and your wives, and get your father and come. ²⁰Never mind about your belongings, because the best of all Egypt will be yours." ²¹So the sons of Israel did this. Joseph gave them carts, as Pharaoh had commanded, and he also gave them provisions for their journey. ²²To each of them he gave new clothing, but to Benjamin he gave three hundred shekels of silver and five sets of clothes. ²³And this is what he sent to his father: ten donkeys loaded with the best things of Egypt, and ten female donkeys loaded with grain and bread and other provisions for his journey. ²⁴Then he sent his brothers away, and as they were leaving he said to them, "Don't quarrel on the way!" ²⁵So they went up out of Egypt and came to their father Jacob in the land of Canaan. ²⁶They told him, "Joseph is still alive! In fact, he is ruler of all Egypt." Jacob was stunned; he did not believe them. ²⁷But when they told him everything Joseph had said to them, and when he saw the carts Joseph had sent to carry him back, the spirit of their father Jacob revived. ²⁸And Israel said, "I'm convinced! My son Joseph is still alive. I will go and see him before I die."

Bible Reference: Genesis 46:7 ⁷Jacob brought with him to Egypt his sons and grandsons and his daughters and granddaughters—all his offspring.

Noah's Ark

Bible Reference: Genesis 6 ¹When men began to increase in number on the earth and daughters were born to them, ²the sons of God saw that the daughters of men were beautiful, and they married any of them they chose. ³Then the LORD said, "My Spirit will not contend with man forever, for he is mortal; his days will be a hundred and twenty years."

⁴The Nephilim were on the earth in those days—and also afterward—when the sons of God went to the daughters of men and had children by them. They were the heroes of old, men of renown.

⁵The LORD saw how great man's wickedness on the earth had become, and that every inclination of the thoughts of his heart was only evil all the time. ⁶ The LORD was grieved that he had made man on the earth, and his heart was filled with pain. ⁷So the LORD said, "I will wipe mankind, whom I have created, from the face of the earth—men and animals, and creatures that move along the ground, and birds of the air—for I am grieved that I have made them." ⁸But Noah found favor in the eyes of the LORD.

⁹This is the account of Noah.

Noah was a righteous man, blameless among the people of his time, and he walked with God. ¹⁰Noah had three sons: Shem, Ham and Japheth.

¹¹Now the earth was corrupt in God's sight and was full of violence. ¹²God saw how corrupt the earth had become, for all the people on earth had corrupted their ways. ¹³So God said to Noah, "I am going to put an end to all people, for the earth is filled with violence because of them. I am surely going to destroy both them and the earth. ¹⁴So make yourself an ark of cypress wood; make rooms in it and coat it with pitch inside and out. ¹⁵This is how you are to build it: The ark is to be 450 feet long, 75 feet wide and 45 feet high. ¹⁶Make a roof for it and finish the ark to within 18 inches of the top. Put a door in the side of the ark and make lower, middle and upper decks. ¹⁷I am going to bring floodwaters on the earth to destroy all life under the heavens, every creature that has the breath of life in it. Everything on earth will perish. ¹⁸But I will establish my covenant with you, and you will enter the ark—you and your sons and your wife and your sons' wives with you. ¹⁹You are to bring into the ark two of all living creatures, male and female, to keep them alive with you. ²⁰Two of every kind of bird, of every kind of animal and of every kind of creature that moves along the ground will come to you to be kept alive. ²¹You are to take every kind of food that is to be eaten and store it away as food for you and for them."

²²Noah did everything just as God commanded him.

Bible Reference: Genesis 7 ¹The LORD then said to Noah, "Go into the ark, you and your whole family, because I have found you righteous in this generation. ²Take with you seven of every kind of clean animal, a male and its mate, and two of every kind of unclean animal, a male and its mate, ³and also seven of every kind of bird, male and female, to keep their various kinds alive throughout the earth. ⁴Seven days from now I will send rain on the earth for forty days and forty nights, and I will wipe from the face of the earth every living creature I have made."

⁵And Noah did all that the LORD commanded him.

⁶Noah was six hundred years old when the floodwaters came on the earth. ⁷And Noah and his sons and his wife and his sons' wives entered the ark to escape the waters of the flood. ⁸Pairs of clean and unclean animals, of birds and of all creatures that move along the ground, ⁹male and female, came to Noah and entered the ark, as God had commanded Noah. ¹⁰And after the seven days the floodwaters came on the earth.

¹¹In the six hundredth year of Noah's life, on the seventeenth day of the second month—on that day all the springs of the great deep burst forth, and the floodgates of the heavens were opened. ¹²And rain fell on the earth forty days and forty nights.

¹³On that very day Noah and his sons, Shem, Ham and Japheth, together with his wife and the wives of his three sons, entered the ark. ¹⁴They had with them every wild animal according to its kind, all livestock according to their kinds, every creature that moves along the ground according to its kind and every bird according to its kind, everything with wings. ¹⁵Pairs of all creatures that have the breath of life in them came to Noah and entered

the ark. ¹⁶The animals going in were male and female of every living thing, as God had commanded Noah. Then the LORD shut him in.

¹⁷For forty days the flood kept coming on the earth, and as the waters increased they lifted the ark high above the earth. ¹⁸The waters rose and increased greatly on the earth, and the ark floated on the surface of the water. ¹⁹They rose greatly on the earth, and all the high mountains under the entire heavens were covered. ²⁰The waters rose and covered the mountains to a depth of more than twenty feet. ²¹Every living thing that moved on the earth perished—birds, livestock, wild animals, all the creatures that swarm over the earth, and all mankind. ²²Everything on dry land that had the breath of life in its nostrils died. ²³Every living thing on the face of the earth was wiped out; men and animals and the creatures that move along the ground and the birds of the air were wiped from the earth. Only Noah was left, and those with him in the ark.

²⁴The waters flooded the earth for a hundred and fifty days.

Bible Reference: Genesis 8 ¹But God remembered Noah and all the wild animals and the livestock that were with him in the ark, and he sent a wind over the earth, and the waters receded. ²Now the springs of the deep and the floodgates of the heavens had been closed, and the rain had stopped falling from the sky. ³The water receded steadily from the earth. At the end of the hundred and fifty days the water had gone down, ⁴and on the seventeenth day of the seventh month the ark came to rest on the mountains of Ararat. ⁵The waters continued to recede until the tenth month, and on the first day of the tenth month the tops of the mountains became visible.

⁶After forty days Noah opened the window he had made in the ark ⁷ and sent out a raven, and it kept flying back and forth until the water had dried up from the earth. ⁸Then he sent out a dove to see if the water had receded from the surface of the ground. ⁹But the dove could find no place to set its feet because there was water over all the surface of the earth; so it returned to Noah in the ark. He reached out his hand and took the dove and brought it back to himself in the ark. ¹⁰He waited seven more days and again sent out the dove from the ark. ¹¹When the dove returned to him in the evening, there in its beak was a freshly plucked olive leaf! Then Noah knew that the water had receded from the earth. ¹²He waited seven more days and sent the dove out again, but this time it did not return to him.

¹³By the first day of the first month of Noah's six hundred and first year, the water had dried up from the earth. Noah then removed the covering from the ark and saw that the surface of the ground was dry. ¹⁴ By the twenty-seventh day of the second month the earth was completely dry.

¹⁵Then God said to Noah, ¹⁶"Come out of the ark, you and your wife and your sons and their wives. ¹⁷Bring out every kind of living creature that is with you—the birds, the animals, and all the creatures that move along the ground—so they can multiply on the earth and be fruitful and increase in number upon it."

¹⁸So Noah came out, together with his sons and his wife and his sons' wives. ¹⁹All the animals and all the creatures that move along the ground and all the birds—everything that moves on the earth—came out of the ark, one kind after another.

²⁰Then Noah built an altar to the LORD and, taking some of all the clean animals and clean birds, he sacrificed burnt offerings on it. ²¹The LORD smelled the pleasing aroma and said in his heart: "Never again will I curse the ground because of man, even though every inclination of his heart is evil from childhood. And never again will I destroy all living creatures, as I have done.

²² "As long as the earth endures,
seedtime and harvest,
cold and heat,
summer and winter,
day and night
will never cease."

Bible Reference: Genesis 9 ¹ Then God blessed Noah and his sons, saying to them, "Be fruitful and increase in number and fill the earth. ² The fear and dread of you will fall upon all the beasts of the earth and all the birds of the air, upon every creature that moves along the ground, and upon all the fish of the sea; they are given into your hands. ³ Everything that lives and moves will be food for you. Just as I gave you the green plants, I now give you everything.

⁴ "But you must not eat meat that has its lifeblood still in it. ⁵ And for your lifeblood I will surely demand an accounting. I will demand an accounting from every animal. And from each man, too, I will demand an accounting for the life of his fellow man.

⁶ "Whoever sheds the blood of man,
by man shall his blood be shed;
for in the image of God
has God made man.

⁷ As for you, be fruitful and increase in number; multiply on the earth and increase upon it."

⁸ Then God said to Noah and to his sons with him: ⁹ "I now establish my covenant with you and with your descendants after you ¹⁰ and with every living creature that was with you—the birds, the livestock and all the wild animals, all those that came out of the ark with you—every living creature on earth. ¹¹ I establish my covenant with you: Never again will all life be cut off by the waters of a flood; never again will there be a flood to destroy the earth."

¹² And God said, "This is the sign of the covenant I am making between me and you and every living creature with you, a covenant for all generations to come: ¹³ I have set my rainbow in the clouds, and it will be the sign of the covenant between me and the earth. ¹⁴ Whenever I bring clouds over the earth and the rainbow appears in the clouds, ¹⁵ I will remember my covenant between me and you and all living creatures of every kind. Never again will the waters become a flood to destroy all life. ¹⁶ Whenever the rainbow appears in the clouds, I will see it and remember the everlasting covenant between God and all living creatures of every kind on the earth."

¹⁷ So God said to Noah, "This is the sign of the covenant I have established between me and all life on the earth."

The Sons of Noah

¹⁸ The sons of Noah who came out of the ark were Shem, Ham and Japheth. (Ham was the father of Canaan.) ¹⁹ These were the three sons of Noah, and from them came the people who were scattered over the earth.

²⁰ Noah, a man of the soil, proceeded to plant a vineyard. ²¹ When he drank some of its wine, he became drunk and lay uncovered inside his tent. ²² Ham, the father of Canaan, saw his father's nakedness and told his two brothers outside. ²³ But Shem and Japheth took a garment and laid it across their shoulders; then they walked in backward and covered their father's nakedness. Their faces were turned the other way so that they would not see their father's nakedness.

²⁴ When Noah awoke from his wine and found out what his youngest son had done to him, ²⁵ he said,
"Cursed be Canaan!
The lowest of slaves
will he be to his brothers."
²⁶ He also said,
"Blessed be the LORD, the God of Shem!
May Canaan be the slave of Shem.
²⁷ May God extend the territory of Japheth;
may Japheth live in the tents of Shem,
and may Canaan be his slave."

²⁸ After the flood Noah lived 350 years. ²⁹ Altogether, Noah lived 950 years, and then he died.

Pharaoh's Dreams

Bible Reference: Genesis 41 ¹ When two full years had passed, Pharaoh had a dream: He was standing by the Nile, ² when out of the river there came up seven cows, sleek and fat, and they grazed among the reeds. ³ After them, seven other cows, ugly and gaunt, came up out of the Nile and stood beside those on the riverbank. ⁴ And the cows that were ugly and gaunt ate up the seven sleek, fat cows. Then Pharaoh woke up.

⁵ He fell asleep again and had a second dream: Seven heads of grain, healthy and good, were growing on a

single stalk. ⁶ After them, seven other heads of grain sprouted—thin and scorched by the east wind. ⁷ The thin heads of grain swallowed up the seven healthy, full heads. Then Pharaoh woke up; it had been a dream.

⁸ In the morning his mind was troubled, so he sent for all the magicians and wise men of Egypt. Pharaoh told them his dreams, but no one could interpret them for him.

⁹ Then the chief cupbearer said to Pharaoh, "Today I am reminded of my shortcomings. ¹⁰ Pharaoh was once angry with his servants, and he imprisoned me and the chief baker in the house of the captain of the guard. ¹¹ Each of us had a dream the same night, and each dream had a meaning of its own. ¹² Now a young Hebrew was there with us, a servant of the captain of the guard. We told him our dreams, and he interpreted them for us, giving each man the interpretation of his dream. ¹³ And things turned out exactly as he interpreted them to us: I was restored to my position, and the other man was hanged."

¹⁴ So Pharaoh sent for Joseph, and he was quickly brought from the dungeon. When he had shaved and changed his clothes, he came before Pharaoh.

¹⁵ Pharaoh said to Joseph, "I had a dream, and no one can interpret it. But I have heard it said of you that when you hear a dream you can interpret it."

¹⁶ "I cannot do it," Joseph replied to Pharaoh, "but God will give Pharaoh the answer he desires."

¹⁷ Then Pharaoh said to Joseph, "In my dream I was standing on the bank of the Nile, ¹⁸ when out of the river there came up seven cows, fat and sleek, and they grazed among the reeds. ¹⁹ After them, seven other cows came up—scrawny and very ugly and lean. I had never seen such ugly cows in all the land of Egypt. ²⁰ The lean, ugly cows ate up the seven fat cows that came up first. ²¹ But even after they ate them, no one could tell that they had done so; they looked just as ugly as before. Then I woke up."

²² "In my dreams I also saw seven heads of grain, full and good, growing on a single stalk. ²³ After them, seven other heads sprouted—withered and thin and scorched by the east wind. ²⁴ The thin heads of grain swallowed up the seven good heads. I told this to the magicians, but none could explain it to me."

²⁵ Then Joseph said to Pharaoh, "The dreams of Pharaoh are one and the same. God has revealed to Pharaoh what he is about to do. ²⁶ The seven good cows are seven years, and the seven good heads of grain are seven years; it is one and the same dream. ²⁷ The seven lean, ugly cows that came up afterward are seven years, and so are the seven worthless heads of grain scorched by the east wind: They are seven years of famine."

²⁸ "It is just as I said to Pharaoh: God has shown Pharaoh what he is about to do. ²⁹ Seven years of great abundance are coming throughout the land of Egypt, ³⁰ but seven years of famine will follow them. Then all the abundance in Egypt will be forgotten, and the famine will ravage the land. ³¹ The abundance in the land will not be remembered, because the famine that follows it will be so severe. ³² The reason the dream was given to Pharaoh in two forms is that the matter has been firmly decided by God, and God will do it soon."

³³ "And now let Pharaoh look for a discerning and wise man and put him in charge of the land of Egypt. ³⁴ Let Pharaoh appoint commissioners over the land to take a fifth of the harvest of Egypt during the seven years of abundance. ³⁵ They should collect all the food of these good years that are coming and store up the grain under the authority of Pharaoh, to be kept in the cities for food. ³⁶ This food should be held in reserve for the country, to be used during the seven years of famine that will come upon Egypt, so that the country may not be ruined by the famine."

³⁷ The plan seemed good to Pharaoh and to all his officials. ³⁸ So Pharaoh asked them, "Can we find anyone like this man, one in whom is the spirit of God."

³⁹ Then Pharaoh said to Joseph, "Since God has made all this known to you, there is no one so discerning and wise as you. ⁴⁰ You shall be in charge of my palace, and all my people are to submit to your orders. Only with respect to the throne will I be greater than you."

Joseph in Charge of Egypt

⁴¹ So Pharaoh said to Joseph, "I hereby put you in charge of the whole land of Egypt." ⁴² Then Pharaoh took his signet ring from his finger and put it on Joseph's finger. He dressed him in robes of fine linen and put a gold chain around his neck. ⁴³ He had him ride in a chariot as his second-in-command, and men shouted before him, "Make way!" Thus he put him in charge of the whole land of Egypt.

⁴⁴ Then Pharaoh said to Joseph, "I am Pharaoh, but without your word no one will lift hand or foot in all

Egypt." ⁴⁵ Pharaoh gave Joseph the name Zaphenath-Paneah and gave him Asenath daughter of Potiphera, priest of On, to be his wife. And Joseph went throughout the land of Egypt.

⁴⁶ Joseph was thirty years old when he entered the service of Pharaoh king of Egypt. And Joseph went out from Pharaoh's presence and traveled throughout Egypt. ⁴⁷ During the seven years of abundance the land produced plentifully. ⁴⁸ Joseph collected all the food produced in those seven years of abundance in Egypt and stored it in the cities. In each city he put the food grown in the fields surrounding it. ⁴⁹ Joseph stored up huge quantities of grain, like the sand of the sea; it was so much that he stopped keeping records because it was beyond measure.

⁵⁰ Before the years of famine came, two sons were born to Joseph by Asenath daughter of Potiphera, priest of On.⁵¹Joseph named his firstborn Manasseh and said, "It is because God has made me forget all my trouble and all my father's household." ⁵² The second son he named Ephraim and said, "It is because God has made me fruitful in the land of my suffering."

⁵³ The seven years of abundance in Egypt came to an end, ⁵⁴ and the seven years of famine began, just as Joseph had said. There was famine in all the other lands, but in the whole land of Egypt there was food. ⁵⁵ When all Egypt began to feel the famine, the people cried to Pharaoh for food. Then Pharaoh told all the Egyptians, "Go to Joseph and do what he tells you."

⁵⁶ When the famine had spread over the whole country, Joseph opened the storehouses and sold grain to the Egyptians, for the famine was severe throughout Egypt. ⁵⁷ And all the countries came to Egypt to buy grain from Joseph, because the famine was severe in all the world.

Parable of the Sower

This famous parable is found in the gospels of Matthew, Mark and Luke. The parable tells of a farmer who scatters seed which enters different kinds of soil. Some falls by a path, some on rocky ground and again, some among thorns. Some, however falls into rich soil. Predictably, in the first three cases, there was no lasting crop, but in the final case the yield is plentiful. The point of the parable was to illustrate different sorts of hearers of the gospel: " the hearer represented by rocky ground is someone who hears readily enough, but has no staying power 'those represented as shallow soil and or choked by weeds are listeners whose lives produce nothing of lasting worth' only the rich soil produces a bountiful harvest."

Bible Reference: Mark 4:2-20 ²He taught them many things by parables, and in his teaching said: ³ "Listen! A farmer went out to sow his seed. ⁴As he was scattering the seed, some fell along the path, and the birds came and ate it up. ⁵Some fell on rocky places, where it did not have much soil. It sprang up quickly, because the soil was shallow. ⁶But when the sun came up, the plants were scorched, and they withered because they had no root. ⁷Other seed fell among thorns, which grew up and choked the plants, so that they did not bear grain. ⁸Still other seed fell on good soil. It came up, grew and produced a crop, some multiplying thirty, some sixty, some a hundred times." ⁹Then Jesus said, "Whoever has ears to hear, let them hear." ¹⁰When he was alone, the Twelve and the others around him asked him about the parables. ¹¹He told them, "The secret of the kingdom of God has been given to you. But to those on the outside everything is said in parables ¹²so that, ""they may be ever seeing but never perceiving, and ever hearing but never understanding; otherwise they might turn and be forgiven!" ¹³Then Jesus said to them, "Don't you understand this parable? How then will you understand any parable? ¹⁴The farmer sows the word. ¹⁵Some people are like seed along the path, where the word is sown. As soon as they hear it, Satan comes and takes away the word that was sown in them. ¹⁶Others, like seed sown on rocky places, hear the word and at once receive it with joy. ¹⁷But since they have no root, they last only a short time. When trouble or persecution comes because of the word, they quickly fall away. ¹⁸Still others, like seed sown among thorns, hear the word; ¹⁹but the worries of this life, the deceitfulness of wealth and the desires for other things come in and choke the word, making it unfruitful. ²⁰Others, like seed sown on good soil, hear the word, accept it, and produce a crop—some thirty, some sixty, some a hundred times what was sown."

Peter Denies He Knows Jesus

The soldiers seized Jesus in the Garden of Gethsemane and dragged him off to the High Priest's house for questioning. The night was cold and a group of servants and officials gathered round a fire in the house's courtyard. Peter crept in amongst them, desperate to know what was happening but afraid to identify himself.

Suddenly, a servant girl asked,

"You're not one of that man's followers, are you?"

Peter was afraid and quickly denied being a follower. But another asked him the same question. Again, Peter said he wasn't.

But a third person said,

"Surely I've just seen you with Jesus in the Garden?"

Peter was really frightened then and said he did not know Jesus and at that moment he heard a cockerel crowing. He remembered what Jesus had predicted—that Peter would deny knowing him before the cockerel crowed—and he realised what he had done.

Bible Reference: John 18:15-18 [15]Simon Peter and another disciple were following Jesus. Because this disciple was known to the high priest, he went with Jesus into the high priest's courtyard, [16]but Peter had to wait outside at the door. The other disciple, who was known to the high priest, came back, spoke to the servant-girl on duty there and brought Peter in. [17] "You aren't one of this man's disciples too, are you?" she asked Peter. He replied, "I am not." [18]It was cold, and the servants and officials stood round a fire they had made to keep warm. Peter also was standing with them, warming himself.

Bible Reference: John 18:25-27 [25]Meanwhile, Simon Peter was still standing there warming himself. So they asked him, "You aren't one of his disciples too, are you?" He denied it, saying, "I am not." [26]One of the high priest's servants, a relative of the man whose ear Peter had cut off, challenged him, "Didn't I see you with him in the garden?" [27]Again Peter denied it, and at that moment a cock began to crow.

The Ascension

The disciples saw Jesus several times after they found out he was alive again following his death on the Cross. He often talked to them about God and the Kingdom of Heaven. One day, during a meal, he told them that they were not to leave Jerusalem until the promised gift the Holy Spirit had come to them.

Forty days after his Resurrection, Jesus met them and said,

"When the Holy Spirit comes to you, you will receive power and you will be able to be my messengers, both here in this country and throughout the world."

As soon as he had finished speaking, he was taken up into the sky while they watched, until a cloud hid him from their view. While they stood there, trying to see where he had gone, two men appeared before them and asked why they were still looking into the sky.

"This Jesus," they said, "who has just left you will come back to you in the same way."

Bible Reference: Acts 1:1-11 [1]In my former book, Theophilus, I wrote about all that Jesus began to do and to teach [2]until the day he was taken up to heaven, after giving instructions through the Holy Spirit to the apostles he had chosen. [3]After his suffering, he presented himself to them and gave many convincing proofs that he was alive. He appeared to them over a period of forty days and spoke about the kingdom of God. [4]On one occasion, while he was eating with them, he gave them this command: "Do not leave Jerusalem, but wait for the gift my Father promised, which you have heard me speak about. [5]For John baptized with water, but in a few days you will be baptized with the Holy Spirit." [6]So when they met together, they asked him, "Lord, are you at this time going to restore the kingdom to Israel?" [7]He said to them: "It is not for you to know the times or dates the Father has set by his own authority. [8]But you will receive power when the Holy Spirit comes on you; and you will be my witnesses in Jerusalem, and in all Judea and Samaria, and to the ends of the earth." [9]After he said this, he was taken up before their very eyes, and a cloud hid him from their sight. [10]They were looking intently up into the sky as he was going, when suddenly two men dressed in white stood beside them. [11] "Men of Galilee," they said, "why do you stand here looking into the sky? This same Jesus, who has been taken from you into heaven, will come back in the same way you have seen him go into heaven."

The Baptism of Jesus

John the Baptist was baptizing people in the River Jordan as a sign that they were sorry for the things they had done which had displeased God and that they wanted to obey God from then on. John told the people that someone very important was coming to them from God, the common name for this special person being the Messiah.

One day, John saw Jesus coming to him to be baptized. John objected, saying that he needed to be baptized by Jesus, not the other way round. However Jesus said that this was the right thing to do. So John baptized Jesus, immersing him in the water of the River Jordan. As Jesus came up out of the water, he saw the Spirit of God coming down to him as a dove. Then a voice from Heaven said,

"This is my Son. I love him and I am pleased with everything he does."

Bible Reference: <u>Matthew 3:1-17</u> ¹In those days John the Baptist came, preaching in the wilderness of Judea ²and saying, "Repent, for the kingdom of heaven has come near." ³This is he who was spoken of through the prophet Isaiah: "A voice of one calling in the wilderness, 'Prepare the way for the Lord, make straight paths for him.'" ⁴John's clothes were made of camel's hair, and he had a leather belt round his waist. His food was locusts and wild honey. ⁵People went out to him from Jerusalem and all Judea and the whole region of the Jordan. ⁶Confessing their sins, they were baptized by him in the River Jordan. ⁷But when he saw many of the Pharisees and Sadducees coming to where he was baptizing, he said to them: "You brood of vipers! Who warned you to flee from the coming wrath? ⁸Produce fruit in keeping with repentance. ⁹And do not think you can say to yourselves, 'We have Abraham as our father.'" I tell you that out of these stones God can raise up children for Abraham. ¹⁰The axe has been laid to the root of the trees, and every tree that does not produce good fruit will be cut down and thrown into the fire. ¹¹ "I baptize you with water for repentance. But after me comes one who is more powerful than I, whose sandals I am not worthy to carry. He will baptize you with the Holy Spirit and fire. ¹²His winnowing fork is in his hand, and he will clear his threshing-floor, gathering his wheat into the barn and burning up the chaff with unquenchable fire." ¹³Then Jesus came from Galilee to the Jordan to be baptized by John. ¹⁴But John tried to deter him, saying, "I need to be baptized by you, and do you come to me?" ¹⁵Jesus replied, "Let it be so now; it is proper for us to do this to fulfil all righteousness." Then John consented. ¹⁶As soon as Jesus was baptized, he went up out of the water. At that moment heaven was opened, and he saw the Spirit of God descending like a dove and alighting on him. ¹⁷And a voice from heaven said, "This is my Son, whom I love; with him I am well pleased."

The biblical Account of Creation

In the beginning, before there was anything, God made the heavens and the earth. The earth was empty and dark but the Spirit of God was over the deep water. Then God said, "Let there be light!"

and light shone out. God saw the light was good, and he separated it from the darkness. He called the light "day" and the darkness "night". That was the first evening and the first morning.

Then God created the sky and separated the waters above the sky from the waters below it. This was the second day. On the third day, God gathered the waters below the sky into seas and oceans and the dry land appeared. God created plants of all kinds to grow on the land. He was very pleased with all he had done.

On the fourth day, God made the sun to light the day and the stars and the moon to light the night. Again, he was pleased by what he saw. On the next day, he called into existence all the creatures of the seas and all the birds of the air.

Now it was the sixth day. God created all the creatures of the land: the dry land was filled with animals of all kinds. Now the Earth was ready: God made people in his own image. He made them male and female and put them in charge of the Earth and of every other creature on it and told them that all the green plants were theirs for food. God saw that all he had made was very good. On the next day he made nothing more because everything was completed. This seventh day God made holy, because on it he rested from his work.

Bible Reference: <u>Genesis 1:1-31</u> ¹In the beginning God created the heavens and the earth. ²Now the earth was formless and empty, darkness was over the surface of the deep, and the Spirit of God was hovering over the waters. ^{3}And God said, "Let there be light," and there was light. ^{4}God saw that the light was good, and he separated the light from the darkness. ^{5}God called the light "day", and the darkness he called "night". And there was evening, and there was morning - the first day. ^{6}And God said, "Let there be a vault between the waters to separate water from water." ^{7}So God made the vault and separated the water under the vault from the water above it. And it was so. ^{8}God called the vault "sky". And there was evening, and there was morning - the second day. ^{9}And God said, "Let the water under the sky be gathered to one place, and let dry ground appear." And it was so. ^{10}God called the dry ground "land", and the gathered waters he called "seas". And God saw that it was good. ^{11}Then God said, "Let the land produce vegetation: seed-bearing plants and trees on the land that bear fruit with seed in it, according to their various kinds." And it was so. ^{12}The land produced vegetation: plants bearing seed according to their kinds and trees bearing fruit with seed in it according to their kinds. And God saw that it was good. ^{13}And there was evening, and there was morning—the third day. ^{14}And God said, "Let there be lights in the vault of the sky to separate the day from the night, and let them serve as signs to mark seasons and days and years, ^{15}and let them be lights in the vault of the sky to give light on the earth." And it was so. ^{16}God made two great lights—the greater light to govern the day and the lesser light to govern the night. He also made the stars. ^{17}God set them in the vault of the sky to give light on the earth, ^{18}to govern the day and the night, and to separate light from darkness. And God saw that it was good. ^{19}And there was evening, and there was morning—the fourth day. ^{20}And God said, "Let the water teem with living creatures, and let birds fly above the earth across the vault of the sky." ^{21}So God created the great creatures of the sea and every living and moving thing with which the water teems, according to their kinds, and every winged bird according to its kind. And God saw that it was good. ^{22}God blessed them and said, "Be fruitful and increase in number and fill the water in the seas, and let the birds increase on the earth." ^{23}And there was evening, and there was morning—the fifth day. ^{24}And God said, "Let the land produce living creatures according to their kinds: livestock, creatures that move along the ground, and wild animals, each according to its kind." And it was so. ^{25}God made the wild animals according to their kinds, the livestock according to their kinds, and all the creatures that move along the ground according to their kinds. And God saw that it was good. ^{26}Then God said, "Let us make human beings in our image, in our likeness, so that they may rule over the fish in the sea and the birds in the sky, over the livestock and all the wild animals, and over all the creatures that move along the ground." ^{27}So God created human beings in his own image, in the image of God he created them; male and female he created them. ^{28}God blessed them and said to them, "Be fruitful and increase in number; fill the earth and subdue it. Rule over the fish in the sea and the birds in the sky and over every living creature that moves on the ground." ^{29}Then God said, "I give you every seed-bearing plant on the face of the whole earth and every tree that has fruit with seed in it. They will be yours for food. ^{30}And to all the beasts of the earth and all the birds in the sky and all the creatures that move on the ground - everything that has the breath of life in it - I give every green plant for food." And it was so. ^{31}God saw all that he had made, and it was very good. And there was evening, and there was morning - the sixth day.

Bible Reference: Genesis 2:1-4 ^{1}Thus the heavens and the earth were completed in all their vast array. ^{2}By the seventh day God had finished the work he had been doing; so on the seventh day he rested from all his work. ^{3}Then God blessed the seventh day and made it holy, because on it he rested from all the work of creating that he had done. ^{4}This is the account of the heavens and the earth when they were created, when the LORD God made the earth and the heavens.

The Birth of Jesus

The story of the birth of <u>Jesus</u> is perhaps the best known of the <u>gospel</u> stories because of its celebration at <u>Christmas</u>. The story is told in different forms in the gospels of <u>Matthew</u> and <u>Luke</u>. In Matthew's account, the events are seen through the eyes of <u>Joseph</u>, a man who is horrified to discover that <u>Mary</u>, to whom he is engaged, is pregnant before their marriage. In a <u>dream</u>, Joseph is assured that this is <u>God</u>'s doing and that he should marry her at once. He does so, but does not sleep with her. After Jesus is born in Joseph's ancestral town of <u>Bethlehem</u>, the family flees from the fury of <u>King Herod</u>, who has had news of the birth of another "king" from some <u>wise men</u> from the east. These <u>magi</u> have followed a <u>star</u> seeking out Jesus, to present him with gifts of <u>gold</u>,

frankincense and myrrh. Luke tells Mary's side of the story. It is announced to Mary by an angel named Gabriel that she is to become pregnant by the power of God's Holy Spirit, even though she is a virgin. She assents to this. Later, she and Joseph travel to Bethlehem for a Roman census and the baby is born in the squalor of a stable. But this is an event of "great joy" proclaimed by angels to lowly shepherds, who immediately leave their sheep to pay the baby homage. Jesus is no ordinary baby, but God's son who will bring salvation to the world. This story is called the incarnation because God involved himself directly in the messiness of human life by becoming a human being in the person of Jesus.

Bible Reference: Matthew 1:18-2:12 ¹⁸This is how the birth of Jesus the Messiah came about: his mother Mary was pledged to be married to Joseph, but before they came together, she was found to be pregnant through the Holy Spirit. ¹⁹Because Joseph her husband was a righteous man and did not want to expose her to public disgrace, he had in mind to divorce her quietly. ²⁰But after he had considered this, an angel of the Lord appeared to him in a dream and said, "Joseph son of David, do not be afraid to take Mary home as your wife, because what is conceived in her is from the Holy Spirit. ²¹She will give birth to a son, and you are to give him the name Jesus, because he will save his people from their sins." ²²All this took place to fulfil what the Lord had said through the prophet: ²³ "The virgin will conceive and give birth to a son, and they will call him Immanuel" (which means "God with us"). ²⁴When Joseph woke up, he did what the angel of the Lord had commanded him and took Mary home as his wife. ²⁵But he had no union with her until she gave birth to a son. And he gave him the name Jesus. ¹After Jesus was born in Bethlehem in Judea, during the time of King Herod, Magi from the east came to Jerusalem ²and asked, "Where is the one who has been born king of the Jews? We saw his star when it rose and have come to worship him." ³When King Herod heard this he was disturbed, and all Jerusalem with him. ⁴When he had called together all the people's chief priests and teachers of the law, he asked them where the Messiah was to be born. ⁵"In Bethlehem in Judea," they replied, "for this is what the prophet has written: ⁶" "But you, Bethlehem, in the land of Judah, are by no means least among the rulers of Judah; for out of you will come a ruler who will shepherd my people Israel." ⁷Then Herod called the Magi secretly and found out from them the exact time the star had appeared. ⁸He sent them to Bethlehem and said, "Go and make a careful search for the child. As soon as you find him, report to me, so that I too may go and worship him." ⁹After they had heard the king, they went on their way, and the star they had seen when it rose went ahead of them until it stopped over the place where the child was. ¹⁰When they saw the star, they were overjoyed. ¹¹On coming to the house, they saw the child with his mother Mary, and they bowed down and worshipped him. Then they opened their treasures and presented him with gifts of gold, frankincense and myrrh. ¹²And having been warned in a dream not to go back to Herod, they returned to their country by another route.

Bible Reference: Luke 2:1-20 ¹In those days Caesar Augustus issued a decree that a census should be taken of the entire Roman world. ²(This was the first census that took place while Quirinius was governor of Syria.) ³And everyone went to their own town to register. ⁴So Joseph also went up from the town of Nazareth in Galilee to Judea, to Bethlehem the town of David, because he belonged to the house and line of David. ⁵He went there to register with Mary, who was pledged to be married to him and was expecting a child. ⁶While they were there, the time came for the baby to be born, ⁷and she gave birth to her firstborn, a son. She wrapped him in cloths and placed him in a manger, because there was no guest room available for them. ⁸And there were shepherds living out in the fields near by, keeping watch over their flocks at night. ⁹An angel of the Lord appeared to them, and the glory of the Lord shone around them, and they were terrified. ¹⁰But the angel said to them, "Do not be afraid. I bring you good news of great joy that will be for all the people. ¹¹Today in the town of David a Saviour has been born to you; he is the Messiah, the Lord. ¹²This will be a sign to you: you will find a baby wrapped in cloths and lying in a manger." ¹³Suddenly a great company of the heavenly host appeared with the angel, praising God and saying, ¹⁴ "Glory to God in the highest heaven, and on earth peace to those on whom his favour rests." ¹⁵When the angels had left them and gone into heaven, the shepherds said to one another, "Let's go to Bethlehem and see this thing that has happened, which the Lord has told us about." ¹⁶So they hurried off and found Mary and Joseph, and the baby, who was lying in the manger. ¹⁷When they had seen him, they spread the word concerning what had been told them about this child, ¹⁸and all who heard it were amazed at what the shepherds said to them. ¹⁹But Mary treasured up all these things and pondered them in her heart. ²⁰The shepherds returned, glorifying and praising God for all the things they had heard and seen, which were just as they had been told.

Moses and the Burning Bush

Bible Reference: Exodus 3: 1-22 ¹ Now Moses was tending the flock of Jethro his father-in-law, the priest of Midian, and he led the flock to the far side of the desert and came to Horeb, the mountain of God. ² There the angel of the LORD appeared to him in flames of fire from within a bush. Moses saw that though the bush was on fire it did not burn up. ³ So Moses thought, "I will go over and see this strange sight—why the bush does not burn up."

⁴ When the LORD saw that he had gone over to look, God called to him from within the bush, "Moses! Moses!"

And Moses said, "Here I am."

⁵ "Do not come any closer," God said. "Take off your sandals, for the place where you are standing is holy ground." ⁶ Then he said, "I am the God of your father, the God of Abraham, the God of Isaac and the God of Jacob." At this, Moses hid his face, because he was afraid to look at God.

⁷ The LORD said, "I have indeed seen the misery of my people in Egypt. I have heard them crying out because of their slave drivers, and I am concerned about their suffering. ⁸ So I have come down to rescue them from the hand of the Egyptians and to bring them up out of that land into a good and spacious land, a land flowing with milk and honey—the home of the Canaanites, Hittites, Amorites, Perizzites, Hivites and Jebusites. ⁹ And now the cry of the Israelites has reached me, and I have seen the way the Egyptians are oppressing them. ¹⁰ So now, go. I am sending you to Pharaoh to bring my people the Israelites out of Egypt."

¹¹ But Moses said to God, "Who am I, that I should go to Pharaoh and bring the Israelites out of Egypt?"

¹² And God said, "I will be with you. And this will be the sign to you that it is I who have sent you: When you have brought the people out of Egypt, you will worship God on this mountain."

¹³ Moses said to God, "Suppose I go to the Israelites and say to them, 'The God of your fathers has sent me to you,' and they ask me, 'What is his name?' Then what shall I tell them?"

¹⁴ God said to Moses, "I am who I am. This is what you are to say to the Israelites: 'I am has sent me to you.'"

¹⁵ God also said to Moses, "Say to the Israelites, 'The LORD, the God of your fathers—the God of Abraham, the God of Isaac and the God of Jacob—has sent me to you.'" This is my name forever, the name by which I am to be remembered from generation to generation.

¹⁶ "Go, assemble the elders of Israel and say to them, 'The LORD, the God of your fathers—the God of Abraham, Isaac and Jacob—appeared to me and said: I have watched over you and have seen what has been done to you in Egypt. ¹⁷ And I have promised to bring you up out of your misery in Egypt into the land of the Canaanites, Hittites, Amorites, Perizzites, Hivites and Jebusites—a land flowing with milk and honey.'"

¹⁸ "The elders of Israel will listen to you. Then you and the elders are to go to the king of Egypt and say to him, "The LORD, the God of the Hebrews, has met with us. Let us take a three-day journey into the desert to offer sacrifices to the LORD our God." ¹⁹ But I know that the king of Egypt will not let you go unless a mighty hand compels him. ²⁰ So I will stretch out my hand and strike the Egyptians with all the wonders that I will perform among them. After that, he will let you go.

²¹ "And I will make the Egyptians favorably disposed toward this people, so that when you leave you will not go empty-handed. ²² Every woman is to ask her neighbor and any woman living in her house for articles of silver and gold and for clothing, which you will put on your sons and daughters. And so you will plunder the Egyptians."

The Coming of the Holy Spirit

After the Ascension, the disciples stayed in Jerusalem, as Jesus had told them to do. Mary, Jesus' mother, his brothers and the other women who had travelled with them joined the disciples each day in prayer as they waited for Jesus' promise to them to be fulfilled.

Suddenly one day, when they were all together, there was a loud noise in the room, like a strong wind rushing down from the sky. They all saw what seemed to be flames which came to rest on each of them. Immediately, the Holy Spirit made them all able to speak in languages they had never learned.

At the time, there were Jews in Jerusalem from all over the world, for the Feast of Pentecost. These people were amazed to hear the disciples and the others with them praising God in their own languages!

Later, after Peter had explained to the crowd what this event meant, many became followers of Jesus.

Bible Reference: Acts 2: 1-12 ¹When the day of Pentecost came, they were all together in one place. ²Suddenly a sound like the blowing of a violent wind came from heaven and filled the whole house where they were sitting. ³They saw what seemed to be tongues of fire that separated and came to rest on each of them. ⁴All of them were filled with the Holy Spirit and began to speak in other tongues as the Spirit enabled them. ⁵Now there were staying in Jerusalem God-fearing Jews from every nation under heaven. ⁶When they heard this sound, a crowd came together in bewilderment, because each one heard their own language being spoken. ⁷Utterly amazed, they asked: "Aren't all these who are speaking Galileans? ⁸Then how is it that each of us hears them in our native language? ⁹Parthians, Medes and Elamites; residents of Mesopotamia, Judea and Cappadocia, Pontus and Asia, ¹⁰Phrygia and Pamphylia, Egypt and the parts of Libya near Cyrene; visitors from Rome ¹¹(both Jews and converts to Judaism); Cretans and Arabs - we hear them declaring the wonders of God in our own tongues!" ¹²Amazed and perplexed, they asked one another, "What does this mean?"

The Death and Resurrection of Jesus

Jesus "death on the Cross and resurrection on the third day form the climax of the gospel story. All four gospels devote several chapters to the arrest, trial, crucifixion and resurrection of Jesus. These events are seen as taking place in both the human and divine spheres. Jesus is caught up in the machinations of Jewish and imperial politics and at the same time he believed to be the Son of God who dies for the sins of the world. Paul later summarises the meaning of these events like this: "God was in Christ reconciling the world to himself". The gospels all report that Jesus' tomb was found empty on the first Easter Sunday and describe subsequent appearances to his disciples and others in a form which was both tangible yet other-worldly. The resurrection is seen as God's vindication of Jesus and the triumph of life over death.

Bible Reference: Luke 23:23-46 ²³But with loud shouts they insistently demanded that he be crucified, and their shouts prevailed. ²⁴So Pilate decided to grant their demand. ²⁵He released the man who had been thrown into prison for insurrection and murder, the one they asked for, and surrendered Jesus to their will. ²⁶As the soldiers led him away, they seized Simon from Cyrene, who was on his way in from the country, and put the cross on him and made him carry it behind Jesus. ²⁷A large number of people followed him, including women who mourned and wailed for him. ²⁸Jesus turned and said to them, "Daughters of Jerusalem, do not weep for me; weep for yourselves and for your children. ²⁹For the time will come when you will say, "Blessed are the childless women, the wombs that never bore and the breasts that never nursed!" ³⁰Then "they will say to the mountains," "Fall on us!" and to the hills "Cover us!" ³¹ "For if people do these things when the tree is green, what will happen when it is dry?" ³²Two other men, both criminals, were also led out with him to be executed. ³³When they came to the place called the Skull, they crucified him there, along with the criminals—one on his right, the other on his left. ³⁴Jesus said, "Father, forgive them, for they do not know what they are doing." And they divided up his clothes by casting lots. ³⁵The people stood watching, and the rulers even sneered at him. They said, "He saved others; let him save himself if he is God's Messiah, the Chosen One." ³⁶The soldiers also came up and mocked him. They offered him wine vinegar ³⁷and said, "If you are the king of the Jews, save yourself." ³⁸There was a written notice above him, which read: THIS IS THE KING OF THE JEWS. ³⁹One of the criminals who hung there hurled insults at him: "Aren't you the Messiah? Save yourself and us!" ⁴⁰But the other criminal rebuked him. "Don't you fear God," he said, "since you are under the same sentence? ⁴¹We are punished justly, for we are getting what our deeds deserve. But this man has done nothing wrong." ⁴²Then he said, "Jesus, remember me when you come into your kingdom." ⁴³Jesus answered him, "Truly I tell you, today you will be with me in paradise." ⁴⁴It was now about noon, and darkness came over the whole land until three in the afternoon, ⁴⁵for the sun stopped shining. And the curtain of the temple was torn in two. ⁴⁶Jesus called out with a loud voice, "Father, into your hands I commit my spirit." When he had said this, he breathed his last.

Bible Reference: John 20:1-18 ¹Early on the first day of the week, while it was still dark, Mary Magdalene went to the tomb and saw that the stone had been removed from the entrance. ²So she came running to Simon Peter and the other disciple, the one Jesus loved, and said, "They have taken the Lord out of the tomb, and we don't know where they have put him!" ³So Peter and the other disciple started for the tomb. ⁴Both were running, but the other disciple outran Peter and reached the tomb first. ⁵He bent over and looked in at the strips of linen lying there but did not go in. ⁶Then Simon Peter came along behind him and went straight into the tomb. He saw the strips of linen lying there, ⁷as well as the cloth that had been wrapped round Jesus' head. The cloth was still lying in its place, separate from the linen. ⁸Finally the other disciple, who had reached the tomb first, also went inside. He saw and believed. ⁹(They still did not understand from Scripture that Jesus had to rise from the dead.) ¹⁰Then the disciples went back to where they were staying. ¹¹Now Mary stood outside the tomb crying. As she wept, she bent over to look into the tomb ¹²and saw two angels in white, seated where Jesus' body had been, one at the head and the other at the foot. ¹³They asked her, "Woman, why are you crying?" "They have taken my Lord away," she said, "and I don't know where they have put him." ¹⁴At this, she turned round and saw Jesus standing there, but she did not realize that it was Jesus. ¹⁵He asked her, "Woman, why are you crying? Who is it you are looking for?" Thinking he was the gardener, she said, "Sir, if you have carried him away, tell me where you have put him, and I will get him." ¹⁶Jesus said to her, "Mary." She turned towards him and cried out in Aramaic, "Rabboni!" (which means "Teacher"). ¹⁷Jesus said, "Do not hold on to me, for I have not yet ascended to the Father. Go instead to my brothers and tell them, 'I am ascending to my Father and your Father, to my God and your God.'" ¹⁸Mary Magdalene went to the disciples with the news: "I have seen the Lord!" And she told them that he had said these things to her.

The First Passover

God sent Moses the Israelite to the Egyptian Pharaoh to warn him about the last plague. In it, every first-born son of Egyptian families would die. God predicted that the Egyptians would be so glad to see the Israelites leave that they would send them away with riches. But Pharaoh refused to give in.

So God told Moses how his people (the Israelites) were to prepare for the plague. Each family was to get dressed ready for a journey, then eat a meal of lamb, with bitter herbs and unleavened bread. They were to daub blood from the lamb onto the doorposts of their homes. When the angel bringing death to the Egyptians came, he would pass over these houses, sparing the sons within. This was the first Passover for the Israelites.

During that night, every first-born son of the Egyptians died, but the Israelites were safe. (Each year, God said, they were to commemorate this event, eating unleavened bread to recall that they had no time to allow the bread to rise before they set off See Big Ideas: Passover). There was great mourning throughout the land and the Egyptians begged the Israelites to leave quickly. Moses led them out, towards the Red Sea. God guided them by a pillar of cloud during the day and by a pillar of fire at night. The Israelites were leaving after 430 years in Egypt. However, then Pharaoh changed his mind again.

Bible Reference: Exodus 11:1-10 ¹Now the LORD said to Moses, "I will bring one more plague on Pharaoh and on Egypt. After that, he will let you go from here, and when he does, he will drive you out completely. ²Tell the people that men and women alike are to ask their neighbours for articles of silver and gold." ³(The LORD made the Egyptians favourably disposed towards the people, and Moses himself was highly regarded in Egypt by Pharaoh's officials and by the people.) ⁴So Moses said, "This is what the LORD says: 'About midnight I will go throughout Egypt. ⁵Every firstborn son in Egypt will die, from the firstborn son of Pharaoh, who sits on the throne, to the firstborn son of the female slave, who is at her hand mill, and all the firstborn of the cattle as well. ⁶There will be loud wailing throughout Egypt—worse than there has ever been or ever will be again. ⁷But among the Israelites not a dog will bark at any person or animal.'" Then you will know that the LORD makes a distinction between Egypt and Israel. ⁸All these officials of yours will come to me, bowing down before me and saying, 'Go, you and all the people who follow you!' After that I will leave." Then Moses, hot with anger, left Pharaoh. ⁹The LORD had said to Moses, "Pharaoh will refuse to listen to you—so that my wonders may be multiplied in Egypt." ¹⁰Moses and Aaron performed all these wonders before Pharaoh, but the LORD hardened Pharaoh's heart, and he would not let the Israelites go out of his country.

Bible Reference:Exodus 12:1-51 ¹The LORD said to Moses and Aaron in Egypt, ² "This month is to be for you the first month, the first month of your year. ³Tell the whole commUnity of Israel that on the tenth day of this month each man is to take a lamb for his family, one for each household. ⁴If any household is too small for a whole lamb, they must share one with their nearest neighbour, having taken into account the number of people there are. You are to determine the amount of lamb needed in accordance with what each person will eat. ⁵The animals you choose must be year-old males without defect, and you may take them from the sheep or the goats. ⁶Take care of them until the fourteenth day of the month, when all the members of the commUnity of Israel must slaughter them at twilight. ⁷Then they are to take some of the blood and put it on the sides and tops of the door-frames of the houses where they eat the lambs. ⁸That same night they are to eat the meat roasted over the fire, along with bitter herbs, and bread made without yeast. ⁹Do not eat the meat raw or boiled in water, but roast it over a fire—with the head, legs and internal organs. ¹⁰Do not leave any of it till morning; if some is left till morning, you must burn it. ¹¹This is how you are to eat it: with your cloak tucked into your belt, your sandals on your feet and your staff in your hand. Eat it in haste; it is the LORD's Passover. ¹² "On that same night I will pass through Egypt and strike down every firstborn of both people and animals, and I will bring judgment on all the gods of Egypt. I am the LORD. ¹³The blood will be a sign for you on the houses where you are, and when I see the blood, I will pass over you. No destructive plague will touch you when I strike Egypt." ¹⁴This is a day you are to commemorate; for the generations to come you shall celebrate it as a festival to the LORD—a lasting ordinance. ¹⁵For seven days you are to eat bread made without yeast. On the first day remove the yeast from your houses, for whoever eats anything with yeast in it from the first day until the seventh must be cut off from Israel. ¹⁶On the first day hold a sacred assembly, and another one on the seventh day. Do no work at all on these days, except to prepare food for everyone to eat; that is all you may do. ¹⁷ "Celebrate the Festival of Unleavened Bread, because it was on this very day that I brought your divisions out of Egypt. Celebrate this day as a lasting ordinance for the generations to come. ¹⁸In the first month you are to eat bread made without yeast, from the evening of the fourteenth day until the evening of the twenty-first day. ¹⁹For seven days no yeast is to be found in your houses. And anyone, whether foreigner or native-born, who eats anything with yeast in it must be cut off from the commUnity of Israel. ²⁰Eat nothing made with yeast. Wherever you live, you must eat unleavened bread." ²¹Then Moses summoned all the elders of Israel and said to them, "Go at once and select the animals for your families and slaughter the Passover lamb. ²²Take a bunch of hyssop, dip it into the blood in the basin and put some of the blood on the top and on both sides of the door-frame. None of you shall go out of the door of your house until morning. ²³When the LORD goes through the land to strike down the Egyptians, he will see the blood on the top and sides of the door-frame and will pass over that doorway, and he will not permit the destroyer to enter your houses and strike you down." ²⁴Obey these instructions as a lasting ordinance for you and your descendants. ²⁵When you enter the land that the LORD will give you as he promised, observe this ceremony. ²⁶And when your children ask you, "What does this ceremony mean to you?" ²⁷then tell them, "It is the Passover sacrifice to the LORD, who passed over the houses of the Israelites in Egypt and spared our homes when he struck down the Egyptians." Then the people bowed down and worshipped. ²⁸The Israelites did just what the LORD commanded Moses and Aaron. ²⁹At midnight the LORD struck down all the firstborn in Egypt, from the firstborn of Pharaoh, who sat on the throne, to the firstborn of the prisoner, who was in the dungeon, and firstborn of all the livestock as well. ³⁰Pharaoh and all his officials and all the Egyptians got up during the night, and there was loud wailing in Egypt, for there was not a house without someone dead. ³¹During the night Pharaoh summoned Moses and Aaron and said, "Up! Leave my people, you and the Israelites! Go, worship the LORD as you have requested. ³²Take your flocks and herds, as you have said, and go. And also bless me." ³³The Egyptians urged the people to hurry and leave the country. "For otherwise," they said, "we will all die!" ³⁴So the people took their dough before the yeast was added, and carried it on their shoulders in kneading troughs wrapped in clothing. ³⁵The Israelites did as Moses instructed and asked the Egyptians for articles of silver and gold and for clothing. ³⁶The LORD had made the Egyptians favourably disposed towards the people, and they gave them what they asked for; so they plundered the Egyptians. ³⁷The Israelites journeyed from Rameses to Sukkoth. There were about six hundred thousand men on foot, besides women and children. ³⁸Many other people went up with them, and also large droves of livestock, both flocks and herds. ³⁹With the dough the Israelites had brought from Egypt, they baked loaves of unleavened bread. The dough was without yeast because they had been driven out of Egypt and did not have time to prepare food for themselves. ⁴⁰Now the length of time the Israelite people lived in Egypt was 430 years. ⁴¹At the end of the 430 years, to the very day, all the LORD's divisions left Egypt. ⁴²Because the LORD kept vigil that night to bring them out of Egypt, on this night all the Israelites are to keep vigil to honour the LORD for the generations to come. ⁴³The LORD said to Moses and Aaron, "These are the regulations for the Passover: 'No foreigner is to eat of it. ⁴⁴Any slave you have bought may eat of it after you have circumcised him, ⁴⁵but a temporary resident or a hired worker may not eat of it.'" ⁴⁶It must be eaten inside one house; take none of the meat outside the house. Do not break any of the bones. ⁴⁷The whole commUnity of Israel must celebrate it. ⁴⁸"A foreigner residing among you who wants to celebrate the LORD's Passover must have all the males in his household circumcised; then he may take part like one born in the land. No uncircumcised male may eat of it. ⁴⁹The same law applies both to the native-born and to the foreigner residing among you." ⁵⁰All the Israelites did just what the LORD had commanded Moses and Aaron. ⁵¹And on that very day the LORD brought the Israelites out of Egypt by their divisions.

Bible Reference: Exodus 13:1-22 ¹The LORD said to Moses, ² "Consecrate to me every firstborn male. The first offspring of every womb among the Israelites belongs to me, whether human or animal." ³Then Moses said to the people, "Commemorate this day, the day you came out of Egypt, out of the land of slavery, because the LORD brought you out of it with a mighty hand. Eat nothing containing yeast. ⁴Today, in the month of Aviv, you are leaving. ⁵When the LORD brings you into the land of the Canaanites, Hittites, Amorites, Hivites and Jebusites—the land he swore to your ancestors to give you, a land flowing with milk and honey—you are to observe this ceremony in this month: ⁶for seven days eat bread made without yeast and on the seventh day hold a festival to the LORD. ⁷Eat unleavened bread during those seven days; nothing with yeast in it is to be seen among you, nor shall any yeast be seen anywhere within your borders. ⁸On that day tell your children, 'I do this because of what the LORD did for me when I came out of Egypt.' ⁹This observance will be for you like a sign on your hand and a reminder on your forehead that this law of the LORD is to be on your lips. For the LORD brought you out of Egypt with his mighty hand. ¹⁰You must keep this ordinance at the appointed time year after year. ¹¹"After the LORD brings you into the land of the Canaanites and gives it to you, as he promised on oath to you and your ancestors, ¹²you are to give over to the LORD the first offspring of every womb. All the firstborn males of your livestock belong to the LORD. ¹³Redeem with a lamb every firstborn donkey, but if you do not redeem it, break its neck. Redeem every firstborn among your sons. ¹⁴ "In days to come when your children ask you, "What does this mean?" say to them, "With a mighty hand the LORD brought us out of Egypt, out of the land of slavery. ¹⁵When Pharaoh stubbornly refused to let us go, the LORD killed the firstborn of both people and animals in Egypt. This is why I sacrifice to the LORD the first male offspring of every womb and redeem each of my firstborn sons. ¹⁶And it will be like a sign on your hand and a symbol on your forehead that the LORD brought us out of Egypt with his mighty hand." ¹⁷When Pharaoh let the people go, God did not lead them on the road through the Philistine country, though that was shorter. For God said, "If they face war, they might change their minds and return to Egypt." ¹⁸So God led the people around by the desert road towards the Red Sea. The Israelites went up out of Egypt ready for battle. ¹⁹Moses took the bones of Joseph with him because Joseph had made the Israelites swear an oath. He had said, "God will surely come to your aid, and then you must carry my bones up with you from this place." ²⁰After leaving Sukkoth they camped at Etham on the edge of the desert. ²¹By day the LORD went ahead of them in a pillar of cloud to guide them on their way and by night in a pillar of fire to give them light, so that they could travel by day or night. ²²Neither the pillar of cloud by day nor the pillar of fire by night left its place in front of the people.

The Good Samaritan

This story, found only in Luke's gospel, was told by Jesus in response to a question posed by a lawyer:

"who is my neighbour?" The lawyer, no doubt expecting to be told that he should be neighbourly towards his fellow <u>Jews</u> would not have found this story at all comfortable. A man attacked by bandits and left for dead on the road to Jericho is ignored by a passing <u>priest</u>, then by a Levite, both of whom would have feared <u>ritual</u> <u>uncleanness</u>. Instead, the one who comes to his aid is a <u>Samaritan</u>, whom the other two would have despised. A sense of outrage is implied that such a figure could be held up by Jesus as a model of neighbourliness to a <u>pious</u> <u>Jew</u>. The point of the story was Jesus' challenging of such artificial barriers.

Bible Reference: <u>Luke 10:25-37</u> ²⁵On one occasion an expert in the law stood up to test Jesus. "Teacher," he asked, "what must I do to inherit eternal life?" ²⁶ "What is written in the Law?" he replied. "How do you read it?" ²⁷He answered, "Love the Lord your God with all your heart and with all your soul and with all your strength and with all your mind"; and, "Love your neighbour as yourself." ²⁸ "You have answered correctly," Jesus replied. "Do this and you will live." ²⁹But he wanted to justify himself, so he asked Jesus, "And who is my neighbour?" ³⁰In reply Jesus said: "A man was going down from Jerusalem to Jericho, when he fell into the hands of robbers. They stripped him of his clothes, beat him and went away, leaving him half-dead. ³¹A priest happened to be going down the same road, and when he saw the man, he passed by on the other side. ³²So too, a Levite, when he came to the place and saw him, passed by on the other side. ³³But a Samaritan, as he travelled, came where the man was; and when he saw him, he took pity on him. ³⁴He went to him and bandaged his wounds, pouring on oil and wine. Then he put the man on his own donkey, brought him to an inn and took care of him. ³⁵The next day he took out two denarii and gave them to the innkeeper. "Look after him," he said, "and when I return, I will reimburse you for any extra expense you may have." ³⁶ "Which of these three do you think was a neighbour to the man who fell into the hands of robbers?" ³⁷The expert in the law replied, "The one who had mercy on him." Jesus told him, "Go and do likewise."

The Good Shepherd

Jesus said, "I am the good shepherd. A good shepherd is willing to die for his sheep because he loves them so much. Someone who is paid to look after the sheep will not be willing to face danger for them. If such a person sees a wolf coming, he will leave the sheep to their fate and save himself. What are the sheep to him? He is just paid to look after them. He does not love and cherish them."

"I am the good shepherd. I know all of my sheep and each one of them knows me. In the same way, my Father knows me and I know him. I lay down my life for the sheep—willingly and knowingly."

Bible Reference: <u>John 10:11-15</u> ¹¹ "I am the good shepherd. The good shepherd lays down his life for the sheep. ¹²The hired hand is not the shepherd and does not own the sheep. So when he sees the wolf coming, he abandons the sheep and runs away. Then the wolf attacks the flock and scatters it. ¹³The man runs away because he is a hired hand and cares nothing for the sheep." ¹⁴I am the good shepherd; I know my sheep and my sheep know me—¹⁵just as the Father knows me and I know the Father - and I lay down my life for the sheep.

The Last Supper

Bible Reference: <u>Luke 22: 7-38</u> ⁷Then came the day of Unleavened Bread on which the Passover lamb had to be sacrificed. ⁸Jesus sent Peter and John, saying, "Go and make preparations for us to eat the Passover."

⁹ "Where do you want us to prepare for it?" they asked.

¹⁰He replied, "As you enter the city, a man carrying a jar of water will meet you. Follow him to the house that he enters, ¹¹and say to the owner of the house, 'The Teacher asks: Where is the guest room, where I may eat the Passover with my disciples?' ¹²He will show you a large upper room, all furnished. Make preparations there."

¹³They left and found things just as Jesus had told them. So they prepared the Passover.

¹⁴When the hour came, Jesus and his apostles reclined at the table. ¹⁵And he said to them, "I have eagerly desired to eat this Passover with you before I suffer. ¹⁶For I tell you, I will not eat it again until it finds fulfillment in the kingdom of God."

[17] After taking the cup, he gave thanks and said, "Take this and divide it among you. [18] For I tell you I will not drink again of the fruit of the vine until the kingdom of God comes."

[19] And he took bread, gave thanks and broke it, and gave it to them, saying, "This is my body given for you; do this in remembrance of me."

[20] In the same way, after the supper he took the cup, saying, "This cup is the new covenant in my blood, which is poured out for you. [21] But the hand of him who is going to betray me is with mine on the table. [22] The Son of Man will go as it has been decreed, but woe to that man who betrays him." [23] They began to question among themselves which of them it might be who would do this.

[24] Also a dispute arose among them as to which of them was considered to be greatest. [25] Jesus said to them, "The kings of the Gentiles lord it over them; and those who exercise authority over them call themselves Benefactors. [26] But you are not to be like that. Instead, the greatest among you should be like the youngest, and the one who rules like the one who serves. [27] For who is greater, the one who is at the table or the one who serves? Is it not the one who is at the table? But I am among you as one who serves. [28] You are those who have stood by me in my trials. [29] And I confer on you a kingdom, just as my Father conferred one on me, [30] so that you may eat and drink at my table in my kingdom and sit on thrones, judging the twelve tribes of Israel."

[31] "Simon, Simon, Satan has asked to sift you as wheat. [32] But I have prayed for you, Simon, that your faith may not fail. And when you have turned back, strengthen your brothers."

[33] But he replied, "Lord, I am ready to go with you to prison and to death."

[34] Jesus answered, "I tell you, Peter, before the rooster crows today, you will deny three times that you know me."

[35] Then Jesus asked them, "When I sent you without purse, bag or sandals, did you lack anything?"

"Nothing," they answered.

[36] He said to them, "But now if you have a purse, take it, and also a bag; and if you don't have a sword, sell your cloak and buy one. [37] It is written: 'And he was numbered with the transgressors'; and I tell you that this must be fulfilled in me. Yes, what is written about me is reaching its fulfillment."

[38] The disciples said, "See, Lord, here are two swords."

"That is enough," he replied.

The Lost Sheep and the Lost Coin

The Pharisees and the teachers of the Law were annoyed when they saw tax-collectors and other people of whom they disapproved listening to Jesus' teaching.

"This man welcomes sinners and even eats with them!" they muttered to each other.

Jesus heard them and told them these parables.

"Imagine that a man has one hundred sheep. If one goes missing, he doesn't just forget about it, does he? No, that one sheep is too valuable to him. He leaves the others and searches the hills and valleys until he finds the missing sheep. Then he picks it up and carries it home on his shoulders. He is so pleased, in fact, that he invites all his friends to join him in a party to celebrate with him."

"I tell you," Jesus told them, "there is more rejoicing in heaven when one sinner says sorry and becomes God's follower than over ninety-nine right-living people who do not need to say sorry."

Then he said, "What if a woman loses one of her ten precious silver coins? You know what she does—she searches carefully in every possible place until she finds it. Then, when she does find it, she asks her friends to help her celebrate because she is so pleased. In the same way," Jesus said, "the angels rejoice greatly over each sinner who says sorry."

Bible Reference: Luke 15:1-10 [1] Now the tax collectors and sinners were all gathering round to hear Jesus. [2] But the Pharisees and the teachers of the law muttered, "This man welcomes sinners, and eats with them." [3] Then Jesus told them this parable: [4] "Suppose one of you has a hundred sheep and loses one of them. Doesn't he leave the ninety-nine in the open country and go after the lost sheep until he finds it? [5] And when he finds it, he joyfully puts it on his shoulders [6] and goes home. Then he calls his friends and neighbours together and says, 'Rejoice with me; I have found my lost sheep.'" ⁷I tell you that in the same way there will be more rejoicing in heaven over one sinner who repents than over ninety-nine righteous people who do not need to repent. ⁸ "Or suppose a woman has ten silver coins and loses one. Doesn't she light a lamp, sweep the house and search carefully until she finds it? ⁹And when she finds it, she calls her friends and neighbours together and says, 'Rejoice with me; I have found my lost coin.'" ¹⁰In the same way, I tell you, there is rejoicing in the presence of the angels of God over one sinner who repents."

The Parable of the Talents

Jesus said, "The kingdom of God is like this. A man was going on a long journey. He shared out his wealth among his three servants, according to their ability. He gave one five talents of money (an amount worth several hundred pounds), one two talents and just one talent to the third. The first two servants each doubled their money through care and work. The third servant, however, just hid his talent in the ground."

"When their master came back, the first two servants eagerly showed him what they had achieved. Their master congratulated them and told them that he would entrust them with even more as they had been faithful and careful with just a little of his wealth."

"Then the third servant came. He explained that, as he knew how hard and strict his master was, he had been afraid of losing the talent with which he had been entrusted, so he had buried it. His master was furious."

"You are a lazy and wicked servant!" he shouted.

Then he ordered his men to take the one talent from him and to give it to the man who now had ten.

"Whoever has much will be given more. But he who has nothing will have even what he has taken away from him."

Then he told them to throw the third servant out of the master's house.

Bible Reference: Matthew 25:14-30 ¹⁴ "Again, it will be like a man going on a journey, who called his servants and entrusted his wealth to them. ¹⁵To one he gave five bags of gold, to another two bags, and to another one bag, each according to his ability. Then he went on his journey. ¹⁶The man who had received five bags of gold went at once and put his money to work and gained five bags more. ¹⁷So also, the one with two bags of gold gained two more. ¹⁸But the man who had received one bag went off, dug a hole in the ground and hid his master's money. ¹⁹After a long time the master of those servants returned and settled accounts with them. ²⁰The man who had received five bags of gold brought the other five. "Master," he said, "you entrusted me with five bags of gold. See, I have gained five more." ²¹His master replied, "Well done, good and faithful servant! You have been faithful with a few things; I will put you in charge of many things. Come and share your master's happiness!" ²²The man with two bags of gold also came. "Master," he said, "you entrusted me with two bags of gold: see, I have gained two more." ²³His master replied, "Well done, good and faithful servant! You have been faithful with a few things; I will put you in charge of many things. Come and share your master's happiness!" ²⁴Then the man who had received one bag of gold came. "Master," he said, "I knew that you are a hard man, harvesting where you have not sown and gathering where you have not scattered seed. ²⁵So I was afraid and went out and hid your gold in the ground. See, here is what belongs to you." ²⁶His master replied, "You wicked, lazy servant! So you knew that I harvest where I have not sown and gather where I have not scattered seed? ²⁷Well then, you should have put my money on deposit with the bankers, so that when I returned I would have received it back with interest." ²⁸ "Take the bag of gold from him and give it to the one who has ten bags. ²⁹For those who have will be given more, and they will have an abundance. As for those who do not have, even what they have will be taken from them. ³⁰And throw that worthless servant outside, into the darkness, where there will be weeping and gnashing of teeth."

The Plagues

Moses returned to Egypt and asked Pharaoh to let the Israelites go into the desert to worship God. But Pharaoh refused. To keep the slaves under control, he ordered that they should make the same number of bricks each day for his building projects as previously, yet also had to gather their own straw from which to make the bricks. The Israelite foremen were furious with Moses: they now had even more work to do.

God said to Moses,

"Tell the people that I will rescue them!"

Then God sent a series of plagues on the Egyptians to persuade them to let his people go.

- First, God turned all the water in Egypt into blood
- Then swarms of frogs covered the land
- Next, gnats filled the air
- Flies settled everywhere
- The Egyptians' livestock died — but no Israelite animal
- Boils erupted on the Egyptians' bodies
- Hail flattened the crops
- Then locusts ate all that was left
- Darkness covered the Egyptians — but the Israelites enjoyed normal daylight.

Several times, Pharaoh said the Israelites could go, but each time he refused once the plague was over.

So God sent the final plague.

Bible Reference: Exodus 5:1-23 [1]Afterwards Moses and Aaron went to Pharaoh and said, "This is what the LORD, the God of Israel, says: "Let my people go, so that they may hold a festival to me in the wilderness." [2]Pharaoh said, "Who is the LORD, that I should obey him and let Israel go? I do not know the LORD and I will not let Israel go." [3]Then they said, "The God of the Hebrews has met with us. Now let us take a three-day journey into the wilderness to offer sacrifices to the LORD our God, or he may strike us with plagues or with the sword." [4]But the king of Egypt said, "Moses and Aaron, why are you taking the people away from their labour? Get back to your work!" [5]Then Pharaoh said, "Look, the people of the land are now numerous, and you are stopping them from working." [6]That same day Pharaoh gave this order to the slave drivers and overseers in charge of the people: [7] "You are no longer to supply the people with straw for making bricks; let them go and gather their own straw. [8]But require them to make the same number of bricks as before; don't reduce the quota. They are lazy; that is why they are crying out, 'Let us go and sacrifice to our God.' [9]Make the work harder for them so that they keep working and pay no attention to lies." [10]Then the slave drivers and the overseers went out and said to the people, "This is what Pharaoh says: "I will not give you any more straw. [11]Go and get your own straw wherever you can find it, but your work will not be reduced at all." [12]So the people scattered all over Egypt to gather stubble to use for straw. [13]The slave drivers kept pressing them, saying, "Complete the work required of you for each day, just as when you had straw." [14]And Pharaoh's slave drivers beat the Israelite overseers they had appointed, demanding, "Why haven't you met your quota of bricks yesterday or today, as before?" [15]Then the Israelite overseers went and appealed to Pharaoh: "Why have you treated your servants this way? [16]Your servants are given no straw, yet we are told, 'Make bricks!' Your servants are being beaten, but the fault is with your own people." [17]Pharaoh said, "Lazy, that's what you are—lazy! That is why you keep saying, 'Let us go and sacrifice to the LORD.' [18]Now get to work. You will not be given any straw, yet you must produce your full quota of bricks." [19]The Israelite overseers realized they were in trouble when they were told, "You are not to reduce the number of bricks required of you for each day." [20]When they left Pharaoh, they found Moses and Aaron waiting to meet them, [21]and they said, "May the LORD look on you and judge you! You have made us obnoxious to Pharaoh and his officials and have put a sword in their hand to kill us." [22]Moses returned to the LORD and said, "Why, Lord, why have you brought trouble on this people? Is this why you sent me? [23]Ever since I went to Pharaoh to speak in your name, he has brought trouble on this people, and you have not rescued your people at all."

Bible Reference: Exodus 6:1-30 [1]Then the LORD said to Moses, "Now you will see what I will do to Pharaoh: because of my mighty hand he will let them go; because of my mighty hand he will drive them out of his country." [2]God also said to Moses, "I am the LORD. [3]I appeared to Abraham, to Isaac and to Jacob as God Almighty, but by my name the LORD I did not make myself known to them. [4]I also established my covenant with them to give them the land of Canaan, where they resided as foreigners. [5]Moreover, I have heard the

groaning of the Israelites, whom the Egyptians are enslaving, and I have remembered my covenant. ⁶ "Therefore, say to the Israelites: "I am the LORD, and I will bring you out from under the yoke of the Egyptians. I will free you from being slaves to them, and I will redeem you with an outstretched arm and with mighty acts of judgment. ⁷I will take you as my own people, and I will be your God. Then you will know that I am the LORD your God, who brought you out from under the yoke of the Egyptians. ⁸And I will bring you to the land I swore with uplifted hand to give to Abraham, to Isaac and to Jacob. I will give it to you as a possession. I am the LORD." ⁹Moses reported this to the Israelites, but they did not listen to him because of their discouragement and harsh labour. ¹⁰Then the LORD said to Moses, ¹¹ "Go, tell Pharaoh king of Egypt to let the Israelites go out of his country." ¹²But Moses said to the LORD, "If the Israelites will not listen to me, why would Pharaoh listen to me, since I speak with faltering lips?" ¹³Now the LORD spoke to Moses and Aaron about the Israelites and Pharaoh king of Egypt, and he commanded them to bring the Israelites out of Egypt. ¹⁴These were the heads of their families: The sons of Reuben the firstborn son of Israel were Hanok and Pallu, Hezron and Karmi. These were the clans of Reuben. ¹⁵The sons of Simeon were Jemuel, Jamin, Ohad, Jakin, Zohar and Shaul the son of a Canaanite woman. These were the clans of Simeon. ¹⁶These were the names of the sons of Levi according to their records: Gershon, Kohath and Merari. Levi lived 137 years. ¹⁷The sons of Gershon, by clans, were Libni and Shimei. ¹⁸The sons of Kohath were Amram, Izhar, Hebron and Uzziel. Kohath lived 133 years. ¹⁹The sons of Merari were Mahli and Mushi. These were the clans of Levi according to their records. ²⁰Amram married his father's sister Jochebed, who bore him Aaron and Moses. Amram lived 137 years. ²¹The sons of Izhar were Korah, Nepheg and Zikri. ²²The sons of Uzziel were Mishael, Elzaphan and Sithri. ²³Aaron married Elisheba, daughter of Amminadab and sister of Nahshon, and she bore him Nadab and Abihu, Eleazar and Ithamar. ²⁴The sons of Korah were Assir, Elkanah and Abiasaph. These were the Korahite clans. ²⁵Eleazar son of Aaron married one of the daughters of Putiel, and she bore him Phinehas. These were the heads of the Levite families, clan by clan. ²⁶It was this Aaron and Moses to whom the LORD said, "Bring the Israelites out of Egypt by their divisions." ²⁷They were the ones who spoke to Pharaoh king of Egypt about bringing the Israelites out of Egypt—this same Moses and Aaron. ²⁸Now when the LORD spoke to Moses in Egypt, ²⁹he said to him, "I am the LORD. Tell Pharaoh king of Egypt everything I tell you." ³⁰But Moses said to the LORD, "Since I speak with faltering lips, why would Pharaoh listen to me?"

Bible Reference: Exodus 7:1-24 ¹Then the LORD said to Moses, "See, I have made you like God to Pharaoh, and your brother Aaron will be your prophet. ²You are to say everything I command you, and your brother Aaron is to tell Pharaoh to let the Israelites go out of his country. ³But I will harden Pharaoh's heart, and though I multiply my signs and wonders in Egypt, ⁴he will not listen to you. Then I will lay my hand on Egypt and with mighty acts of judgment I will bring out my divisions, my people the Israelites. ⁵And the Egyptians will know that I am the LORD when I stretch out my hand against Egypt and bring the Israelites out of it." ⁶Moses and Aaron did just as the LORD commanded them. ⁷Moses was eighty years old and Aaron eighty-three when they spoke to Pharaoh. ⁸The LORD said to Moses and Aaron, ⁹"When Pharaoh says to you, 'Perform a miracle,' then say to Aaron, 'Take your staff and throw it down before Pharaoh,' and it will become a snake." ¹⁰So Moses and Aaron went to Pharaoh and did just as the LORD commanded. Aaron threw his staff down in front of Pharaoh and his officials, and it became a snake. ¹¹Pharaoh then summoned the wise men and sorcerers, and the Egyptian magicians also did the same things by their secret arts: ¹²each one threw down his staff and it became a snake. But Aaron's staff swallowed up their staffs. ¹³Yet Pharaoh's heart became hard and he would not listen to them, just as the LORD had said. ¹⁴Then the LORD said to Moses, "Pharaoh's heart is unyielding; he refuses to let the people go. ¹⁵Go to Pharaoh in the morning as he goes out to the river. Wait on the bank of the Nile to meet him, and take in your hand the staff that was changed into a snake." ¹⁶Then say to him, "The LORD, the God of the Hebrews, has sent me to say to you: let my people go, so that they may worship me in the wilderness. But until now you have not listened. ¹⁷This is what the LORD says: by this you will know that I am the LORD: with the staff that is in my hand I will strike the water of the Nile, and it will be changed into blood. ¹⁸The fish in the Nile will die, and the river will stink; the Egyptians will not be able to drink its water." ¹⁹The LORD said to Moses, "Tell Aaron, 'Take your staff and stretch out your hand over the waters of Egypt—over the streams and canals, over the ponds and all the reservoirs—and they will turn to blood.' Blood will be everywhere in Egypt, even in the wooden buckets and stone jars." [20]Moses and Aaron did just as the LORD had commanded. He raised his staff in the presence of Pharaoh and his officials and struck the water of the Nile, and all the water was changed into blood. [21]The fish in the Nile died, and the river smelled so bad that the Egyptians could not drink its water. Blood was everywhere in Egypt. [22]But the Egyptian magicians did the same things by their secret arts, and Pharaoh's heart became hard; he would not listen to Moses and Aaron, just as the LORD had said. [23]Instead, he turned and went into his palace, and did not take even this to heart. [24]And all the Egyptians dug along the Nile to get drinking water, because they could not drink the water of the river.

Bible Reference: <u>Exodus 8:1-32</u> [1]Then the LORD said to Moses, "Go to Pharaoh and say to him, 'This is what the LORD says: let my people go, so that they may worship me. [2]If you refuse to let them go, I will send a plague of frogs on your whole country. [3]The Nile will teem with frogs. They will come up into your palace and your bedroom and onto your bed, into the houses of your officials and on your people, and into your ovens and kneading troughs. [4]The frogs will come up on you and your people and all your officials.'" [5]Then the LORD said to Moses, "Tell Aaron, 'Stretch out your hand with your staff over the streams and canals and ponds, and make frogs come up on the land of Egypt.'" [6]So Aaron stretched out his hand over the waters of Egypt, and the frogs came up and covered the land. [7]But the magicians did the same things by their secret arts; they also made frogs come up on the land of Egypt. [8]Pharaoh summoned Moses and Aaron and said, "Pray to the LORD to take the frogs away from me and my people, and I will let your people go to offer sacrifices to the LORD." [9]Moses said to Pharaoh, "I leave to you the honour of setting the time for me to pray for you and your officials and your people that you and your houses may be rid of the frogs, except for those that remain in the Nile." [10]"Tomorrow," Pharaoh said. Moses replied, "It will be as you say, so that you may know there is no-one like the LORD our God. [11]The frogs will leave you and your houses, your officials and your people; they will remain only in the Nile." [12]After Moses and Aaron left Pharaoh, Moses cried out to the LORD about the frogs he had brought on Pharaoh. [13]And the LORD did what Moses asked. The frogs died in the houses, in the courtyards and in the fields. [14]They were piled into heaps, and the land reeked of them. [15]But when Pharaoh saw that there was relief, he hardened his heart and would not listen to Moses and Aaron, just as the LORD had said. [16]Then the LORD said to Moses, "Tell Aaron, 'Stretch out your staff and strike the dust of the ground,' and throughout the land of Egypt the dust will become gnats." [17]They did this, and when Aaron stretched out his hand with the staff and struck the dust of the ground, gnats came on people and animals. All the dust throughout the land of Egypt became gnats. [18]But when the magicians tried to produce gnats by their secret arts, they could not. Since the gnats were on people and animals everywhere, [19]the magicians said to Pharaoh, "This is the finger of God." But Pharaoh's heart was hard and he would not listen, just as the LORD had said. [20]Then the LORD said to Moses, "Get up early in the morning and confront Pharaoh as he goes to the river and say to him, 'This is what the LORD says: let my people go, so that they may worship me. [21]If you do not let my people go, I will send swarms of flies on you and your officials, on your people and into your houses. The houses of the Egyptians will be full of flies; even the ground will be covered with them.'" [22]But on that day I will deal differently with the land of Goshen, where my people live; no swarms of flies will be there, so that you will know that I, the LORD, am in this land. [23]I will make a distinction between my people and your people. This sign will occur tomorrow." [24]And the LORD did this. Dense swarms of flies poured into Pharaoh's palace and into the houses of his officials; throughout Egypt the land was ruined by the flies. [25]Then Pharaoh summoned Moses and Aaron and said, "Go, sacrifice to your God here in the land." [26]But Moses said, "That would not be right. The sacrifices we offer the LORD our God would be detestable to the Egyptians. And if we offer sacrifices that are detestable in their eyes, will they not stone us? [27]We must take a three-day journey into the wilderness to offer sacrifices to the LORD our God, as he commands us." [28]Pharaoh said, "I will let you go to offer sacrifices to the LORD your God in the wilderness, but you must not go very far. Now pray for me." [29]Moses answered, "As soon as I leave you, I will pray to the LORD, and tomorrow the flies will leave Pharaoh and his officials and his people. Only let Pharaoh be sure that he does not act deceitfully again by not letting the people go to offer sacrifices to the LORD." [30]Then Moses left Pharaoh and prayed to the LORD, [31]and the LORD did what Moses asked. The flies left Pharaoh and his officials and his people; not a fly remained. [32]But this time also Pharaoh hardened his heart and would not let the people go.

Bible Reference: Exodus 9:1-35 ¹Then the LORD said to Moses, "Go to Pharaoh and say to him, This is what the LORD, the God of the Hebrews, says: 'Let my people go, so that they may worship me.' ²If you refuse to let them go and continue to hold them back, ³the hand of the LORD will bring a terrible plague on your livestock in the field—on your horses, donkeys and camels and on your cattle, sheep and goats. ⁴But the LORD will make a distinction between the livestock of Israel and that of Egypt, so that no animal belonging to the Israelites will die." ⁵The LORD set a time and said, "Tomorrow the LORD will do this in the land." ⁶And the next day the LORD did it: all the livestock of the Egyptians died, but not one animal belonging to the Israelites died. ⁷Pharaoh investigated and found that not even one of the animals of the Israelites had died. Yet his heart was unyielding and he would not let the people go. ⁸Then the LORD said to Moses and Aaron, "Take handfuls of soot from a furnace and let Moses toss it into the air in the presence of Pharaoh. ⁹It will become fine dust over the whole land of Egypt, and festering boils will break out on people and animals throughout the land." ¹⁰So they took soot from a furnace and stood before Pharaoh. Moses tossed it into the air, and festering boils broke out on people and animals. ¹¹The magicians could not stand before Moses because of the boils that were on them and on all the Egyptians. ¹²But the LORD hardened Pharaoh's heart and he would not listen to Moses and Aaron, just as the LORD had said to Moses. ¹³Then the LORD said to Moses, "Get up early in the morning, confront Pharaoh and say to him, 'This is what the LORD, the God of the Hebrews, says: let my people go, so that they may worship me, ¹⁴or this time I will send the full force of my plagues against you and against your officials and your people, so you may know that there is no-one like me in all the earth. ¹⁵For by now I could have stretched out my hand and struck you and your people with a plague that would have wiped you off the earth. ¹⁶But I have raised you up for this very purpose, that I might show you my power and that my name might be proclaimed in all the earth. ¹⁷You still set yourself against my people and will not let them go. ¹⁸Therefore, at this time tomorrow I will send the worst hailstorm that has ever fallen on Egypt, from the day it was founded till now. ¹⁹Give an order now to bring your livestock and everything you have in the field to a place of shelter, because the hail will fall on every person and animal that has not been brought in and is still out in the field, and they will die.'" ²⁰Those officials of Pharaoh who feared the word of the LORD hurried to bring their slaves and their livestock inside. ²¹But those who ignored the word of the LORD left their slaves and livestock in the field. ²²Then the LORD said to Moses, "Stretch out your hand towards the sky so that hail will fall all over Egypt—on people and animals and on everything growing in the fields of Egypt." ²³When Moses stretched out his staff towards the sky, the LORD sent thunder and hail, and lightning flashed down to the ground. So the LORD rained hail on the land of Egypt; ²⁴hail fell and lightning flashed back and forth. It was the worst storm in all the land of Egypt since it had become a nation. ²⁵Throughout Egypt hail struck everything in the fields—both people and animals; it beat down everything growing in the fields and stripped every tree. ²⁶The only place it did not hail was the land of Goshen, where the Israelites were. ²⁷Then Pharaoh summoned Moses and Aaron. "This time I have sinned," he said to them. "The LORD is in the right, and I and my people are in the wrong. ²⁸Pray to the LORD, for we have had enough thunder and hail. I will let you go; you don't have to stay any longer." ²⁹Moses replied, "When I have gone out of the city, I will spread out my hands in prayer to the LORD. The thunder will stop and there will be no more hail, so you may know that the earth is the LORD's. ³⁰But I know that you and your officials still do not fear the LORD God." ³¹(The flax and barley were destroyed, since the barley was in the ear and the flax was in bloom. ³²The wheat and spelt, however, were not destroyed, because they ripen later.) ³³Then Moses left Pharaoh and went out of the city. He spread out his hands towards the LORD; the thunder and hail stopped, and the rain no longer poured down on the land. ³⁴When Pharaoh saw that the rain and hail and thunder had stopped, he sinned again: he and his officials hardened their hearts. ³⁵So Pharaoh's heart was hard and he would not let the Israelites go, just as the LORD had said through Moses.

The Prodigal Son

This story, again found only in Luke is one of three all illustrating the theme of God's mercy: the lost sheep, the lost coin and the lost/ prodigal son. The story centres on the younger of two sons who demands his inheritance early then squanders it on a life of debauchery, until he finds himself penniless in a famine-stricken land. Eventually, he comes to his senses and returns home to ask his father's forgiveness, hoping to be taken on as a servant. Instead, his father greets him rapturously and throws a huge party to celebrate his homecoming. The elder brother, meanwhile, on hearing the noise of merrymaking is outraged at his father's action and refuses to go in. His father urges him to do so, reminding him that he is equally loved. The story illustrates the joy of <u>God</u> the father at the return of a <u>repentant</u> child from the "far country" of <u>sin</u> and alienation.

Bible Reference: Luke 15:11-32 [11]Jesus continued: "There was a man who had two sons. [12]The younger one said to his father, 'Father, give me my share of the estate.' So he divided his property between them." [13]Not long after that, the younger son got together all he had, set off for a distant country and there squandered his wealth in wild living. [14]After he had spent everything, there was a severe famine in that whole country, and he began to be in need. [15]So he went and hired himself out to a citizen of that country, who sent him to his fields to feed pigs. [16]He longed to fill his stomach with the pods that the pigs were eating, but no-one gave him anything. [17] "When he came to his senses, he said, "How many of my father's hired servants have food to spare, and here I am starving to death! [18]I will set out and go back to my father and say to him: Father, I have sinned against heaven and against you. [19]I am no longer worthy to be called your son; make me like one of your hired servants." [20]So he got up and went to his father. "But while he was still a long way off, his father saw him and was filled with compassion for him; he ran to his son, threw his arms round him and kissed him." [21]The son said to him, "Father, I have sinned against heaven and against you. I am no longer worthy to be called your son." [22] "But the father said to his servants, "Quick! Bring the best robe and put it on him. Put a ring on his finger and sandals on his feet. [23]Bring the fattened calf and kill it. Let's have a feast and celebrate. [24]For this son of mine was dead and is alive again; he was lost and is found." So they began to celebrate." [25]Meanwhile, the elder son was in the field. When he came near the house, he heard music and dancing. [26]So he called one of the servants and asked him what was going on. [27] "Your brother has come," he replied, "and your father has killed the fattened calf because he has him back safe and sound." [28]The elder brother became angry and refused to go in. So his father went out and pleaded with him. [29]But he answered his father, "Look! All these years I've been slaving for you and never disobeyed your orders. Yet you never gave me even a young goat so I could celebrate with my friends. [30]But when this son of yours who has squandered your property with prostitutes comes home, you kill the fattened calf for him!" [31] "My son," the father said, "you are always with me, and everything I have is yours. [32]But we had to celebrate and be glad, because this brother of yours was dead and is alive again; he was lost and is found."

The Temptation of Jesus

Mark's <u>gospel</u> records very briefly that after his <u>baptism</u>, <u>Jesus</u> spent forty days in the <u>wilderness</u> being tempted by <u>Satan</u>. He is shown overcoming the <u>temptations</u> and then begins his <u>ministry</u>. <u>Matthew</u> and <u>Luke</u> build on Mark and in vivid fashion record three specific challenges by the <u>devil</u> that Jesus uses his <u>miraculous</u> powers: "if you are the <u>Son of God</u>," then "The supreme challenge was for Jesus to worship Satan in return for which, he is promised control of all the kingdoms of the world. In response to this and the other tests Jesus quotes <u>scripture</u> to repel his adversary: "You must worship the <u>Lord</u> your <u>God</u>, and serve him alone". The point of the story is that: "Jesus triumphed in resisting temptation, where human beings had previously failed" he was thus equipped "in the power of the <u>Spirit</u>" to overthrow the powers of <u>evil</u>.

Bible Reference: Luke 4: 1-15 [1]Jesus, full of the Holy Spirit, left the Jordan and was led by the Spirit into the wilderness, [2]where for forty days he was tempted by the devil. He ate nothing during those days, and at the end of them he was hungry. [3]The devil said to him, "If you are the Son of God, tell this stone to become bread." [4]Jesus answered, "It is written: "People do not live on bread alone." [5]The devil led him up to a high place and showed him in an instant all the kingdoms of the world. [6]And he said to him, "I will give you all their authority and splendour; it has been given to me, and I can give it to anyone I want to. [7]If you worship me, it will all be yours." [8]Jesus answered, "It is written: 'Worship the Lord your God and serve him only.'" [9]The devil led him to Jerusalem and had him stand on the highest point of the temple. "If you are the Son of God," he said, "throw yourself down from here. [10]For it is written: "He will command his angels concerning you to guard you carefully; [11]they will lift you up in their hands, so that you will not strike your foot against a stone." [12]Jesus

answered, "It is said: 'Do not put the Lord your God to the test.'" ¹³When the devil had finished all this tempting, he left him until an opportune time. ¹⁴Jesus returned to Galilee in the power of the Spirit, and news about him spread through the whole countryside. ¹⁵He was teaching in their synagogues, and everyone praised him.

The Ten Commandments Given to Moses

The giving of the Ten Commandments is a story within a larger story, which tells of God's deliverance of the people of Israel from captivity in Egypt. He enters into a covenant relationship with them whereby they undertake to be faithful to God's law. The actual giving of the commandments at Mount Sinai is described as a terrifying experience in which God "comes down" to talk with Moses and inscribes the ten points of his law for humankind on tablets of stone. These summarize God's covenant with his people and set out a basic ethical norm applicable to people in all ages. The first four concern humankind's relationship to God, the remaining six people's relationship to others. The commandments: "show God's concern for the whole of life" set out standards governing family relationships, regard for human life, sex, property, speech and thought "illustrate that, as creator, God alone can show his creatures how to behave."

Bible Reference: Exodus 20:1-17 ¹And God spoke all these words: ² "I am the LORD your God, who brought you out of Egypt, out of the land of slavery." ³You shall have no other gods before me. ⁴ "You shall not make for yourself an image in the form of anything in heaven above or on the earth beneath or in the waters below. ⁵You shall not bow down to them or worship them; for I, the LORD your God, am a jealous God, punishing the children for the sin of the parents to the third and fourth generation of those who hate me, ⁶but showing love to a thousand generations of those who love me and keep my commandments." ⁷You shall not misuse the name of the LORD your God, for the LORD will not hold anyone guiltless who misuses his name. ⁸ "Remember the Sabbath day by keeping it holy. ⁹Six days you shall labour and do all your work, ¹⁰but the seventh day is a Sabbath to the LORD your God. On it you shall not do any work, neither you, nor your son or daughter, nor your male or female servant, nor your animals, nor any foreigner residing in your towns. ¹¹For in six days the LORD made the heavens and the earth, the sea, and all that is in them, but he rested on the seventh day. Therefore the LORD blessed the Sabbath day and made it holy." ¹²Honour your father and your mother, so that you may live long in the land the LORD your God is giving you. ¹³ "You shall not murder." ¹⁴You shall not commit adultery. ¹⁵ "You shall not steal." ¹You shall not give false testimony against your neighbour. ¹⁷ "You shall not covet your neighbour's house. You shall not covet your neighbour's wife, or his male or female servant, his ox or donkey, or anything that belongs to your neighbour."

The Word Becomes Flesh

At the beginning of all things, the Word was there. The Word was with God and the Word was in fact God. Everything was made through him. There was nothing made without him. In the Word was life, and that life lit the way for people. This light shines through the darkness and the darkness has not defeated it.

A man called John (known as John the Baptist) came from God to tell people about this light that was coming to them, this light that would light the way to God for everyone. This Word, this man, was part of the world, but the world did not recognize him for who he was. He came to his own people—but they did not accept him. But those few who did accept him, those who believed in him, he made them children of God through him: children born not by human choice or desire but by God's will.

This Word became flesh and blood and lived among people. They saw his glory—the glory belonging solely to the only Son of the Father, filled with truth and grace.

Bible Reference: John 1:1-14 ¹In the beginning was the Word, and the Word was with God, and the Word was God. ²He was with God in the beginning. ³Through him all things were made; without him nothing was made that has been made. ⁴In him was life, and that life was the light of all people. ⁵The light shines in the darkness, and the darkness has not overcome it. ⁶There was a man sent from God whose name was John. ⁷He came as a witness to testify concerning that light, so that through him all might believe. ⁸He himself was not the light; he came only as a witness to the light. ⁹The true light that gives light to everyone was coming into the world. ¹⁰He was in the world, and though the world was made through him, the world did not recognize him. ¹¹He came to that which was his own, but his own did not receive him. ¹²Yet to all who did receive him, to those who believed in his name, he gave the right to become children of God—¹³children born not of natural descent, nor of human decision or a husband's will, but born of God. ¹⁴The Word became flesh and made his dwelling among us. We have seen his glory, the glory of the one and only Son, who came from the Father, full of grace and truth.

Zacchaeus

In Jericho, there was a chief tax-collector called Zacchaeus. He worked for the Roman army so was unpopular with his Jewish countrymen. He heard about Jesus and wanted to see him for himself.

So when he found out Jesus was in town, he joined the people milling around him. But there was a problem: Zacchaeus was not very tall and, try as he might, he could not see Jesus above the heads of the crowd. So he climbed a tree by the side of the road.

But when Jesus came, he stopped, looked up and said,

"Come down Zacchaeus! I am coming to your house!"

The tax-collector scrambled down and gladly took Jesus to his house.

The people around were not so glad. They said,

"Jesus is going to be the guest of a sinner!"

Then Zacchaeus said,

"Lord, right now I am giving to the poor half of all I own, and I promise to pay back four times over any money I have obtained dishonestly!"

People were amazed. This man was rich because of the extra tax he had taken from them—and he was offering to pay back more than the Jewish law demanded!

Jesus said that he had come to find and save the people who were not yet living as God wanted them to.

Bible Reference: Luke 19:1-10 ¹Jesus entered Jericho and was passing through. ²A man was there by the name of Zacchaeus; he was a chief tax collector and was wealthy. ³He wanted to see who Jesus was, but because he was short he could not see over the crowd. ⁴So he ran ahead and climbed a sycamore-fig tree to see him, since Jesus was coming that way. ⁵When Jesus reached the spot, he looked up and said to him, "Zacchaeus, come down immediately. I must stay at your house today." ⁶So he came down at once and welcomed him gladly. ⁷All the people saw this and began to mutter, "He has gone to be the guest of a "sinner". ⁸But Zacchaeus stood up and said to the Lord, "Look, Lord! Here and now I give half of my possessions to the poor, and if I have cheated anybody out of anything, I will pay back four times the amount." ⁹Jesus said to him, "Today salvation has come to this house, because this man, too, is a son of Abraham. ¹⁰For the Son of Man came to seek and to save what was lost."

Appendix IV
参考的主要文献和网站

[1] Barton, John & Muddiman, John. The Oxford Bible Commentary (Ed) 2001.
[2] Fields, Wilbur. Old Testament History: An Overview of Sacred History & Truth[M]College Press Publishing Co. 1996.
[3] Gabel, John. The Bible as Literature an Introduction 5ed. Oxford University Press, 2001.
[4] Greenlee, J. Harold. Introduction to New Testament Textual Criticism, Revised Edition[M]Hendrickson Publishers, 1995 .
[5] Jeffrey, David Lyle. A Dictionary of Biblical Tradition in English Literature [M].Grand Rapids, Michigan: William B. Eerdmans Publishing Company, 1992.
[6] Lowth, Robert. Lectures on the Sacred Poetry of the Hebrews[M]. London: Routledge/Thoemmes press, 1995.
[7] Ryken, Leland. Words of Delight: A Literary Introduction to the Bible[M]. Grand Rapids, Michigan: Baker Book House, 1987.
[8] Shaheen, Nasseb. Biblical Reference in Shakespeare's Plays[M].London: Associated University Press, 1999.
[9] White, E.G. Patriarchs and Prophets [M] Pacific Press Publishing Association, 1993.
[10] 何乃英.旧约文学特征刍议[J].外国文学研究,1994(2).
[11] 梁　工,卢龙光.圣经与文学阐释[M].北京:人民文学出版社, 2003.
[12] 梁　工.仅次于莎士比亚戏剧的文学经典[J].外国文学评论, 2008(4).
[13] 梁　工.莎士比亚与圣经[M].北京:商务印书馆,2005.
[14] 梁　工.圣经文学研究:第一辑[M].北京:人民文学出版社, 2008.
[15] 梁　工.西方圣经批评引论[M].北京:商务印书馆,2005.
[16] 梁　工.跨文化视域中的圣经文学研究[J].解放军外国语学院学报, 2003(5).
[17] 梁　工.简论该隐形象在欧洲文学中的演变[J].国外文学, 1997(3).
[18] 梁　工.圣经文学导读[M].漓江出版社, 1990.
[19] 梁　工.《希伯来文学中上帝形象的演变》[J],《南开学报》,1989(5).
[20] 刘洪一.犹太圣经的世界性及与现代文明的联结[J].外国文学研究,2004(6).
[21] 刘连祥.《圣经》伊甸园神话和母亲原型[J].外国文学评论, 1990(1).
[22] 刘连祥.试论《圣经》的神话结构[J].上海师范大学学报, 1992(4).
[23] 刘意青.简约、含蓄的《圣经》叙事艺术[J].外国文学, 2001,(01) .
[24] 刘意青.圣经的文学阐释[M].北京:北京大学出版社,2004.
[25] 舒　天.基督教与中世纪的西方文学发展[J].国外文学,1993(3).
[26] 孙彩霞.西方现代派文学与圣经[M].北京:中国社会科学出版社,2005.
[27] 肖明翰.《失乐园》中的自由意志与人的堕落和再生 [J].外国文学评论, 1999(1).
[28] 肖明翰.试论弥尔顿的《斗士参孙》[J].外国文学评论, 1996(2).
[29] 杨慧林.基督教的底色与文化延伸[M].哈尔滨:黑龙江人民出版社, 2002.
[30] 游　斌.希伯来圣经的文本、历史与思想世界[M].北京:宗教文化出版社, 2007.
[31] 张浩达.文庸、荒原视觉《圣经》—西方艺术中的基督教 [M].北京:社会科学文献出版社,2001.
[32] 张思齐.《论以斯帖形象的美学意义》[J].东方丛刊,1999 (2).
[33] 朱维之.圣经文学十二讲[M].人民文学出版社, 1989.
[34] 邹　溱.《老人与海》中的圣经隐喻[J].国外文学, 1993 (4).
[35] Bible Life: http://www.biblelife.org/biblediet.htm
[36] Bible People: http://www.bible-people.info/Joseph.htm
[37] Elijah Project: http://www.elijahproject.net/modestyquiz.html
[38] Learn the Bble: http://www.learnthebible.org/water-in-the-bible.html
[39] Religion Online: http://www.religion-online.org/showarticle.asp?title=3218
[40] Study Light: http://www.studylight.org/dic/hbd/view.cgi?number=T1737